Dawson, James W.

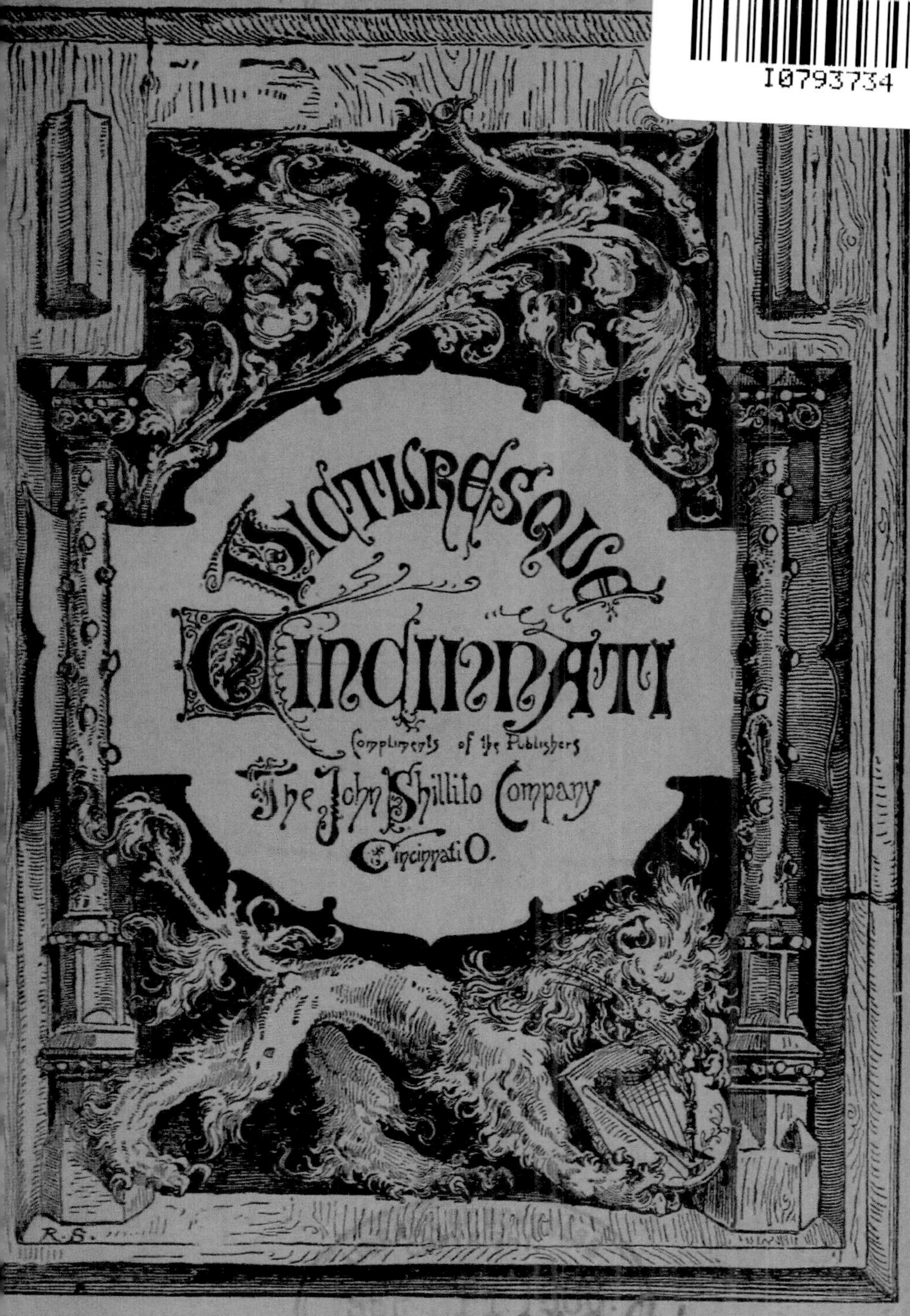

Marula

An imprint of Arcadia Publishing

Picturesque Cincinnati
by James W. Dawson
The John Shillito Company

A Marula Historical Reprint
Originally published in 1883

Published by Arcadia Publishing
Charleston SC

ISBN 978-0-7385-9475-0

Printed in the United States of America

For all general information contact Arcadia Publishing at:
Telephone 843-853-2070
Fax 843-853-0044
E-mail sales@arcadiapublishing.com
For customer service and orders:
Toll-Free 1-888-313-2665

Visit us on the Internet at www.arcadiapublishing.com

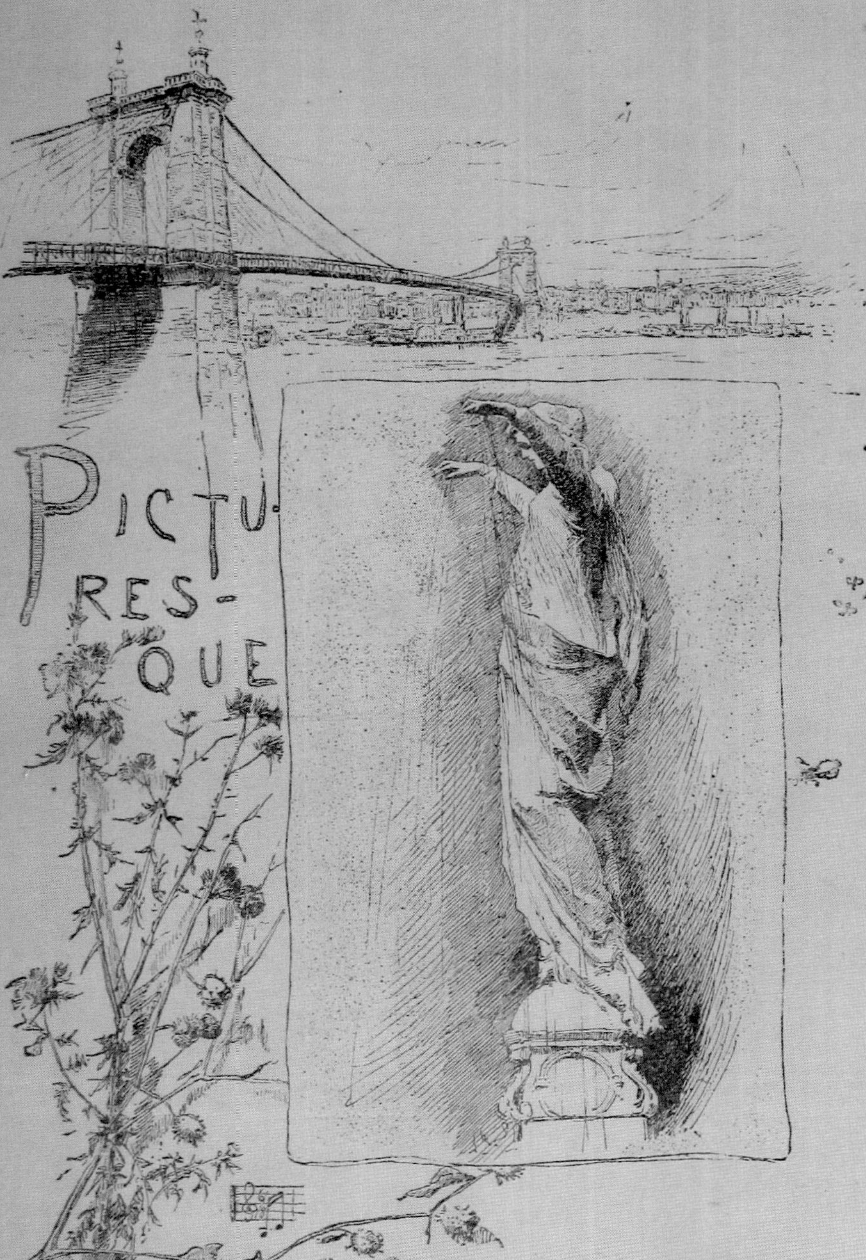
PICTU-
RES-
QUE
CINCINNATI.

PICTURESQUE CINCINNATI.

A **Bit of History.** — Cincinnati, or Losanteville as the place was first named (l'os-ante-ville, the town opposite the mouth), was settled in the latter part of 1788 or beginning of 1789 by a party under Israel Ludlow. The ground on which the city stands was purchased by Matthias Denman, who associated with himself Robert Patterson and John Filson. The latter was killed by Indians on a visit to the site of the proposed settlement, and Ludlow took his place in the enterprise. The date of the settlement is involved in doubt; although Dec. 28, 1788, is generally celebrated as the birthday of the town. While no especial incident marks the early history of the city, the Indians gave more than the usual trouble; and it was not until after Harmar and St. Clair had been successively defeated by them, that Wayne secured, as the result of a decisive victory in 1794, a peace which was signed at Greenville in 1795. The progress of the settlement, delayed and crippled by Indian wars until the peace, was rapid afterwards. The site of the city was well chosen, for climate, natural advantages, river communication, and was probably selected principally as being on the Indian trail between Detroit, the Great Lakes, and Lexington, Ky., where it crossed the Ohio River. The tide of Western emigration, as soon as it became safe, quickly peopled Cincinnati with a thrifty, energetic, and enterprising population. The growth of the city, though rapid, has been healthy. No back-set has ever seriously affected the onward march of the place. Neither epidemic, commercial disaster, fire, war, nor wild speculation has roughly disturbed her course. What advance has been made has been maintained, and in this fact lies the explanation and cause of the city's present position.

The name of Cincinnati was given in 1790, when St. Clair came to the place as governor of the North-west Territory. Cincinnati was incorporated as a city in 1819, and from that time has been a great centre, and holds a high rank among American cities in every department of trade, culture, influence, and wealth.

A single lifetime has covered the existence of Cincinnati; for the first white child born in the place (William Moody, March 17, 1790) died in 1879.

By the annexation of Columbia, the city has obtained the right to date back its settlement to November, 1788, as a party had landed and settled there previous to the coming of the party under Ludlow to Losanteville; but five years' annexation has not overcome the history of the previous eighty-five years, and Cincinnati still dates its existence from Dec. 28, 1788. — *Julius Dexter.*

Academies. — See Schools.

Academy of Medicine, the Cincinnati, was established in 1857; and its membership at present comprises about one hundred and twenty physicians of the regular school, principally alumni of the Medical College of Ohio. In 1874 a division was the result of a dispute about some point of medical ethics; and about twenty members withdrew, and formed the Cincinnati Medical Society. During the spring, autumn, and winter months, the Academy holds weekly meetings, on Monday evenings, in the amphitheatre of the Ohio College of Dental Surgery. Membership fee, $3; annual subscription, $2.

Ætna Insurance Company, of Hartford, Conn., is the largest and strongest American fire-insurance company. Its cash capital is $4,000,000, and its gross assets almost $10,000,000. It has paid nearly $75,000,000 for losses. Its Western business, built up through the department located at Cincinnati, has played a most important part in the growth of this gigantic corporation. The Ætna owns the building, No. 171 Vine Street, and is considered to some extent a local institution.

Aldermen and Aldermanic Districts. — The twenty-five wards of the city are equally divided into five aldermanic districts, from each of which six aldermen are elected to serve four years without compensation. The board, known also as the Upper House, meets regularly on the second and fourth Fridays of every month in the Council Chamber, City Building. The districts are as follows: First district: 1st, 2d, 3d, 4th, and 7th wards; Second district: 5th, 6th, 8th, 9th, and 10th wards; Third district: 11th, 12th, 23d, 24th, and 25th wards; Fourth district: 13th, 14th, 15th, 16th, and 22d wards; Fifth district: 17th, 18th, 19th, 20th, and 21st wards. The following are the names of the present board of aldermen: Michael Ryan, president; Samuel R. Smith, vice-president; Edwin Henderson, clerk. *First District:* Michael Kary, Charles M. Devitt, William L. Pettit, George N. Stone, Frank Vormohr. *Second District:* John T. Jones, Julius Reis, Samuel Mains, William Loder, James B. Wilson, George A. Schneider. *Third District:* Cassimir Baumann, Edward Felix, George W. Hill, Philip Nuber, Albert Williamson, William M. McGary. *Fourth District:* H. Riedemann, Jackson A. Armstrong, Charles Hess, Edward N. Wilson, W. M. Ampt, Washington T. Porter. *Fifth District:* William H. Hodgson, J. D. Holcomb, Thomas T. Shay, Jeremiah Mahony, Moses Clinton, Samuel R. Smith.

Allemania Club, organized in 1849, occupies the beautiful freestone building erected for the club in 1879, on the north-west corner of Fourth Street and Central Avenue. The building and its elaborate furnishings cost nearly $100,000. In the third story is the Allemania Hall, with seating capacity of 500. There is a library of 1,500 volumes; and parlors, reading, billiard, card, and chess rooms, besides a restaurant and bar. The club, comprising 200 Israelites, gives during the year many entertainments, to which none but members and a few persons invited by those taking part in the entertainment are admitted. At other times strangers can, upon invitation of a member, visit the club-house. The membership fees are: initiation, $25, and dues $3 a month. Non-residents introduced by members are granted the privileges of the club at $5 a month.

Alençon, Point-Lace (or Point d'Alençon). — Its first appearance in France was in the year 1665, and it was first made by Madame Gilbert, a native of Alençon. This lace is made entirely by hand with a fine needle, upon a parchment pattern, in small pieces, afterward united by invisible seams. Each part is executed by a special workman. Formerly it required eighteen different hands to complete a piece of lace: the number, we believe, is now reduced to twelve. The design, engraved upon a copper plate, is printed off in divisions upon pieces of parchment ten inches long, each numbered according to their order. They are then passed from one worker to another until the different operations are completed; and then remains the great work of uniting all these segments imperceptibly together. This is done by a seam following as closely as possible the outlines of the pattern. Point d'Alençon is of a solidity which defies time and washing, and has been justly called the "Queen of Lace." For the largest assortment of fine point-laces in all the best makes, visit The John Shillito Company.

American Protestant Association, as its name implies, is composed of men whose principles are opposed to the tenets of the Roman Catholic Church. It partakes largely of a political character, but is ostensibly a social organization. There are 15 lodges and encampments in the city, with an aggregate membership of 2,500.

American Sunday-school Union, organized in Philadelphia in 1824, has two prime objects, — to establish and maintain Sunday schools, and to publish and circulate moral and religious literature. The Union is non-sectarian, ten different denominations being represented in the board of managers. It employs missionaries who devote their whole time to establishing Bible-schools throughout the country.

American Tract Society, instituted in New York in 1825, has for its object the diffusion of "a knowledge of our Lord Jesus Christ as the Redeemer of sinners, and to promote the interests of vital godliness and sound morality by the circulation of religious tracts calculated to meet the approbation of all evangelical Christians." The Western Tract Society and Presbyterian Board of Publication are located at 176 Elm Street.

Amusements. — See Bellevue House, Coliseum, Esher's New Palace, Grand Opera House, Heuck's Opera House, Highland House, Lookout Opera House, Price's Hill, Robinson's Opera House, Vine-street Opera House, Zoölogical Society.

Arbeiter Halle, No. 474 Walnut Street, north of Thirteenth Street, belongs to the Arbeiter Bund (workingmen's society). The building contains a large hall, two small halls, and eight large committee-rooms, besides a large bar and billiard-room. The association has been in existence twenty-eight years, and the hall was erected to meet its wants. Twenty-seven trades-unions, benevolent associations, and singing societies, make this building their place of meeting. The hall is sustained by receipts from rents and the proceeds of the bar and billiard-room.

Arcade. — See Emery Arcade.

Archery has established itself as a permanent and prominent feature of amusements in Cincinnati. The Westwood was the first club to begin shooting, and had been doing so for some time before Maurice Thompson aroused the country by his stirring magazine-articles in 1877. In July of that year was started the Sagittarian Club of Walnut Hills, and also about the same time the College-hill Archery Club. These three clubs were organized by adoption of constitutions, election of officers and members, and are still leading clubs. The College-hill Club kept for two years its original members; but in 1879 a part of them withdrew, and with other persons organized the Waverley Archery Club of College Hill. The clubs named, and the Ivanhoe Archery Club of East Walnut Hills, organized in 1878, include the best shots of this city and its vicinity. The Westwood meets every Wednesday afternoon, on the grounds of Jas. N. Gamble at Westwood, and shoots ten rounds of three arrows each at a forty-eight-inch target; ladies shooting at a distance of thirty yards, and gentlemen at forty yards. The College-hill meets every Tuesday, and the Waverley every Wednesday afternoon, on the grounds of some members at College Hill, and shoots the regulation round. The Ivanhoe meets Friday afternoon, on the grounds of members at East Walnut Hills. The Sagittarian meets on Saturday, on its grounds, called Ashland Range, at Walnut Hills, and begins shooting at 4 P.M. The regular round is shot at same distances as those of the Westwood. Visitors interested in archery can easily get an invitation to witness the games through an acquaintance with a member of some club. There is a long list of other archery-clubs, which are scattered throughout the city and its suburbs.

Area of Cincinnati for twenty-five years previous to 1870, when the first annexation was made, was 4,480 acres, or seven square miles. The territory annexed in 1870 amounted to 8,085 acres, or 12.75 square miles. The last annexation, in 1873, brought in 2,695 acres, or 4.25 square miles. Total number of acres, 15,260; total square miles, 24. The Ohio-river frontage of the city, from Columbia on the east to Riverside on the west, is 11 miles.

Army, the. — The military protection of the city consists of five companies of the First Regiment of Ohio National Guards, under command of Col. C. B. Hunt. The regiment is organized under the militia laws of the State, and is uniformed in the United-States regulation uniform.

The Second Battery Light Artillery, Ohio National Guards, organized under the State militia laws, consists of eighty young men, with an armament of four six-pound bronze guns, with caissons, battery, wagon and equipments complete, sabres and revolvers. The company is under command of Capt. W. H. Murphy, with armory located at Power Hall, Exposition Buildings.

The police-force is also drilled in the manual of arms. The military companies will average about 60 men, rank and file, the artillery 80, and the drilled police 325; making a total of 705 available soldiers. The city owns a Gatling gun, bought during the railroad riots of 1877, which is in charge of the superintendent of police.

Art. — Cincinnati is making rapid strides towards becoming one of the American art-centres; and, although the public art institutions are but few, there are a number of valuable and extensive collections owned by the citizens, and the visitor who obtains the privilege of seeing some of these collections will probably be surprised to find so many art-treasures stored away in this city. A realizing sense of the importance of having permanent buildings for an Art Museum caused to be incorporated in 1879 a Women's Art-Museum Association, with power to receive and hold gifts for such a building and its contents. From various sources, such as lectures, loan exhibitions, private donations, and bequests, several thousand dollars have been realized.

The amount required to accomplish the desired end was large, and the prospect of immediate success very small. At this juncture another of Cincinnati's generous millionnaires, Mr. Charles W. West, came forward with a formal donation of $150,000 for the purpose of founding a museum, upon condition that the citizens subscribe a like amount; which was at once done. Mr. West also donated $150,000 as an endowment for the museum.

The acquisitions of rare and valuable objects have been much larger in number than could well have been anticipated so early in the history of the enterprise. The present location of the museum is in the south wing of Music Hall. The permanent building will be located in Eden Park, and will be of the Florentine Romanesque style.

The other art-institutions are the School of Design, the Ohio Mechanics' Institute, and Fry's Carving School, all of which are noticed in their alphabetical places. Among the many noteworthy private collections are the paintings of Joseph Longworth, Henry Probasco, George Hoadly, George K. Shoenberger, Reuben R. Springer, William S. Groesbeck, John L. Stettinius, L. B. Harrison, W. W. Scarborough, and Nathaniel F. Baker; the bronzes of Erasmus Gest; the engravings of William Karrmann, J. Le Boutillier, S. C. Tatem, William Henry Davis, and George McLaughlin. The hall of William Hooper's residence at East Walnut Hills has been carved throughout by pupils of the School of Design and Henry L. Fry. The principal and oldest art-store is that of William Wiswell, No. 70 West Fourth Street, who has been engaged in the art-business in this city for forty-seven years. The other chief art-stores are those of P. Smith & Co., No. 141 West Fifth Street, and A. B. Closson, jun., No. 186 West Fourth Street, both having very pretty art-galleries. (See Etching Club, Painters, Pottery, Sculptors.)

Astronomical Society, the Cincinnati, was organized in May, 1842; and on the 16th of June next Prof. O. M. Mitchel was sent to Europe, under the auspices of the society, to obtain such information as might facilitate the building of an observatory, and to make arrangements for the purchase of astronomical instruments. At Munich he contracted for an object-glass, celebrated throughout Europe for its clearness and accuracy. It was placed in the Cincinnati Observatory, and cost when mounted $9,500. The amount needed for this purchase, and also for the building, was raised by shares of $25 each, to which all classes of persons subscribed. The corner-stone of the observatory was laid by John Quincy Adams, Nov. 9, 1843, on a four-acre lot, situated on the summit of Mount Adams, and donated by Nicholas Longworth. In 1872, the old site on Mount Adams having become unsuitable by reason of the noise and smoke of the city, the Longworth heirs joined with the Astronomical Society in an agreement to give the grounds to the city, to be sold, and the proceeds to be donated to the School of Drawing and Design; the city agreeing, on its part, to sustain an observatory in connection with the University of Cincinnati. The building, with the grounds, was sold in 1872 to the Passionists Fathers, and is now used as a monastery. John

Kilgour gave four acres of land on Mount Lookout as a site for the new building; and the Astronomical Society donated all their instruments and reports, and became extinct. (See Observatory.)

Athletic Club, the Cincinnati, is an amateur association formed by a number of respectable young men of Cincinnati to encourage all manly sports, and to promote physical culture. It was organized in 1879, and has its headquarters at the rooms of the Cincinnati Gymnasium. All members of the club are also members of the gymnasium. Its officers are Frank Wright, president; and Ed. Lucius, secretary.

Aurora Fire and Marine Insurance Company of Cincinnati was incorporated in 1871. Its cash capital is $100,000; total assets, $146,441. Since its organization it has paid for losses $471,020. The company has about 100 agencies scattered through six States. The office is No. 6 West Fourth Street, where it has been for the past twelve years. The president is C. J. Krebiel, and the secretary is F. Goulé.

Avenue, the, is the popular name of Spring-grove Avenue, which begins at Harrison Avenue opposite the northern terminus of McLean Avenue, and runs north past United Railroads Stock-yards, through Cumminsville, past Spring Grove, Chester Park, and Spring Lake, to its junction with the Carthage Pike, — a distance of five miles. The roadway is a hundred feet wide, each side being occupied by a horse-railway track as far as Cumminsville. A single track extends from Cumminsville to Spring Grove. Noble silver poplars, on both sides, give generous shade nearly the whole day; and part of the way a double row of trees covers the car-track on either side. The grade is almost level the entire distance. The centre roadway, thirty feet wide, is made of screened gravel; and on both sides of the roadway is a loam and sand track twenty-five feet wide. It is the popular evening drive, and the most favorable test-road around the city for fast horses. Toll is collected at two gates. The Seventh-street, John-street, and Baymiller-street horse-cars connect with the horse-cars on the Avenue.

Avondale is a suburb of Cincinnati, joining the city on the north, and lying east of Clifton. Its southern boundary is two miles and a half from Fountain Square. The Cincinnati Northern Narrow-gauge Railway has a branch road running to this suburb. There are also two lines of street-cars, — one *viâ* the inclined plane at Mount Adams, and the other up Broadway and Lebanon Turnpike. It is one of the most beautiful of the suburbs, many of Cincinnati's wealthiest business-men having elegant residences therein.

Banks, State and National. — First National, north-west corner Third and Walnut; Fourth National, north-east corner Third and Walnut; Merchants' National, 75 West Third; National Lafayette and Bank of Commerce, 18 West Third; Second National, north-west corner Court and Main; Third National, 65 West Third; Bank of Cincinnati, 31 West Third; Commercial Bank, 132 Main; Franklin Bank, 14 West Third; German National Bank, south-west corner Third and Walnut; Western German Bank, north-east corner Twelfth and Vine; Citizens' National Bank, 51 West Third; Exchange National Bank, 34 West Third; Metropolitan National Bank, 25 West Third; Union National Bank, 90 West Third; Queen City National Bank, 53 West Third; Cincinnati National Bank, 90 West Third.

Baptist Churches. — See Churches.

Bar Association, the Cincinnati, was organized for the advancement of legal knowledge, and the better and more convenient discharge of professional duties connected therewith. George Hoadly is the president, and nearly all the prominent lawyers of the city are members. Besides having an annual banquet, the association meets at the Literary-club Rooms whenever any business is to be transacted. The assessment is $5 a year.

Barracks, the Newport, owned by the United-States Government, are situated on the point of Newport, Ky., where the Licking River empties into the Ohio. The grounds once included five acres and a half, but a part have since been washed away. The river-front is protected by a wall of masonry. The permanent buildings occupy the outer portions of the square. They enclose a parade-ground, and have accommodations for three companies, although six hundred men have been quartered there. At present it is the headquarters for the Department of the South. The barracks are reached most conveniently by the Newport Ferry, which has a landing about three hundred yards from the main gates.

Base Ball. — There is one professional club and innumerable amateur clubs in Cincinnati. The professional club, named after our city, is incorporated, holds membership in the American Alliance, and has enclosed grounds at the foot of Bank Street, about two miles from

Fountain Square. They are accessible by means of all the west-end lines of street-cars. The amateur clubs play their games both at the Cincinnati grounds and at the old Ball Park on the Avenue, while innumerable games are played in every available vacant lot in the city or its suburbs. Cincinnati is a great city for base-ball. Some of the games frequently bring out an attendance of upwards of ten thousand people.

Baths, Public. — There is one public swimming-bath in the city, moored in the summer in the Ohio River at the foot of Broadway. It consists of a boat 200 by 50 feet, with 86 dressing-rooms. A current of water 4½ feet in depth constantly passes through it. There is a swimming-school attached; the basin being 20 feet square, and the water from 2½ to 3½ feet deep. Price of a single bath, 15 cents; season tickets, $5. Public bath-houses are numerous throughout the city. Most of the hotels have public bathing accommodations. At many of the bath-establishments, Turkish, electric, sea-salt, and medicated baths are furnished. Prices range from 20 cents to $1.50, according to the kind of bath.

Bellevue is a suburb of Newport, Ky., lying directly east of that city, and west of Dayton. It is regularly built, and is inhabited principally by workingmen and men of moderate means, who do business in Cincinnati. It is about three miles from Fountain Square, and is reached by the Newport and Dayton line of street-cars, which start in Cincinnati from Fountain Square.

Bellevue House. — One of the famous hill-top resorts of the city. It is situated at the head of the Cincinnati and Clifton Inclined-plane Railway. The hill on which it stands is an almost abrupt rise of 300 feet above McMicken Avenue. Two beautiful views of the city under the hills can be had from the terrace, — one covering the Mill-creek Valley, the other all that portion of the city west of Mount Adams and north of Fourth Street. The grounds attached comprise about 12 acres, in which are an immense pavilion, a park, and an orchard. The esplanade, overlooking the city, is 500 feet long, and 150 feet wide. This, as well as the main halls and the floor of the pavilion, is covered with chairs and refreshment-tables. As many as ten thousand people can be accommodated, and a much larger number has frequently been entertained in one evening. The grounds are largely used for picnics, balls, and private parties. The entire place is open at all times, and the admission is almost always free. *Horse-cars,* —

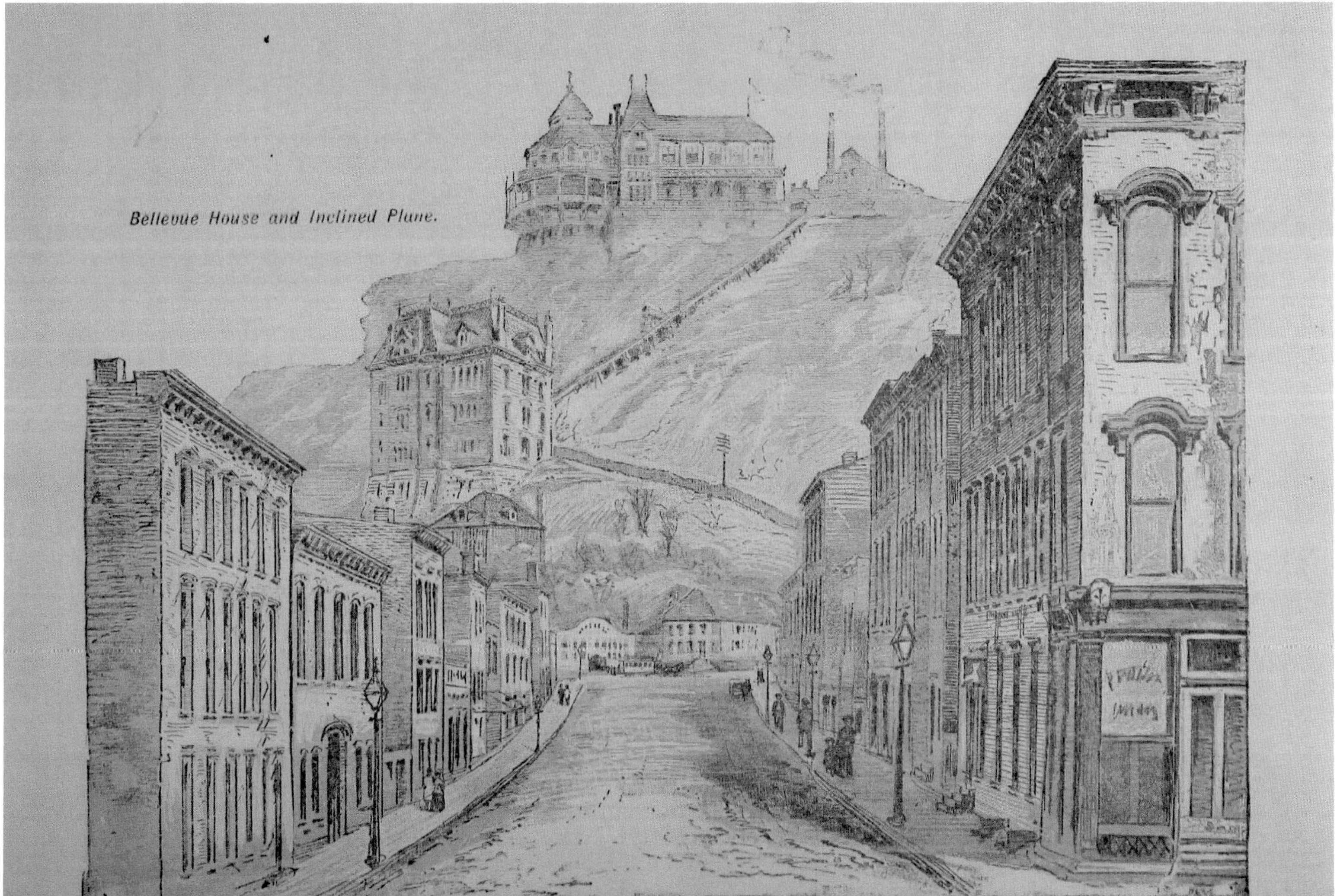

Bellevue House and Inclined Plane.

Elm-street and Vine-street lines, which take passengers to the Inclined Plane. The distance is 1½ miles from Fountain Square.

B'nai B'rith, a mutual-benefit order of Israelites, has seven lodges in Cincinnati, six of which meet weekly in the lodge-room, north-east corner of Fifth Street and Central Avenue. The sick-benefits are $4 a week; the dues do not exceed $25 a year; death assessments, 75 cents each. These fees cover an endowment insurance of $1,000, and are obligatory on all the members. Connected with the order, but not obligatory on the members, is an insurance feature of $2,000, payable at death to the heirs of the deceased. This order instituted the Jewish Orphan Asylum at Cleveland, supported by the lodges throughout District No. 2, which comprises the States of Ohio, Indiana, and Kentucky.

Board of Trade and Transportation collects, preserves, and circulates information relating to the business of Cincinnati, especially the facts relating to its manufacturing interests; encourages wise and needful legislation, and opposes the enactment of laws likely to prove prejudical to the commercial and manufacturing interests. It studies the workings of the system of transportation, and endeavors to remedy its defects and abuses, as well as to secure just rates of freight, the discontinuance of overcharges, and the prompt settlement of damages on goods shipped. It facilitates the adjustment of controversies between its members and others, and strives to promote the industrial interests of the city. Its voting membership is about 300; the annual dues being, for firms, $30; for individuals, $20. Its rooms are No. 55 West Fourth Street, and are open every week-day. Visitors admitted.

Boards, the various, of public offices, will be found under the head expressing the chief idea of the office: e.g., for Board of Aldermen, see Aldermen; for Board of Education, see Education, etc.

Bohemian Benevolent Association. — Composed of about 150 persons, who immigrated to this city from Bohemia, and who have united for mutual benefit. Its meetings are held every second Monday night at Arbeiter Halle.

Boman's is a name given to the former homestead of Gen. M. S. Wade. In its day it was one of the finest villas in Ohio; but it has since degenerated into a lunch, beer, and wine resort for persons driving along the roads in Avondale, Walnut Hills, and the surrounding country.

Bond Hill is a station on the Marietta and Cincinnati Railroad, about nine miles from Cincinnati. It was located in 1870, and has a population of about 600.

Bonds of Cincinnati are regarded by capitalists as securities as safe as those offered by the bonds of any American city. The first bond was issued in 1834; and since that time the city has never failed to promptly pay its bonds at maturity, and has never issued a renewal bond. The following statement shows the security offered by a Cincinnati bond: assessed valuation of real estate and personal property for the year ending June 30, 1882, about \$166,986,000; valuation of property owned by the city, \$35,887,000; amount of sinking-fund, Jan. 1, 1883, \$3,180,398; cash in bank Jan. 1, 1883, \$104,857; total, \$39,172,973; total bonded debt, Jan. 1, 1883, \$27,120,707; balance in favor of the city, \$12,052,266.

Books relating to Cincinnati. — The chief works are: Notices concerning Cincinnati, 1810, by Daniel Drake; Natural and Statistical View of Cincinnati, 1815, by Daniel Drake; Cincinnati in 1826, by Benjamin Drake and E. D. Mansfield; Tales and Sketches from the Queen City, 1838, by Benjamin Drake; Cincinnati in 1841, in 1851, and in 1859 (three volumes), by Charles Cist; The Queen City, 1869, by George E. Stevens; Suburbs of Cincinnati, 1870, by Sidney D. Maxwell; Illustrated Cincinnati, 1875, by Daniel J. Kenny; Cincinnati Illustrated, 1879, by Daniel J. Kenny. "Boston (Mass.) Daily Advertiser," July 28, 1879, published a four-column review of the city, by Moses King. The Encyclopædia Britannica and the American Encyclopædia have long reviews. (The above books and reviews can be seen at the rooms of the Historical and Philosophical Society.)

Bookstores. — The principal general bookstores are those of Robert Clarke & Co., 65 West Fourth Street; Peter G. Thomson, 179 Vine; George E. Stevens, 39 West Fourth; Methodist Book Concern, 190 West Fourth; J. R. Hawley, 164 Vine; Perry & Morton, 162 Vine; and Alfred Warren, 219 Central Avenue.

Bottoms, the. — That portion of the city, principally devoted to business, lying on the plateau between Third Street and the Ohio River, is now known as the "Bottom." What are known as Millcreek Bottoms lie west of McLean Avenue, and south of Cumminsville. Deer-creek Bottom, now occupied by Eggleston Avenue, is a thing of the past.

Boys' Protectory, situated at Delhi, eight miles west of the city, is in charge of the Brotherhood of St. Francis. It is a home for the education and maintenance of orphan and other destitute boys between the ages of five and seventeen years, who are taught the rudiments of an education, and a useful trade. There are about one hundred and twenty children in the institution. The city office is corner of Stone and Longworth Streets.

Bradstreet Company's Mercantile Agency have a branch office at 78 and 80 West Third Street, employing more than thirty clerks under the superintendence of Levi C. Goodale. Bradstreet's issues a "Book of Reports" quarterly, showing the names and standing of every firm and corporation in the United States and Canada, a daily sheet showing failures, dissolutions, judgments, etc., and written reports about any firm or corporation. Over nine thousand inquiries a month are answered at the Cincinnati office, which is one of the forty-four main offices scattered throughout North America.

Breweries. — However favorable to total-abstinence principles a writer may be, he cannot neglect to mention, in a description of Cincinnati, the breweries and distilleries; for they constitute two of the most important industries of the city. In regard to the breweries, it can be said that in the year ending January, 1881, there were twenty-three of them, having a total invested capital of $3,195,000, occupying real estate valued at $2,398,000, giving employment to about 900 persons, and manufacturing $4,740,000 worth of beer. The visitor, whether a total abstainer or not, should surely see some of the great breweries; for in no other way can he comprehend the magnitude of the business done.

Bridges. — Three immense structures span the Ohio River at Cincinnati, the most notable of which is the suspension bridge connecting Cincinnati with Covington. It is the largest single span of its class in the world. The Cincinnati approach begins at Front Street, midway between Walnut and Vine. Water Street is crossed at a height of 15 feet by a bridge of boiler-iron. On the south side of Water Street is the anchor pit; and 300 feet farther on, at the water's edge, is the tower, 230 feet high, over which the gigantic cables pass. The towers are higher, and each contains more stone, than the Bunker-hill Monument. The distance between this tower and the one on the Kentucky shore is 1,057 feet. The bridge is 36 feet wide, and contains two ways for pedestrians, two carriage-ways,

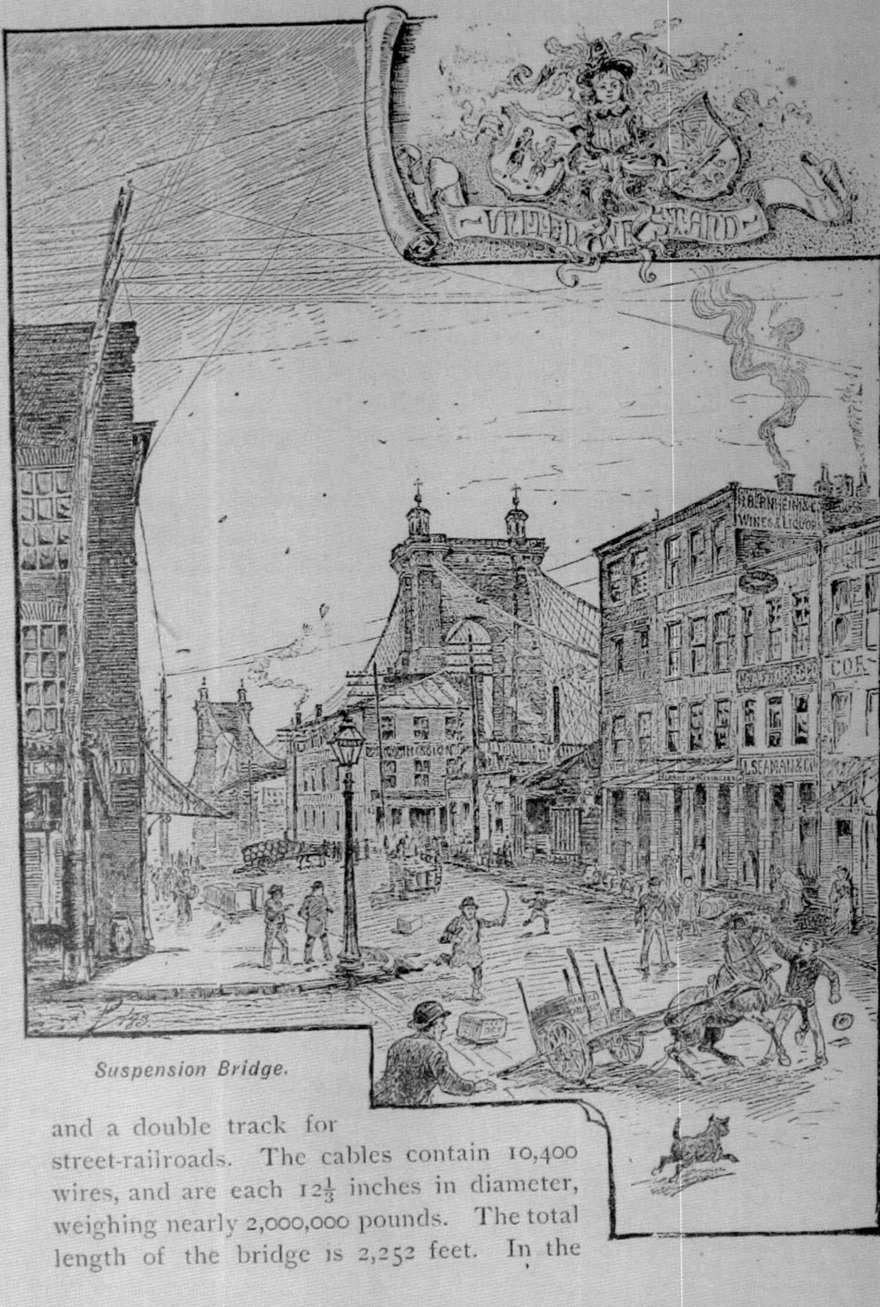

Suspension Bridge.

and a double track for street-railroads. The cables contain 10,400 wires, and are each $12\frac{1}{3}$ inches in diameter, weighing nearly 2,000,000 pounds. The total length of the bridge is 2,252 feet. In the centre it is 103 feet above low-water mark. It was opened to travel in 1867, and cost $1,800,000. The various lines of Covington and one line of Newport street-cars cross the bridge, which is five squares from the esplanade. Toll for foot-passengers, three cents. The bridge connecting Cincinnati with Newport, Ky., is a mile east of the suspension-bridge, and is 100 feet above low-water mark. The channel span is 405 feet in length. The structure is of wrought iron, and rests on 11 piers, and together with its approaches is 3,090 feet long. It was built for the Louisville Short-line Railroad, but contains also two ways for foot-passengers, and a double carriage-way, in which is a street-railroad track for one of the Newport lines of horse-cars. The Cincinnati Southern Railroad Bridge, connecting Cincinnati with Ludlow, Ky., is used exclusively for railway purposes. It is about a mile and a half west of the suspension-bridge. With its approaches, it is over a mile in length. It is of wrought iron, and has five piers in the water; the longest span being 510 feet, and the shortest 300 feet. It is 103 feet above low water.

Brighton is that portion of the city extending from the junction of Freeman Street with Central Avenue, west to Mill Creek. It was originally the site of the former stock-yards: hence its name. The Brighton House, a popular hotel with stock-raisers for many years, but now torn down, was at one time the favorite suburban resort. The encroachments of the city up the valley necessitated the removal of the stock-yards, and with their departure the greatness of the hotel vanished. Ernst Station, also called Brighton Station, is within the limits of Brighton. The horse-car stables of the John-street, Baymiller-street, and Seventh-street lines are located here.

Brotherhood of Locomotive Engineers, organized in 1855, has branches throughout the United States. The Cincinnati branch has about 100 members. It is a secret benevolent order, and since its organization has distributed over $1,000,000 in benefits to sick and disabled members and their families.

Bucktown, a name given to the district lying in the Deer-creek Bottom, east of Broadway. It was formerly wholly inhabited by negroes and the lowest and most depraved class of whites: hence its name. The march of factory improvement, the building of Eggleston Avenue, and filling-up of the old canal, have driven many of its old inhabitants to other sections; and Bucktown will probably, in a few years, exist only in name.

Builders' Exchange occupies rooms 55 West Fourth Street. It was organized in 1878, for "the collection and dissemination of statistics and information of value to any or all of the several trades engaged in the building business; the mutual improvement and advancement of all artisans and tradesmen in their several avocations connected with said business; the peaceable settlement of matters in dispute between contractors, sub-contractors, and employers; the advantages of a general place of meeting for the transaction of business; the establishment and enforcement of such lawful rules and methods of procedure as may be deemed for the best interests of the association and its various members; and to do any and all other things falling within the general scope of the business and procedures of such associations." The dues are $10 a year.

Building Associations, of which there are about 170, receive nearly $100,000 a week in instalments of 25 cents, 50 cents, and $1, on each share of stock. This money is loaned, at six per cent interest, secured by first mortgages or bonds, only to members. The interest is paid weekly, along with the instalments. It is decided to which members to loan the money by one of two systems, known as the "auction" and "drawing" systems. In the "auction," the one bidding the highest premium has the right of asking the first loan, the next-highest bidder the second loan, and so on. In the "drawing," it is decided by lot in what order the loans are to be made. As a rule, only $400 are loaned to the holder of one share of stock, and by law no person can borrow more than $8,000 from any one association. These building associations enable persons of small incomes to build homes, and also to derive a profit from their "deposits;" for when the societies close up, usually every six years, the profits are divided among the members, or "shareholders."

Burial-Places. — See Cemeteries.

Burnet Residence, on the north-west corner of Seventh and Elm Streets, is the old family mansion of the late Judge Jacob Burnet, who is famous among other things for having entertained in a most hospitable manner the distinguished visitors of his time. When the house was built, in 1824, it was the handsomest and most commodious family residence in the city; and the grounds comprised the whole square bounded by Seventh, Elm, Eighth, and Plum Streets. It is to-day one of those comfortable and roomy old-fashioned houses having a wide hall through the centre, and is occupied by a family keeping a few boarders. The grounds now comprise about one-fourth of the square.

Burnet House, on the north-west corner of Third and Vine Streets, has about 300 rooms in all, and accommodations for 600 guests The hotel is on the American plan, the terms being $3 and $4 a day. When built, in 1849, it was one of the grandest and most spacious hotels in the world. The building, including the terrace, fronts 212 feet on Third Street and 210 feet on Vine Street. It is six stories high, and has a dome 42 feet in diameter and 100 feet above the basement floor. In 1875 the whole interior was remodelled, and is now up to the standard required of first-class hotels. The perfect management, the desirable location, and the superior accommodations make it one of the most attractive hotels in the city. The Burnet has always enjoyed the patronage of the most noted personages; and among its guests have been James Buchanan, Abraham Lincoln, U S Grant, Rutherford B. Hayes, the Prince of Wales, Lord Lyons, the Duke of Newcastle, Louis Kossuth, Lewis Cass, John C. Breckenridge, Stephen A. Douglas, Salmon P. Chase, Horace Greeley, John Mitchell, Jefferson Davis, Gens. Sherman, Burnside, Sheridan, and Thomas, Edwin Forrest, Edwin Booth, John E. Owens, Jenny Lind, Ristori, Charlotte Cushman, Carlotta and Adelina Patti, Formes, Grisi, Wachtel, Nilsson, Cary, Roze, Gerster, Mary Anderson, and many others. The numerous daily arrivals show that the Burnet is still a favorite hotel with the best class of travellers. On the Third-street side is the commodious and excellent Burnet-house Restaurant, where about 500 business men are accustomed to take their dinners. The president is J. W. Dunklee, the secretary T. W. Zimmerman, and the treasurer O. G. Barnes.

Burnet-woods Park lies directly north of the city, and about two miles from Fountain Square, and contains 163½ acres, about one-third of which is improved. The purchase was made in 1873, and the improvements begun in 1875 There is a lake of about three acres, used in winter for skating, and in summer for boating. The improvements have cost $63,000. One of the wealthy citizens proposes to erect and stock, in the near future, a museum similar to the famous Kensington Museum in London; and one of the prominent knolls is suggested as the site. Free open-air concerts are given each week, the funds being provided by an endowment of $50,000 made by William S Groesbeck. *Horse-cars*,—Vine-street and Elm-street lines.

Butchers' Melting Association, organized as a joint-stock company by Cincinnati butchers in 1854, and buildings erected at the intersection of John and Findlay Streets, in the region then known as Texas. The association is now in few hands; and the surplus fat, which was formerly rendered into lard and tallow for the butchers, is at present bought by the association, and, after rendering, put on the market for sale. Association wagons collect all refuse fat, bones, and scraps from the numerous butcher-stalls throughout the city.

Caledonian Society, an association for the purpose of assisting destitute Scotchmen and their families residing in this country. It was instituted in 1832, and numbers among its members about forty prominent and wealthy Scots. It has a fund for the relief of members who may become needy. The officers are elected annually, and an annual banquet is held on St. Andrew's Day.

California, a suburb on the east side of the Little Miami River, fronting on the Ohio, is in Hamilton County, eight miles from Fountain Square. It is a manufacturing place to some extent, and the home of a number of Cincinnati business-men. Population about 600.

Camp Washington, now a portion of the twenty-fourth ward, lies between the site of the old Brighton House and Cumminsville, on both sides of the Colerain Pike. It received its name from having been the rendezvous of the First and Second Ohio Regiments at the beginning of the Mexican War in 1846, when it was a grove. It is now thickly settled, having a population of 3,000. The Workhouse and House of Refuge are here located. The Avenue horse-cars traverse its entire length.

Canals. — The Miami and Erie Canal, begun about 1820, and popularly termed the "Rhine," traverses the city in a south-easterly direction from Cumminsville to the Little Miami Railroad Depot, where it empties through an underground tunnel into the Ohio River. From Canal Street and Sycamore Street to the river, it has been converted into an immense sewer, known as Eggleston-avenue Sewer. Through the city proper it runs south from McMicken Avenue on Plum Street to Canal Street, which should properly be called Eleventh Street. A right angle is here made, and an easterly direction is taken to Sycamore Street, where the canal is lost in the sewer. The portion of the city north-east of this angle is settled by Germans, and is the district popularly known as "Over the Rhine."

The Whitewater Canal was abandoned sixteen years ago: and the rails of the Indianapolis, Cincinnati, and Lafayette Railroad now occupy its bed, and the Central Avenue freight-depot is on its basin.

Carthage, a suburban village about eight miles from Fountain Square, on the Cincinnati, Hamilton, and Dayton and the Dayton Short-line Railroads, contains many elegant private residences, and has a population of about 1,500 persons, most of whom do business in the city. It is approached by private conveyance by way of Spring-grove Avenue and the Carthage Pike. Longview Insane Asylum, the city and county infirmaries, and county fair-grounds are on the outskirts of the village; and the Colored Lunatic Asylum is within a short distance of it.

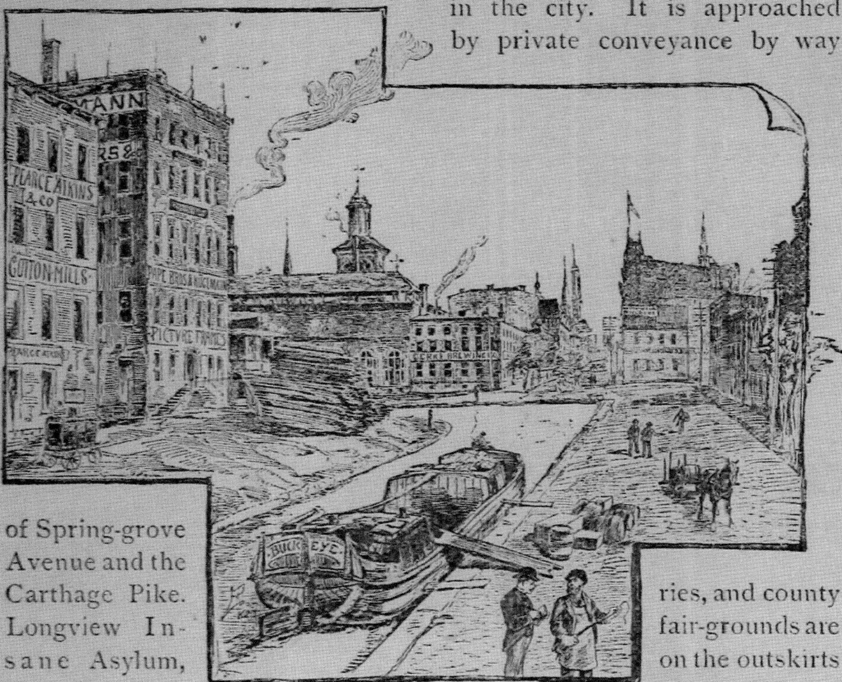

View of the Canal.

Carthage Pike.—Leaving Fountain Square, the traveller passes northward on Vine Street to Hammond Street, in Corryville, which is the beginning of the Carthage Pike proper. Continuing northward, he passes Burnet-woods Park, Clifton, the Zoölogical Gardens, through Mount St. Bernard, on to the junction with Spring-grove Avenue, a distance of five miles. Continuing, he passes Longview Asylum and the Colored Lunatic Asylum before Carthage is reached, a distance of eight miles. North of Carthage he passes the Hamilton-county Fair Grounds, the County Infirmary, through the beautiful suburb of Glendale, and on to Hamilton, in Butler County. It is a beautiful drive. The Vine-street Hill, which is over half a mile in length, can be avoided by taking Spring-grove Avenue to the junction.

Casino is a stone structure on the highest point of land in Eden Park. It is also called the Shelter House and Weather House. Its elevation is 420 feet above the level of the river; and a grand view of the park, the river, the city, Walnut Hills, Mount Auburn, and Avondale, can be had from its balconies. It is used as a place for rest and shelter in the park, and is supplied with chairs and cold water.

Cathedral. — See St. Peter's Cathedral.

Catholic Institute Building, on the north-west corner of Longworth and Vine Streets, is owned by David Sinton, and contains the Grand Opera House on the ground floor, and Mozart Hall in the third story, besides the rooms devoted to the purposes of the institute itself, which are the propagation of the dogmas of the Church of Rome.

Catholics. — This city is the arch-diocese of Cincinnati, comprising all that part of Ohio south of 40° 41′. The first bishop of this diocese was the Rt. Rev. Edward Fenwick, consecrated in 1822; after whom came the Most Rev. J. B. Purcell as bishop in 1833, and archbishop in 1850. In January, 1880, the Holy See appointed the Rt. Rev. William H. Elder coadjutor to Archbishop Purcell. It is claimed, that, of the population of Cincinnati, 100,000 are Catholics. They own 36 churches, besides a number of convents, five academies for girls, two colleges for young men, and about a dozen chapels. There are 31 parochial schools, attended by 15,000 children. For list of their churches and chapels, see Churches.

Catholic Religious Orders. — *Brothers of the Holy Cross* have charge of St. Joseph's College for boys, on Eighth Street, near Central Avenue. *Franciscan Friars* have their principal novitiate corner Vine and Liberty Streets. The brothers of this order have charge of the Boys' Protectory at Delhi. The Fathers have charge of St. Francis, St. John, St. George, and St. Bonaventure churches, and also of a preparatory school having sixty pupils. *Jesuit Fathers* have charge of St. Xavier's church and college. *Passionist Fathers*, an order of monks founded by St. Paul of the Cross, occupy the building on Mount Adams formerly used by the Cincinnati Observatory. *Sisters of Charity* conduct one of the largest and finest young-ladies' academies in this vicinity. It is situated at Cedar Grove, on the Warsaw Pike. They also serve as teachers in the parochial schools, and as nurses in the Good Samaritan and other hospitals, besides having charge of St. Joseph's Orphan Asylum at Cumminsville. Their principal novitiate is at Delhi. *Sisters of Mercy* have a convent on Fourth Street, between Central Avenue and John Street. It was established in 1858. These sisters visit the sick and destitute, the jails and hospitals, and provide a home and instruction for poor girls. *Sisters of Notre Dame* have their chief novitiate, or "mother-house," on Sixth Street, between Sycamore Street and Broadway. Besides conducting academies at the "mother-house," and at the corner Court and Mound Streets, they teach pupils of the parochial schools, and also manage the Mount Notre Dame Academy at Reading. *Sisters of the Good Shepherd* help unfortunate girls and children exposed to temptation. They have a refuge on Bank, between Baymiller and Freeman Streets, and a girls' protectory on Baum Street, between Fifth and Sixth Streets. *Sisters of the Poor of St. Francis*, corner Third and Lytle Streets, take care of the sick in St. Mary's and other hospitals. *Ladies of the Sacred Heart*, composed of highly educated ladies, give instruction to the children of the wealthy class. Recently they bought the handsome Neff place in Clifton, and in it conduct their school. *The Little Sisters of the Poor* have their novitiate on the Montgomery Road. Their special work is the care of destitute old people, and they act as Good Samaritans whenever opportunity offers.

Cemeteries. — *Calvary Catholic*, at East Walnut Hills, on the Madisonville Pike; has about 12 acres. *City*, at Lick Run, three miles from the city. *Colored American*, at Avondale. *Fulton*, at Columbia. *German Catholic*, on the Warsaw Pike, 21st ward; about 12 acres. *German Evangelical Protestant*, Baltimore Pike, 24th ward. *German Protestant*, corner of Park Avenue and Chestnut Street, Walnut Hills. *German Protestant*, Reading Pike, three miles and a half north-east of the city. *Jewish Cemetery*, at Clifton. *Judah Torah*, Reformed Jews, at Lick Run. *K. K. Adath Israel*, Polish Jews, at Lick Run. *K. K. Sherith* belongs to Jewish congregation on Lodge Street, and is situated at Lick Run. *Methodist Protestant*, two miles from the city, on the Avondale Road; about four acres; no further interments. *Odd Fellows*, in Spring-grove Cemetery. *St.*

Bernard's Catholic comprises new and old parts on the Carthage Road, about three miles from the city. *St. Joseph's Catholic* comprises new and old parts, — the old about three miles, and the new about five miles, from the city. Both are near the Warsaw Pike, in the 21st ward, and together include 99 acres. *St. Peter's Catholic*, at Lick Run, on the Harrison Turnpike, three miles north-west of the city. No further interments. *Spring Grove*. See Spring-grove Cemetery. *Union Baptist* (colored), on the Warsaw Turnpike, at Gazlay's Corner. Office, 314 West Court. *United Jewish Cemetery* at East Walnut Hills, at the corner Montgomery Pike and Duck-creek Road, comprises the "old" and "new" divisions, the new being well laid out in 377 family lots, and having room for 300 more; and the old being now reserved for the poor and members of the congregations having no lots. The old part was opened in 1849, and the new in 1860. The Eden-park and Walnut-hills horse-cars pass within a short distance. *Wesleyan*, at Cumminsville, on the Colerain Pike. Office, 190 West Fourth Street. The cemetery belongs to the Methodists, and although small is well improved. It was opened in 1843, contains 25 acres, and has about 25,000 interments. Many pioneer preachers and laymen of the Methodist-Episcopal Church are buried here. *Horse-cars*, — the Avenue line. There are also several burying-grounds within the city, most of the bodies from which have been removed, but some marked graves remain. The old Jewish Cemetery, at the corner of Chestnut Street and Central Avenue, is walled in with buildings on Central Avenue, and a high brick wall on Chestnut Street; in the rear of Wesley Chapel, Fifth Street, between Broadway and Sycamore, the first burying-ground in Cincinnati, are still some old graves; also on Court Street, between Wesley Avenue and Mound Street, — the old Catherine-street burying-ground, — a few graves, surrounded by an iron fence, remain.

Chamber of Commerce and Merchants' Exchange was organized to facilitate the settlement of disagreements between business-men. In 1839 its by-laws were adopted, and the organization perfected. From that time the association has held "a prominent place in the regard of business-men, and a place for the discussion of ali leading questions of mercantile usages, of matters of finance, of laws affecting commerce, and, more than all, contributing to the formation of an elevated tone in business intercourse. It became, indeed, a kind of high court in the adjustment of questions growing out of or affecting commercial transactions, which otherwise would have led to expensive and aggravating litigations." The Chamber of Commerce continues to hold its place as a highly respected deliberative body, and as a court of arbitration; but in 1846, by the appointment of a superintendent of the Exchange, it greatly enhanced its usefulness. The duty of the superintendent is not only to have charge of the rooms, but also to collect information relating to commerce, finances, and industries, that may be of general interest and value, and to keep a record of mercantile transactions, and prepare tables of imports and exports. In 1850 a charter was obtained for the association; and in 1866 sections 6, 7, 8, and 9 of a law enacted in that year by the Legislature of Ohio were adopted, and made part of the charter. There are honorary and active members; the former being elected for life, and exempt from assessments or dues, and only one being elected each year. In March, 1882, a radical change was made from the old corporation, and firm memberships were changed to individual memberships. The initiation fee was increased from $10 to $250, $500, and $1,000 respectively, at the successive periods named for the change; and members of the Chamber, at the time of the change, desiring certificates were permitted to receive them on the payment of $100 each. This was eminently successful, the revenues of the Chamber having so increased that the sum of $392,981 had been accumulated at the close of the quarter ending Feb. 28, 1883. The association has bought for $100,000 the site of the present post-office, but cannot get possession of it until the new post-office is completed. The rooms are in Pike's Building, West Fourth Street, and are open every day, Sundays and holidays excepted, from 9 A.M. till 6 P.M.; and the "Change" hours are from 11.30 A.M. till 1 P.M.

Charities, the, of the city, are too numerous to be described in this book. The most important may be found briefly sketched under their alphabetical headings; and they comprise the Cincinnati, the Good Samaritan, the St. Mary's, and the Jewish hospitals; the Ohio Medical, the Miami Medical, and the Homœopathic college dispensaries; the Home of the Friendless, the Widows' Home, the Old Men's Home, the Children's Home; the Boys' Protectory, the Relief Union, and the Union Bethel; the Cincinnati, the German Protestant, the Cumminsville, and the Colored orphan-asylums; the Longview and the Colored lunatic-asylums; the City and the County infirmaries;

the Women's Christian, the Young Men's Christian, and the Young Men's Hebrew associations. Cincinnati is one of the most liberal cities in the world in dispensing charities. Her citizens not only provide for her own destitute and afflicted, but contribute most generously to the relief of the outside suffering, and distribute her charities in both the United States and abroad.

Chester Driving-Park. — On Spring-grove Avenue, and five miles from Fountain Square, is one of the best-appointed half-mile race-courses in the country. The spring races are devoted to trotting, and the autumn races to running. The annual premiums offered average $30,000. The park is the property of an association, and is well sustained by a large number of contributing members. It is easily reached by Spring-grove and Clifton Avenues, the latter passing through the delightful suburb of Clifton. The Cincinnati, Hamilton, and Dayton, the Marietta and Cincinnati, and the Dayton Short-line Railroads, pass the gates on either side of the park. General admission during races, 50 cents; grand-stand and quarter-stretch privileges, $1. The Avenue horse-cars are run to the park.

Children's Home, 192 West Ninth, provides temporary and permanent homes for neglected and homeless children, and secures suitable and permanent homes for them with Christian people in the country. It is authorized to receive the legal care and control of children properly surrendered to it by parents, guardians, or the mayor; is supported by voluntary subscriptions and contributions; and publishes "The Children's Home Record" monthly. The building and grounds, which are models of neatness and taste, cost $140,000. The average number of inmates is 100.

Chimes. — The only chimes in the city are on the St. Peter's Cathedral, and consist of a set of thirteen bells donated in 1850 by Reuben R. Springer. They strike the quarter-hours with four strokes for each quarter, and play a tune every third hour. The Holy Trinity Church, on Fifth Street, between Smith and Mound, has a set of three bells; but they can scarcely be called chimes.

Christ Church, the oldest Episcopal society in Cincinnati, came into existence May 18, 1817, in the parlor of Dr. David Drake, on East Third Street. Two wardens and five vestrymen were then elected, among whom was William H. Harrison, afterwards president of the United States. At first the small congregation of 15 or 20 met in a room of a cotton-factory in Lodge Alley, close by the Tyler-

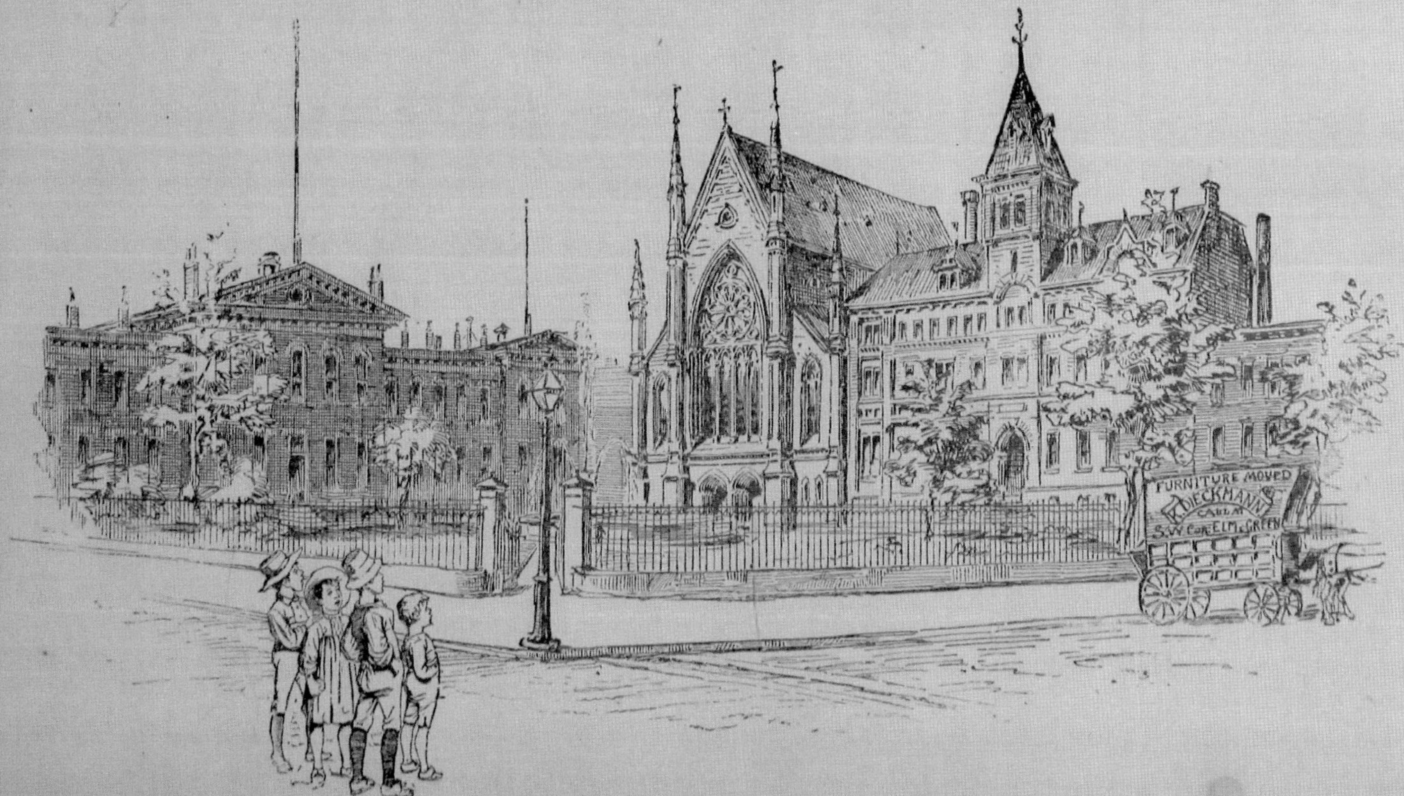

Children's Home.

Davidson Fountain. From there they moved to the corner of Fourth and Main Streets, and occupied a frame building belonging to the First Presbyterian Church. In 1818 they procured the use of a Baptist church on West Sixth Street, which afterwards was bought by the society. Christ Church was incorporated May 17, 1821, under the legal title of "The Episcopal Society of Christ Church, Cincinnati." In 1833 a lot on the north side of Fourth Street, between Sycamore aud Broadway, 100 feet front by 133 feet deep, was bought at $90 per front foot; and in June, 1835, services were held in the new edifice, which is the same the society now occupies. This church is indissolubly linked with much of the history of the Protestant-Episcopal Church in Ohio, and has always been the strongest of the strong families in the diocesan confederation. I. N. Stanger is the rector.

Church Region is a name given to the district in the vicinity of St. Peter's Cathedral, there being no less than ten churches within a radius of one square from the Cathedral.

Church of our Saviour, Protestant-Episcopal, is a pretty little stone church on Evans Street, near Auburn Street, Mount Auburn, which cost $12,000, and was first occupied in 1877. The rector is Dudley W. Rhodes. The following is a complete list of the churches of Cincinnati: —

BAPTIST.

Name.	Organized.	Location.	Clergyman.	Took Ch'ge.
First	1821	Court and Wesley Avenue . .	S. K. Leavitt .	1872
First German . .	1854	Walnut, near Liberty	L. H. Donner .	1878
Mount-Auburn .	1856	Mount Auburn	A. S. Hobart .	1879
Ninth-street . .	1830	S.S. Ninth, bet. Vine and Walnut,	S. W. Duncan .	1875
Third	1843	S.S. Hopkins, nr. Lincoln Park .	E. P. Roberts .	1879
Walnut-hills . .	1872	Kemper Lane, Walnut Hills . .	L. E. Wheeler .	1883
Columbia . . .	1865	Columbia Avenue	W. E. Stevens .	1876
Union (Colored) .	1835	Mound, bet. Ninth and Richm'nd,	Jos. Emery . .	1880
Avondale (Col'd) .	–	Avondale.		
Calvary (Colored),	–	179 West Third Street	Thos. Webb.	
First Cumminsville (Colored) . . .	1870	Cumminsville	P. F. Fossett.	1870
First Walnut-hills (Colored) . . .	–	Walnut Hills	A. F. Darnell.	
Mt.-Zion (Col'd) .	–	152 Cutter Street	Wm. Dortch.	
Shiloh (Colored) .	–	265 Plum Street.		
Willow-st. (Col'd),	–	Walnut Hills	D. Early.	
Zion (Colored). .	–	Ninth, bet. Central Ave. and John,	W. R. Boone.	

CONGREGATIONAL.

Name.	Organized.	Location.	Clergyman.	Took Ch'ge.
Columbia	1867	Columbia	D. F. Harris .	1876
First Orthodox .	1847	Seventh, near Central Avenue.		
Storrs	1872	Cor. River and Mt. Hope Roads.		
Vine-street . . .	1846	Vine, near Ninth	C. H. Daniels.	1878
Welsh	1840	W. S. Lawrence, near Third . .	David Jones.	

DISCIPLES OF CHRIST.

Name.	Organized.	Location.	Clergyman.	Took Ch'ge.
Central	1828	Ninth, near Central Avenue . .	E. T. Williams,	1881
Christian . . .	1871	Fergus Street, 25th Ward . . .	J. B. Crane . .	1882
Fourth	1842	313 Eastern Avenue.		
Richmond-street .	–	Cutter and Richmond	R.T. Matthews.	
Colored Christian .	1846	Harrison, near Broadway . . .	L. Wells . . .	1882

GERMAN EVANGELICAL PROTESTANT.

Name.	Organized.	Location.	Clergyman.	Took Ch'ge.
Camp Washington,	–	Camp Washington	J. A. Voss.	
Emanuel	1865	David, near Jones	J. Kronmueller.	1878
German Evangel'l,	–	Clark, near Freeman	Carl Rumpf.	
St. Peter's . . .	1832	Main and McMicken Avenue .	H. Pohlmeyer .	1867
St. Paul's . . .	1850	Race and Fifteenth	Edward Voss .	1879
St. Jacob's . . .	–	Ninth and Baymiller and Freeman Avenue	G. Kannmacher.	
St. John's . . .	–	Cor. Bellevue Ave. and Fosdick, Mount Auburn	J. Heckmann.	
St. John's (Prot.),	–	Cor. Twelfth and Elm	J. Carl Scholz.	
St. Lucas . . .	1865	Third, opposite Parsons . . .	P. G. Gerber .	1877
St. Martin's . .	–	River Road, 21st Ward . . .	Ernst Guntrum.	
St. Martin's (German Protestant),	–	Saffin Street, St. Petersburg . .	J. A. Voss.	
St. Matthias . .	1861	Cor. Elm and Liberty	Jacob Pister .	1881
Third Evangelical Protestant . .	–	Walnut and Ninth	Charles Truck.	

GERMAN EVANGELICAL UNION.

Name.	Organized.	Location.	Clergyman.	Took Ch'ge.
First Ger'n Evangelical Prot. . .	1854	Apple Street, 25th Ward . . .	Christ. Schenck,	1879
German United Evang'l (Zion) .	1844	Cor. Bremen and Fifteenth . .	Ch. Spathelf.	1880

GERMAN REFORMED.

Name.	Organized.	Location.	Clergyman.	Took Ch'ge.
First	1847	Cor. Elm and Fifteenth . . .	J. Bachmann .	1875
German Evangelical Ref. (Salem),	1857	Cor. Sycamore and Orchard . .	H. I. Stern . .	1882
German Evangelical Ref. (Hope),	–	1847 Eastern Avenue	Anton Seyring.	

HOLLANDISCHE REFORMED.

Name.	Organized.	Location.	Clergyman.	Took Ch'ge.
First	1881	Hughes, near Schiller.		

JEWISH SYNAGOGUES.

Name.	Organized.	Location.	Clergyman.	Took Ch'ge.
Children of Israel,	1819	Eighth and Mound	Raph. Benjamin,	
House of Prayer .	–	184 Longworth	Judah Kaletzky.	
Brotherly Love .	1867	John and Melancthon.		
Children of Jeshurum	1842	Plum and Eighth	Isaac M. Wise .	1854
Orthodox Jewish .	1863	342 Central Avenue	L. Uhlfelder .	1866
K.K. Adath Israel,	–	Walnut and Seventh	Henry Kuttner.	
Sherith Israel . .	1856	Lodge, bet. Sixth and Seventh .	Nathan Moses.	

LUTHERAN.

Name.	Organized.	Location.	Clergyman.	Took Ch'ge.
First	1842	Elm, bet. Ninth and Court . .	H.W.McKnight,	1880
German Evang'l .	–	Race, near Liberty	A. Brochmer.	

METHODIST.

Name.	Organized.	Location.	Clergyman.	Took Ch'ge.
Wesley Chapel . .	1805	Fifth Street, near Broadway . .	T. J. Harris .	1882
Trinity	1837	Ninth, bet. Race and Elm . . .	J. W. Bushong,	1880
St.-Paul	1834	Cor. Seventh and Smith . . .	Isaac W. Joyce,	1880
McKendree . . .	1835	East Front Street	J. S. Whitney .	1882
Asbury	1839	Webster Street	J. W. Gaddis .	1881
Christie	1845	Court, cor. Wesley Avenue . .	H. Tuckley . .	1880
Mount-Auburn .	1851	Auburn Avenue	J. A. Story . .	1881
York street . . .	1847	Cor. York and Baymiller . . .	F. G. Mitchell .	1881
St.-John's . . .	1852	Cor. Park and Longworth . . .	J. R. Shannon .	1883
Walnut-hills . .	1853	McMillan Street	I. H. Bayliss .	1882
Grace	1854	Avondale	J. P. Porter . .	1880
Pearl-street . . .	1845	East Pearl	Silas Bennett .	1881
McLean	1870	Ninth Street, near Freeman . .	W. P. Thirkield,	1881
Fairmount . . .	1870	Fairmount	G. T. Weaver .	1882
Pendleton . . .	1875	Pendleton Street	W. N. Williams,	1883
Columbia . . .	1876	Columbia	C. L. Conger .	1880
Mount-Lookout .	1878	Mount Lookout	Edw. T. Lane .	1882
Wright Chapel . .	1842	Colerain Turnpike, Cumminsville,	C. H. Haines .	1880
Price's hill . . .	1881	Price's Hill	T. M. Dart . .	1882
Camp-Washington, City Mission.	1876	Camp Washington	T. M. Dart .	1882
Finley	1851	Clinton Street	B. D. Hypes .	1882

GERMAN METHODIST.

Name.	Organized.	Location.	Clergyman.	Took Ch'ge.
Race-street . . .	1837	Race, near Thirteenth	John Pfetzing .	1883
Everett-street . .	1846	Everett, near Cutter	F. L. Nazler .	1881
Buckeye	1849	– – – –	L. Allinger . .	1882
Home Mission . .	1864	Spring-grove Avenue	J. Krehbiel . .	1880

METHODIST PROTESTANT.

Name.	Organized.	Location.	Clergyman.	Took Ch'ge.
Grace	–	George, near Linn	C. S. Evans.	

METHODIST (COLORED).

Name.	Organized.	Location.	Clergyman.	Took Ch'ge.
Allen Temple	–	Broadway and Sixth	J. G. Mitchell.	
Brown's Chapel	1862	Walnut Hills	M. R. Wilson	1882
Methodist Church,	–	Twenty-first Ward.		
Mount-Zion	–	Twenty-fifth Ward	Henry Harris.	
Union Chapel	–	Seventh, near Central Avenue	Henry Cardozo.	

PRESBYTERIAN.

Name.	Organized.	Location.	Clergyman.	Took Ch'ge.
First	1793	Fourth, near Main	F. C. Monfort	1881
Second	1816	Eighth and Elm	James Eells	1883
Third	1829	Seventh, near Baymiller	J. P. E. Kumler,	1875
Fourth	–	Orchard, near Main	R. H. Leonard,	1876
Fifth	1831	John and Clark	A. B. Morey	1871
Sixth	–	Eastern Avenue	John Rusk	1878
Seventh	–	Broadway, near Fifth	Jona. Edwards	1881
Mount-Auburn	1868	Mount Auburn	E. D. Ledyard	1874
Walnut-hills	1878	Gilbert Avenue and Seventh St	G. H. Fullerton,	1879
Avondale	1867	Rockdale Avenue, near Main	G. C. Heckman,	1879
Cumminsville	1855	Cumminsville	A. N. Thompson,	1882
Clifton	1882	Clifton	H. Billman	1882
Central	1844	Mound, near Seventh	W. Blackburn	1881
Poplar-street	1860	Poplar, near Freeman	Jas. C. White	1873
First German	1856	Linn, above Findlay	(Vacant.)	
Second German	1867	Liberty, west of Freeman	G. W. Winnes	1867
Welsh	–	College, bet. Sixth and Seventh	M. A. Ellis.	

PRESBYTERIAN UNITED.

Name.	Organized.	Location.	Clergyman.	Took Ch'ge.
First	1834	Sixth, bet. Race and Elm	W. H. French	1870

PRESBYTERIAN REFORMED.

Name.	Organized.	Location.	Clergyman.	Took Ch'ge.
First	1829	Plum, bet. Eighth and Ninth	A. G. Wylie	1882
Second	1840	Clinton, near John	J. M. Foster	1877

PROTESTANT EPISCOPAL.

Name.	Organized.	Location.	Clergyman.	Took Ch'ge.
Christ Church	1817	Fourth, bet. Sycamore and Broadway	I. N. Stanger	1876
Calvary	1854	Clifton	E. Rowland	1878
Chapel of the Nativity	1879	Grand Ave., 21st Ward.	W. B. Melish	1883
Church of the Advent	–	Walnut Hills	Peter Tinsley	1870
Church of the Atonement	–	Riverside	S. H. Boyer	1882
Church of the Redeemer	–	Elm, near Findlay.		
Church of the Resurrect'n	–	Fern Bank	Paul Sterling	1880
Church of our Saviour	1875	Mount Auburn	D. W. Rhodes	1876
Emanuel	–	Eastern Avenue, near Woodburn	J. M. Boyd	1882
Epiphany Mission	–	Walnut Hills	J. D. Stanley	1880
Grace	1867	Avondale	Alfred F. Blake,	1867
St. Matthew's Mission	–	Mount Lookout.		
St. Luke's	–	Findlay and Baymiller	Lewis Brown	1883
St. Philip	–	Twenty-fifth Ward	John Ely	1877
St. Paul's	1828	Seventh and Plum	S. Benedict	1877
Trinity Mission	–	Liberty, near Broadway,	J. M. Boyd	1882

ROMAN CATHOLIC

Name.	Organized.	Location.	Clergyman.	Took Ch'ge.
St.-Peter's	1839	Plum and Eighth	Wm. J. Halley.	1860
All-Saints'	1860	Third, near Collard	Wm. Daly	1880
Church of the Atonement	1873	Third, near John	D. V. Crowley,	1883
Church of the Blessed Sacrament	1874	Twenty-first Ward	F. X. Dutton	1882
Church of the Holy Angels,	1859	Torrence Road	Michael O'Neill,	1865
Church of the Immaculate	1862	Mount Adams	George Basel.	
Church of the Presentation,	1869	Walnut Hills	J. J. Kennedy	1873
Church of the Sac'd Heart,	1869	Bank and Baymiller	Henry Koering.	1865
Holy Trinity (German)	1853	Fifth, near Mound	J. C. Albrinck	1872
Mary of Perpetual Help	1878	Sedamsville	F. X. Wayman,	1882
Our Lady of Victories	1853	Delhi	G. Broering	1881
Passionists' Novitiate	–	Observatory Hill.		
Sacred Heart of Jesus	1873	Camp Washington	Henry Paul	1874
St. Aloysius	1867	Bridgetown	M. Muething	1876
St. Andrew's	1875	Avondale	D. O'Mara	1877
St. Ann's (Colored)	1873	New, east of Broadway,	J. Rumle, S.J.	1882
St. Anthony's (German)	1863	Budd, near Carr	August Meyer	1881
St. Augustine (German)	1854	Bank, near Freeman	A. H. Walburg,	1877
St. Clement's	1839	Taylor Creek	Amb. Sonning	1882
St. Bonaventura	1869	Fairmount	A. Lingmann	1881
St. Boniface	1863	Lakeman Street	B.G.Topmoeller	1866
St. Charles Borromeo	1869	Carthage	St. Franciscan Fathers	1881
St. Edward	1863	Clark, near Mound	R. F. Doyle	1874
St. Xavier	–	Sycamore, near Sixth	Chas. Driscoll	1849
St. Francis de Sales	1879	Woodburn Avenue	Chas. Schmidt	1879
St Francis (Ger)	1859	Liberty and Vine	M. Schaefer	1880
St Gabriel	1859	Glendale	Jas. O'Donnell,	1871
St. George	–	Corryville	Paul Alf.	

ROMAN CATHOLIC, — *Continued.*

Name.	Organized.	Location.	Clergyman.	Took Ch'ge.
St. Henry	1873	Flint Street	J. Schuchardt .	1882
St. James	1849	Mount Airy	J. Schoënfeldt .	1875
St. John's (German). . .	1845	Bremen and Green . .	Otto Jair . .	1855
St. John's	1860	Dry Ridge	Julius Voit . .	1873
St. Joseph (German) . .	1848	Linn and Laurel . . .	E. Stehle . .	1858
St. Ludwig (German) . .	1870	Eighth and Walnut . .	Paul Leopold .	1876
St. Mary's (German) . .	–	Clay and Thirteenth . .	B. Roesener .	1882
St. Patrick's	1874	Twenty-fifth Ward . .	P. B. Mazuret .	1882
St. Patrick's	1850	Third and Mill . . .	J. M. Mackey .	1870
St. Paul's (German) . . .	1850	Spring and Abigail . .	H. Firneding .	1871
St. Vincent de Paul . . .	–	Sedamsville	Jos. Benning.	
St. Philomena (German) .	1848	Pearl, near Pike . . .	H. Kemper . .	1876
St. Rosa (German) . . .	1869	Eastern Avenue and Lumber	B. H. Englers .	1880
St. Stanislaus	–	Cutter and Liberty . .	J. Dickhaus .	1882
St. Lawrence	1870	Twenty-first Ward . .	J. Schoënhoeft .	1883
St. Michael's	1850	Twenty-first Ward . .	M. Desalears .	1874
St. Stephen's	1867	Columbia	Jos. A. Myers .	1880

UNITED BRETHREN IN CHRIST.

Name.	Organized.	Location.	Clergyman.	Took Ch'ge.
Second Church	1864	729 Eastern Avenue . .	Gottlieb Fritz .	1882
German United Brethren .	1845	Clinton and Baymiller .	Jacob Ernst . .	1882
United Brethren in Christ .	–	124 Betts.		

UNIVERSALIST.

Name.	Organized.	Location.	Clergyman.	Took Ch'ge.
First Church	1836	Plum, bet. Fourth and Fifth	W. H. Ryder .	1882

MISCELLANEOUS

Name.	Organized.	Location.	Clergyman.	Took Ch'ge.
Unitarian Church . . .	1830	Eighth and Plum.		
Union Bethel	–	31 Public Landing . .	Thomas Lee.	
Berean Brethren in Christ .	–	195 West Fifth	J. E. Morris.	
Swedenborgian Church of New Jerusalem	1818	Fourth and John . . .	John Goddard .	1865

Cincinnati College was established in 1819; and a Lancaster school, organized in 1815, was merged into it. About $40,000 had been subscribed for the foundation of a college and the erection of a college building; but, by reason of bank troubles, much of that subscription was never paid. Although part of the building was completed, and the college opened, yet in 1826 instruction was suspended for want of funds. It was re-opened in 1836, and continued for two years, when it was again closed, and remained so until 1841. The building was burned in 1845, and shortly afterwards rebuilt, largely by aid of the Young Men's Mercantile Library Association, which, in consideration of its aid, holds a perpetual grant of its rooms on the second floor of the building. In 1869, after the building was again damaged by fire, it was remodelled into its present shape. The college holds a very liberal charter, containing a restriction only against the teaching of denominational theology. The government is vested in a board of trustees elected yearly by the shareholders. The capital is $125,000, in shares of $25 each, for which certificates were issued; but, as the stock was of merely nominal value, it is now difficult to learn who are the stockholders. The value of the property is about $200,000. The income is about $10,000, and is used chiefly to support the Cincinnati Law School and its library. The building is popularly known as the College Building, and is described elsewhere. The president is William Howard Neff, and the secretary A. H. McGuffey.

Cincinnati Gymnasium is one of the largest and best-equipped in this country, and for many years there were none to compare with it. The main hall is 120 by 45 feet, and 35 feet high. There are reading and chess rooms, health-lifts, 17 hot and cold water baths, etc. The society, which was organized in 1853, has 1,000 members, each paying $10 a year. The president is M. F. Wilson, and the superintendent Ed. W. Murphy. The rooms are at 102 West Fourth Street, and are open from six A.M. to ten P.M. daily, except Sundays. Visitors admitted.

Cincinnati Hospital, the, is one of the largest, most convenient, attractive, and best-managed hospitals in the country. The building and grounds occupy two entire squares, extending from Twelfth to Ann Streets, between Plum Street and Central Avenue. There are eight buildings, three stories in height, entirely separate from each other, yet connected by open passage-ways and through the basement. The buildings are arranged on each side of the square, leaving in the centre a large court-yard having an elegant lawn and flower-garden with fountain and grotto. The hospital contains 500 beds. It is a city charitable institution, but pay-patients are received in separate rooms. The staff is composed of sixteen physicians and seven undergraduate internes. The latter are given these positions after a competitive examination. In the large amphitheatre, capable of seating 400 persons, daily clinical lectures from September to March are given, which all medical students are allowed to attend on payment of five dollars per session. There is a fine medical library of 4,000 volumes connected with the hospital, open to the medical profession free of charge. Strangers and friends of pay-patients admitted at any time, and friends of charity-patients on Thursdays.

Cincinnati Insurance Company of Cincinnati held its semi-centennial anniversary in April, 1879, and is to-day the oldest joint-stock general fire and marine insurance company organized west of the Allegheny Mountains. At the semi-centennial the late Robert Buchanan, who had been one of the first directors, was present; and in the office of the company, No. 81 West Third Street, hangs an original copy of the Cincinnati "Commercial Daily Advertiser," containing the official announcement that the requisite amount of stock had been subscribed, and therefore the company was ready for business. The Cincinnati Insurance Company has had a remarkable career of prosperity. For fifty years its dividends averaged thirteen per cent; in some years reaching thirty-two per cent. The president, Jacob Burnet, jun., has held the office for the past twelve years; the secretary is Charles A. Farnham.

Carpets.—The John Shillito Company's carpet department occupies the third floor of building, and is reached by elevator. It covers more space, is better arranged and better lighted, than any carpet room in America. Visitors will find exhibited all the newest designs in floor-coverings of all grades, from the finest Turkish rugs of great value, to the low-priced mattings of China. The patterns are the latest and most elegant that taste and ingenuity have been able to devise, the colorings rich and durable, and the brands the best in the market. Buyers should not fail to examine their stock, and compare their prices, before making selections. They will find in every instance a larger variety, better styles, and *lower prices*, than can be found elsewhere.

Cincinnati University.—See University of Cincinnati.

Cisterns and Fire-Plugs.—Two hundred and eighty-nine public cisterns, each having a capacity of 500 barrels, are scattered throughout the city. They offer an advantage of supplying water as fast as the steam fire-engines can use it, and also of providing a supply wholly independent of the water-works. There are 753 fire-plugs for the engines; and the water-pressure on some is so great that water, without the aid of an engine, can be thrown 150 feet high.

Citizens' Insurance Company of Cincinnati was chartered in 1851, under the name of the Clermont-county Fire, Marine, and Life Insurance Company, and was re-organized in 1858 under the present name. Its aggregate premium receipts exceed $900,000, out of which over $450,000 have been paid for losses. Prior to 1875 the company declared dividends out of its net earnings to the amount of $71,731, which was credited on the unpaid capital stock. Since 1875 the cash dividends will average over eleven and two-thirds per cent a year. The cash capital is now $100,000, and the gross assets $126,734.50. The president is Lewis Glenn, elected in 1875; and the secretary is John B. Abernethy, elected in 1867. The office is at No. 79 West Third Street.

City Building, so called, contains all the offices of the city government, with the exception of that of the fire-commissioners. It is located in the centre of the square bounded by Eighth, Ninth, and Plum Streets, and Central Avenue. The Council Chamber occupies the central portion of the second story. The police-court room is on the first floor, at the north end. The north basement is used as a station-house, or place of temporary confinement, and the south basement as a repair-shop for the fire and water-works department. The building is six squares north-west of Fountain Square.

City-Building Park is a small plat of ground, improved, and ornamented with a neat fountain, situated in front of the City Building.

City Infirmary is an institution in which the city's aged and infirm paupers are cared for. The buildings, which are extensive and commodious, are on the Infirmary farm, a quarter-section of land belonging to the city, west of the Carthage Pike, and in the vicinity of Carthage, about eight miles from Fountain Square. The Infirmary is under control of the board of police-commissioners, and is separate and distinct from the County Infirmary, which is in the same neighborhood. The farm is operated by the inmates, and produces a portion of the provisions used by them. The inmates also make most of their own clothing. The net cost of maintaining the Infirmary is about $35,000 a year. There are now about 565 inmates. The nearest railroad-station is Hartwell; which can be reached by the Cincinnati, Hamilton, and Dayton, and Dayton Short-line roads.

City Officers. — The names of the city officers now holding office, who were elected by the people at the general city elections, are: Mayor, Thomas J. Stephens; city solicitor, James M. Dawson; city treasurer, George L. Herancourt; police-judge, A. R. Von Martels; clerk police-court, George E. Richards; prosecuting attorney police-court, John A. Caldwell. All the other city officers are appointees, either by the governor of Ohio, the courts, or the mayor. The several boards appoint their own subordinate officers.

City Physicians. — Of these there are 25, each physician supplying a district corresponding with the number of the wards. Their duty is to visit the sick who are unable to employ a physician or pay for medicine. The latter is furnished by a druggist in each ward, appointed by the health-department, at contract rates, on the prescription of the district physicians. The physicians receive for their services $20 per month each. The number of indigent sick treated will average 8,000 yearly, and the number of visits made yearly will aggregate 50,000. The city physicians are also detailed for quarantine service when necessary, for which they receive extra pay.

Clearing-House Association, the Cincinnati, organized in 1866, to relieve the banks of the necessity of sending messengers from one bank to another to collect and pay drafts and checks. Nowadays 19 banks and bankers send their "messengers" and "settling-clerks" at two o'clock P.M. to the third story of the building No. 70 West Third Street, and there in a few minutes, without danger of loss, transact the whole business that would otherwise require several hours and considerable risk. After the clerks hand to the manager the amounts due them by other banks, he settles with them by his checks on "debit banks," as those are called which have brought in a less amount of checks against other banks than were brought in against them. The clearings will average about $2,000,000 a day, and the balances about $200,000. The initiation-fee is $50, and the dues $20 a year. Any deficit for expenses is made by a *pro-rata* assessment on the amount of clearings for the year. James Espy is president, and Morris M. White vice-president. George P. Bassett, the manager, has held the same position ever since the clearing-house was organized.

Clifton, north of Cincinnati and the Burnet-woods Park, a most beautiful suburb, and an almost continuous landscape garden, was incorporated as a town in the year 1849. It derived its name from the Clifton Farm, comprises about 1,200 acres of land beautifully diversified with hill and dale, and has a population somewhat exceeding 1,000 persons. In its precincts there is neither shop, factory, nor saloon. It has over 17 miles of avenues, lined with fine shade-trees, 2,000 of which were planted in the years 1877 and 1878; and this planting is to be continued from year to year. The Town Hall is a handsome brick structure, surmounted by a tower with clock. This building contains the public offices and the schoolroom. The school, though a public one, is known as the Resor Academy, and was established originally through the enterprise of the late William Resor, one of the earliest residents of Clifton, and always identified with its interests. The main hall of the building is elegantly frescoed in the Pompeian style, and hung with choice photographs from works of the old masters and the modern painters, the gift of Henry Probasco. The Ladies of the Sacred Heart have also a school for girls in a large stone mansion, with spacious and beautiful grounds, purchased at a cost of $160,000. Among the noted residences may be mentioned those of George K. Shoenberger, Henry Probasco, R. B. Bowler, Richard Smith, E. J. Miller, O. J. Wilson, George W. McAlpin, Thomas Sherlock, Isaac Jordan, Theo. Cook, I. B. Resor, and Mrs. William Resor. The latter's grounds are probably the best known in Clifton, being in a high state of cultivation, and containing greenhouses filled with rare tropical plants and a collection of curious orchids. The residence of Mr. Probasco is a grand structure of blue limestone in the Anglo-Norman style. The interior is in unison with the exterior, and is filled with many of the choicest paintings, statuary, rare volumes, illuminated manuscripts, and other art and literary treasures. The owner is noted for his hospitality, and all travellers who visit Clifton find a welcome at his mansion. It is to Mr. Probasco that Cincinnati is indebted for the Tyler-Davidson Fountain, noticed in its proper place. Numerous handsome cottages, with attractive grounds, are scattered throughout the town, among them those of Mrs. James Bugher and A. W. Whelpley. Calvary Episcopal Church is the only edifice for public worship. It is a neatly designed stone building, having a memorial tower. The outside is covered with ivy, and presents a beautiful picture. The interior is well furnished, and handsomely frescoed, and decorated with Scripture mottoes. All persons have the privilege of quietly driving through the private grounds. The most direct route for vehicles is through Vine Street, Clifton Avenue, and Burnet-woods Park. Persons wishing to walk through Clifton can reach it by the Vine-street or Elm-street line of horse-cars connecting with the Cincinnati and Clifton Inclined Plane and the horse-cars. Ask for ticket to Clifton; fare, 10 cents. The Dayton Short-line and Marietta and Cincinnati Railroads pass the northern boundary of Clifton.

Climate. — The climate of the city and surrounding country is similar to that of other localities of the same latitude and altitude in the Mississippi Valley. Meteorological data for the year 1882 are given later in this book. The thermometer within the past six years has been as high as 103 degrees above (July, 1874), and as low as 10 degrees below zero (January, 1879). There has been little variation in general temperature and rainfall during the last decade. The prevailing winds are from the south-west. The north-west wind is short-lived, the forerunner of storms in summer, and the cause of cold in winter. The east and north-east winds have less moisture and more elasticity than similar winds east of the Alleghany Mountains.

Colerain Pike. — A continuation of Central Avenue. At the junction of Central Avenue with Denman Street, the site of the old Brighton House, it takes a northerly direction, passing through Camp Washington, by the Workhouse and House of Refuge, through Cumminsville and Mount Pleasant, on to Colerain township, from which it received its name. Continuing, it passes through Venice and Oxford, in Butler County, where it is known as the Cincinnati Pike. The road is well macadamized.

Coliseum, the. — A variety theatre, situated on the west side of Vine Street, between Twelfth and Thirteenth Streets, in what was formerly known as Loewen Garden. The building, which is of frame, running back to Bremen Street, is one of the "Over-the-Rhine" theatres, where beer and cigars are the chief support of the enterprise. Prices of admission range from 10 to 25 cents. Seating capacity about 1,000. The Vine-street line of horse-cars passes the door. The main entrance is on Vine Street.

College Building, situated on the east side of Walnut Street, between Fourth and Fifth, is owned by the Cincinnati College. It contains a public hall known as College Hall, used for lectures and public meetings of all kinds; and also the rooms of the Young

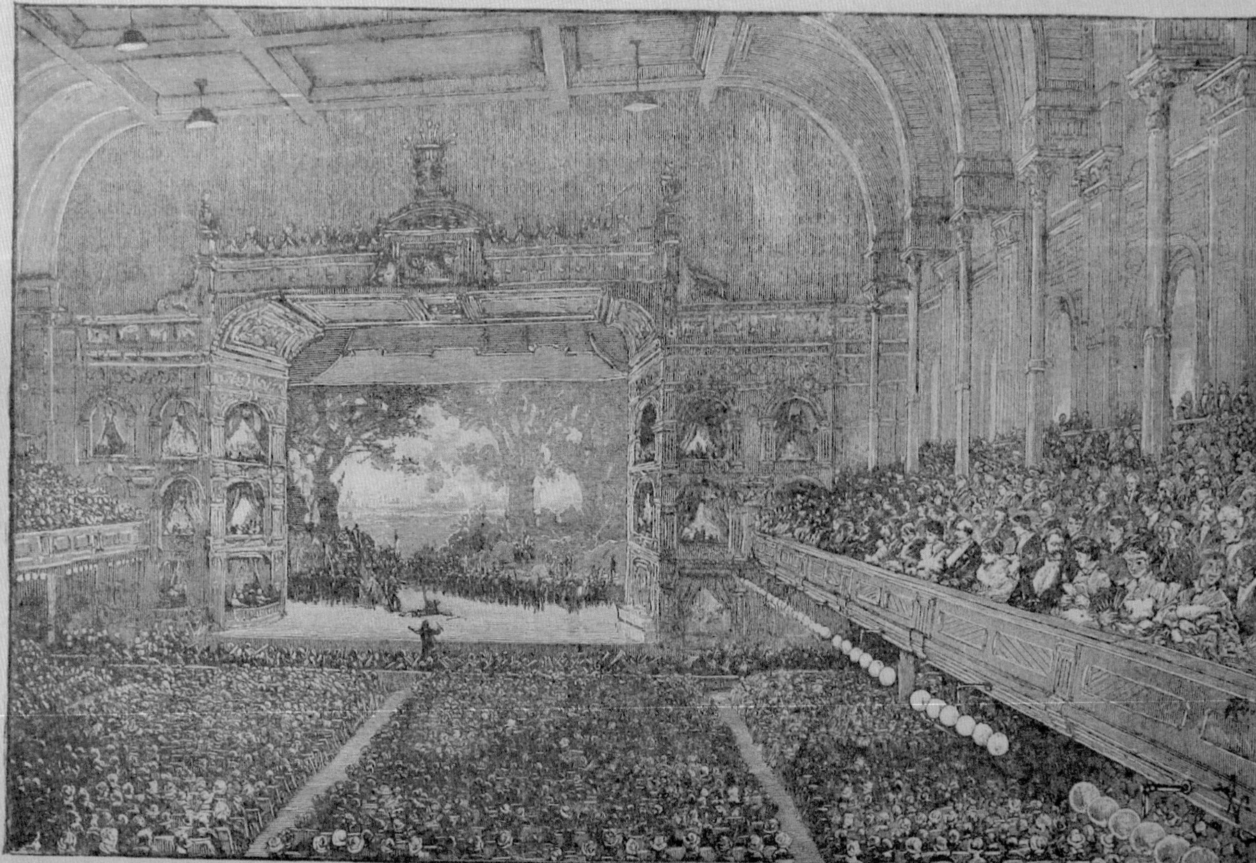

Interior of Music Hall during Opera Festival.

Men's Mercantile Library, of the Cincinnati Law School, of the Historical and Philosophical Society, of the School of Design, besides offices, stores, and private schools.

College Hill, one of the most attractive suburbs of Cincinnati, is inhabited mostly by business-men of the wealthier class. Farmers' College, and also the Sanitarium, are located here. The distance from Fountain Square is about eight miles. By private conveyance it is reached by the Avenue or Colerain Pike to Cumminsville, thence by the College-hill Pike, a beautiful road. A narrow-gauge railroad connects College Hill with the Cincinnati, Hamilton, and Dayton Railroad at Winton Place, adjoining Spring-grove Cemetery. Railway passengers can get on the cars at the Cincinnati, Hamilton, and Dayton Depot, corner of Fifth and Hoadly Streets, at Ernst Station, and at Cumminsville.

College of Medicine and Surgery, the Cincinnati, on the north side of George Street, between John and Smith Streets, is a college of the regular school of medicine. Has two sessions a year, winter and spring. The winter session begins in October, continuing until March; the spring session opening in March, and closing in May. Fees for the course of lectures, $75; matriculation, $5; demonstrators' and hospital ticket, $10; graduation, $25. R. C. Stockton Reed is dean of the faculty.

College of Music of Cincinnati, the. — The College of Music of Cincinnati was incorporated in 1878, with a capital of $50,000. Its originators were among the most important men in the city; and although its stock, like other corporations, permitted the payment of dividends, yet none were ever declared, while the college always stood in the position of a public institution, and was conducted, not for profit, but upon artistic and eleemosynary grounds. At the beginning of the present year a radical change was made in the organization of the college, by reason of a liberal endowment from Mr. Reuben R. Springer. The college grew, in the course of four years, to such proportions that it became necessary to enlarge its quarters for the giving of lessons. A large building adjoining and connecting with the great Music Hall was built, and presented to the college, by Mr. Springer. This gentleman also endowed the college with a gift of some $80,000, and all the stockholders released their right to all but one share of the stock and their right to dividends. This made the college, in a legal sense, an eleemosynary institution,

Steamboats and Hotels.

We are especially well prepared to furnish Hotels and Steamboats with CARPETS, FURNITURE, BEDDING, MATTRESSES, BED-LINEN, TOWELS, TABLE-LINEN, NAPKINS, and all the necessaries for the proper and complete equipment of first-class Hotels or Boats at the lowest prices and with despatch.

Linens with the name of the hotel or boat woven in the goods, a specialty.

The John Shillito Company.

exempt from taxation, and obliged to devote all its resources to musical education. The property of the college is now valued at some $150,000, and it unquestionably stands upon a firm financial footing. It is the object of the College of Music to educate the student upon a well-regulated and scientific plan of instruction. This plan includes instrumental and vocal instruction, with that for theory and musical composition, and direction of chorus and orchestra. Its scheme of instruction is broader probably than that of any other school in the world. It embraces not only vocal studies, but special branches, such as the piano, organ, violin, and other orchestral instruments, with the theory of music. There is also the department of languages, which includes Italian, German, and French, a school for the opera, dramatic training, and elocution. Besides this complete advanced field of technical musical instruction, the College of Music gives weekly concerts, and every year produces the Opera Festivals, which have been the wonder and delight of the musical world. The present board of directors consists of fifteen of the representative men of Cincinnati. This board of officers are George Ward Nichols, president, who was the originator and organizer of the college, and who, from the beginning, has been its presiding officer; Gen. A. T. Goshorn, its vice-president; Peter Rudolph Neff, treasurer; William McAlpin, secretary.

College of Pharmacy, the Cincinnati.—South-west corner Fifth and John Streets. Organized 1870, and one of the ten recognized colleges of pharmacy in the United States. The annual course of instruction consists of six lectures a week, from the first Wednesday in October to the second Wednesday in March. There is also laboratory instruction three afternoons each week during same period. Fees, matriculation, $5; professors' tickets, $30; and graduation, $10.

Colored Orphan Asylum provides an asylum for the protection, care, and education of destitute colored orphan children. The society was incorporated in 1845, and occupied an old house on Ninth Street for twenty years, until it bought four acres of land in Avondale, back of "Boman's," where the asylum still remains. Besides orphans, the society takes care, for a small consideration, of children who cannot be kept at home by their parents. When the children become sufficiently strong, they are apprenticed to responsible parties until they come to their majority. There are at present thirty-one inmates of the asylum, but the number at times is much greater.

Columbia, a village recently annexed to Cincinnati, and forming a part of the First Ward, is the extreme eastern limit of the city, and is at the mouth of the Little Miami River. The pioneer settlers of Cincinnati made their first settlement there, in 1788. It is easiest reached by the Little Miami Railroad, but is connected with the Elm-street horse-cars at Sportsman's Hall by a dummy track. Distance from the Esplanade, five miles.

Commerce. — Cincinnati has from an early period occupied an important position as one of the great commercial cities of the interior. For the year ending Sept. 1, 1881, the approximate value of all receipts was $274,651,218, and of all shipments was $271,973,776; showing an increase over 1879 in receipts of over $50,000,000, and in shipments of over $85,000,000.

Commercial Insurance Company of Cincinnati is one of the oldest and most successful of the local insurance companies. It was organized in 1838, with a capital of $100,000. The gross assets are $236,583, making the surplus greater than the capital itself. The dividends paid will average more than thirteen per cent. The president, J. A. Townley, has been connected with this company for nearly twenty-five years, first as secretary, and since 1875 as president; succeeding M. L. Harbeson, who resigned his position after a service of seventeen years. J. Wilson Johnston has been secretary since 1875. Office, 67 West Third Street.

Common Council, the. — The legislative branch of the city government is composed of a board of aldermen and a board of councilmen. It is presided over by the president of the board of aldermen, and in his absence by the president of the board of councilmen. It has no regular time of meeting, but can be convened any time by call of three aldermen and five councilmen. The principal work of the common council or joint session of the boards is the confirmation of appointments made by the mayor, and the approval of official bonds of city officers. Its meetings are held in the Council Chamber, City Buildings.

Congregationalists. — Seventh-street Church, founded in 1847, Seventh Street between Plum Street and Central Avenue. It was formed by thirty-seven persons, who in 1843 were at their own request dismissed from the Second Presbyterian Church, and organized as the George-street Presbyterian Church. In 1845 it entered the basement of its present edifice, and then took the name of the Seventh-street Presbyterian Church. The corner-stone was laid July 16, 1845, by Rev. Lyman Beecher, D.D.; and the church was dedicated May 10, 1849, and has ever since been occupied by the same congregation. In 1846 action was first taken on the changing of the church discipline; and in the following year a re-organization, under the name of the First Orthodox Congregational Church, took place; but later the name was changed to the Seventh-street Congregational Church. For further information, see Churches.

Consuls of Foreign Countries. — Belgium, P. H. Hartmann, 53 West Second Street; Denmark, P. H. Hartmann, 53 West Second; France, Virgil Gilmore, 110 West Fourth; German Empire, Dr. Ottmar von Mohl (consul for the States of Ohio, Indiana, Kentucky, and West Virginia; secretary, G. G. Wolfram), 260 Vine; Great Britain, R. Knight, 5 West Third; Italy, Dr. R. W. Saunders, north-west corner Fourth and Elm; Netherlands, P. H. Hartmann, 53 West Second; Norway, P. H. Hartmann, 53 West Second; Sweden, P. H. Hartmann, 53 West Second; Switzerland, Jaques Ritchie, 65 East Pearl.

Control, Board of. — The duties of this board are to supervise the work of the county commissioners. It is composed of five members elected by the people. They serve without compensation. The present members are: Max Mosler, president; Theophilus Wilson, Gazzam Gano, George Thompson, Maurice Bauer.

Corryville. — That portion of the 12th ward from the top of Vine-street Hill to the Zoölogical Gardens, between Mount Auburn and Burnet-woods Park.

Cotton is one of the staple articles for which Cincinnati is rapidly becoming a great market. The value of the cotton-crop of the United States is nearly $250,000,000, of which this city receives about $12,000,000; and a good portion of the latter sum is expended here for merchandise of all kinds. There is no doubt that the receipts at this market have very greatly increased since the Southern Railroad was completed. Cincinnati is on the line dividing the North and South, and is conveniently situated between the producers and the consumers. Moreover, the banks have the capital, and desire to encourage this trade; and the Cincinnati people, realizing its great importance, do every thing possible to satisfy both shippers and buyers. The aggregate receipts for the year ending Sept. 1, 1881, were about 325,371 bales; an increase over the preceding year of

Upholstery Department.

ALL KINDS OF GOODS FOR

Furniture Coverings, Lambrequins, Curtains, etc.,

ARE TO BE FOUND IN LARGE VARIETY, INCLUDING

Turcomans, Raw Silks, Terries, Cotolines,
Spun Silks, Satin Damasks, Plain Satins,
Silk Brocatelles, Silk and Mohair Plushes.

And all the richest and most elegant novelties in Silk and Silk-and-Wool Draperies.

Upholstery Cretonnes,

In the choicest English and French designs.

Furniture and Drapery Trimmings,

INCLUDING
Fringes, Gimps, Cord, Loops, Borderings, Tassels, Pendants, and Upholstery Hardware.

Lace Curtains.

A large stock of elegant patterns constantly on hand in all qualities and lengths.

Materials for Loose Covers.

Jacquards, Fancy and Plain Linens, Linen Damasks, etc.

Window Shades

For private dwellings and stores receive our special attention.

ALL KINDS OF LETTERING DONE, AND ANY COLOR DESIRED CAN BE FURNISHED.

The John Shillito Company.

nearly 76,000 bales. The most prominent house in the cotton-trade is J. H. Goodhart & Co., established in 1860, whose office and large warehouse is at Nos. 65 and 67 West Front Street.

Cotton Exchange, the Cincinnati, was established in 1871, to further the interests of the cotton-trade, to establish uniform rules and usages, to adjust controversies between buyers and sellers, and to secure co-operation in all measures thought advantageous to the cotton-trade. The room occupied is one of the Chamber of Commerce rooms; all members of the Cotton Exchange being also members of the Chamber of Commerce. The dues are $5 a year, in addition to the dues of the Chamber of Commerce. The president is C. L. Greene of C. L. Greene & Co.

Councilmen, Board of. — The lower house of the Common Council holds regular meetings on the first and third Fridays of every month in the Council Chamber, City Buildings. It consists of two members from each of the twenty-five wards, one being elected by the voters of the ward each year at the spring election. L. L. Sadler is president, and Charles Winkler vice-president. Following are the names of the present members: 1st ward, W. A. Watkins, D. Blackmore; 2d ward, James Rowe, Benjamin Eggleston; 3d ward, William B. Housman, Henry Wernke; 4th ward, Charles Jeffries, E. T. Harley; 5th ward, Robert Callahan, Eugene Reynolds; 6th ward, Daniel J. Dalton, J. W. Fitzgerald; 7th ward, John Reeder, F. A. Herrmann; 8th ward, W. J. Alexander, John Russell; 9th ward, J. B. Menke, jun., George W. Draper; 10th ward, J. Schrenker, Michael Gramp; 11th ward, C. F. Lohman, Charles Winkler; 12th ward, Dave Billigheimer, I. J. Miller; 13th ward, Emil Ulm, John Maegly; 14th ward, W. T. Marshall, Adam Knorr; 15th ward, Maurice Bauer, H. Knuwener; 16th ward, Peter Fohmer, L. L. Sadler; 17th ward, G. Lowenstein, Jos. M. Rice; 18th ward, Ed. Hudson, George B. Cox; 19th ward, Jas. E. Broderick, John F. Heekin; 20th ward, Charles Steinan, W. N. Forbis; 21st ward, Frank Friend, George Kaiser; 22d ward, R. C. Rohner, Phillip DeWold; 23d ward, Jacob Ungehener, John Weyand; 24th ward, A. B. Engelbrink, F. Pfiester; 25th ward, J. C. Bruckman, Gabriel Dirr.

County Infirmary, the. — On high ground north-east of Carthage. The buildings are new and commodious. The paupers of Hamilton County, outside the city, are there cared for. It can be reached only by private conveyance from Carthage. It is supported by taxation upon the real and personal property in the county, outside of the city.

County Jail, the, on Sycamore Street, between North and South Court Streets, east of the Court House, is in charge of the sheriff of Hamilton County. It is a massive stone structure. All of the inside work, the cells, etc., are made of boiler-iron.

Court House of Hamilton County is on Main Street, at the eastern terminus of Court Street. The structure is 200 feet square, and four stories high. Besides the common pleas, district, superior, and probate court rooms, it contains the offices of all the county officers; to wit, nine judges, the prosecuting attorney, clerks of the courts, auditor, treasurer, sheriff, coroner, commissioners, solicitor, board of control, board of equalization, fee-commissioners, recorder, and the Law Library containing about 15,000 volumes. Notwithstanding all these, the immense building is not all occupied, several offices on Main Street and some back rooms remaining empty.

Courts. — See Law-Courts.

Covington is on the south bank of the Ohio River, opposite Cincinnati, and connected with it by the Suspension Bridge. It is, next to Louisville, the largest city in Kentucky, but it is practically a suburb of Cincinnati. It comprises 1,350 acres, and has 32,000 inhabitants. The principal building is the United-States Court House and Post-Office, completed in 1879, at a cost of nearly $300,000. It is in the Gothic style, and handsomely built of Indiana limestone with Buena Vista sandstone trimmings. In its construction, materials from fifteen States, and five kinds of marble, were used. The Odd Fellows' Hall is a good building. There are one high, four district, and twelve Catholic schools and convents, and also 29 churches, classified as follows: 4 Baptist, 2 Christian, 1 Episcopal, 1 German Protestant, 1 German Reformed, 8 Methodist Episcopal, 2 Presbyterian, and 10 Catholic. The public library has 5,000 volumes. There are four newspapers. Four lines of horse-cars traverse the city; and all stop at Fountain Square, Cincinnati.

Cumminsville, formerly one of the suburbs, is four miles and a half from Fountain Square, but now within the limits of the city, and constitutes its 25th ward. Its name comes from one of the pioneer settlers, who cultivated the ground on which the village stands. The Catholic Orphan Asylum is located here, as well as

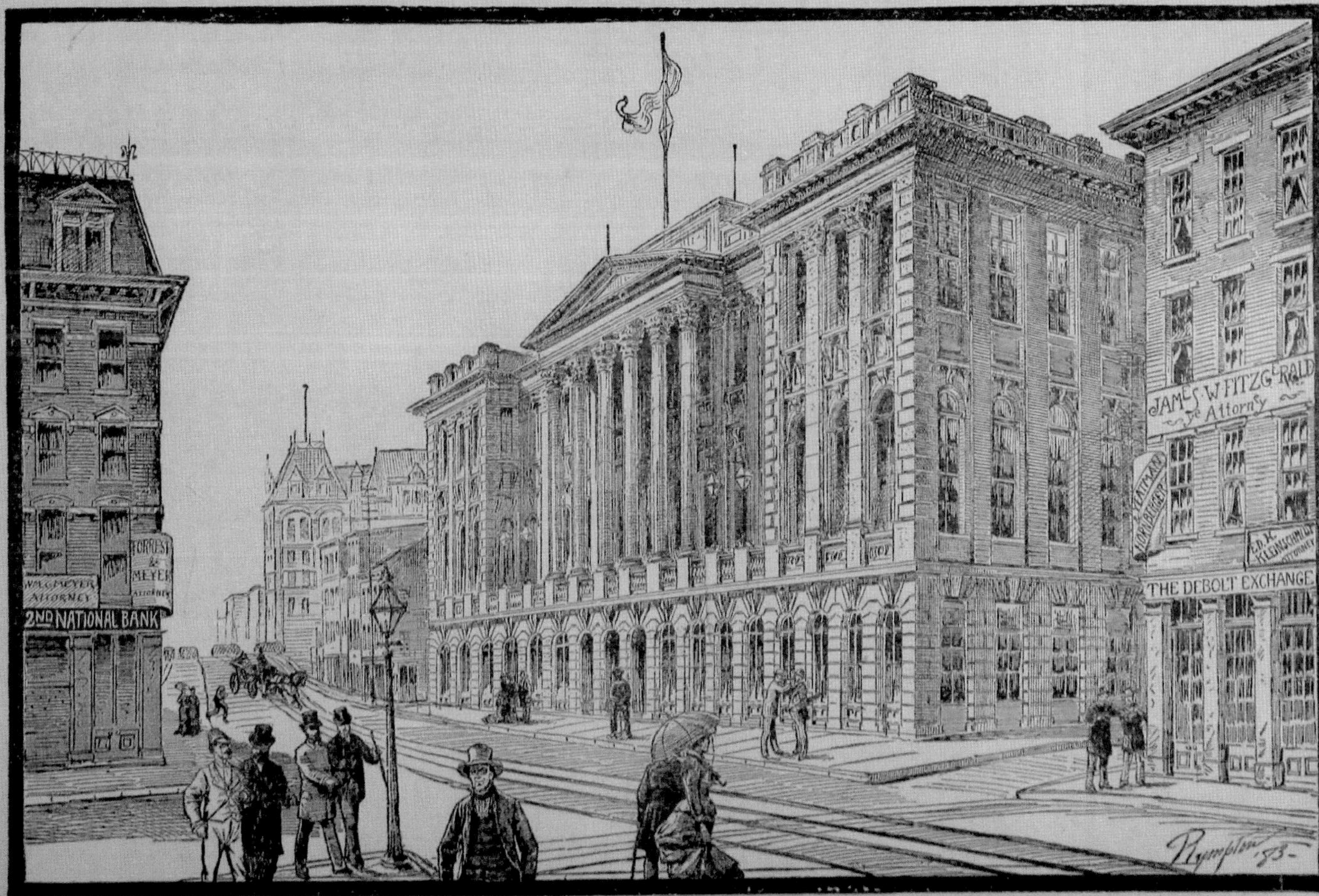
2ND NATIONAL BANK
FORREST & MEYER
THE DEBOLT EXCHANGE
JAMES W. FITZGERALD
Ye Attorney

several large distilleries. Three steam-railroads pass through it,—the Dayton Short-line, Cincinnati, Hamilton, and Dayton, and Marietti and Cincinnati. Spring-grove Avenue and the Colerain Pike also bisect it. The Avenue line of horse-cars passes through Cumminsville to Spring-grove Cemetery.

Custom House, the United States, is on the south-west corner of Fourth and Vine Streets. The building belongs to the United-States Government, and contains the custom-house, post-office, assistant treasurer's office, and United-States courts. It is built of Buena Vista freestone, in the Roman-Corinthian style. It is much too small to supply the growing needs of the city; and the government has now in course of erection a building into which all the departments and courts above mentioned will be removed as soon as it is completed. (See Government Building.)

Cuvier Club, organized in 1874 for the protection of game and fish and for social purposes, has a very fine collection of 3,000 preserved specimens of birds and fish. Its rooms, on Longworth Street, are commodious, and, besides the large display-room, include a small library and reading-room. There are about 400 members, each paying $10 a year. Ladies and children can see the collections every day from nine to one o'clock, free. Visitors at other times are to be introduced by members.

Dayton, Ky., a suburb of Newport, opposite that part of Cincinnati known as Pendleton, is largely inhabited by persons doing business in the city. It is regularly laid out, the houses being for the most part small and neat. Population about 1,000. Distance from Fountain Square by the usually travelled route, three miles. It can be reached by horse-car from the Esplanade.

Deaf Mutes, the School for, is in the Second Intermediate School building, on Ninth Street, between Main and Walnut Streets. The school was established in 1875, and was started with 12 pupils. At the last session 32 pupils were in attendance, requiring the services of two teachers. The method of instruction is by sign language and the manual alphabet. Until recently it was supported wholly by the city, but in 1879 the State made an appropriation toward its support.

Deer Creek, although almost lost to sight by being turned into Eggleston-avenue Sewer, is yet a stream, especially after a heavy rain. Its source is in the ravines of Mount Auburn, about three miles from its mouth. For the distance of a mile or more, the old creek has been transformed into a sewer, and empties into the Ohio immediately east of the Little Miami Depot.

Delhi, a suburb on the river, about nine miles west from Fountain Square, is inhabited by persons doing business in the city, and by farmers from the surrounding country. There are many elegant private residences, churches, schools, and other public buildings. Population, about 2,000. The village can be reached by river, the Lower-river Road, and the Warsaw Pike.

Dental College. — See Ohio College of Dental Surgery.

Depots of Steam-railroads. — There are seven depots, into which all inward trains enter. Below is a list of them, the names being those by which they are most generally known: Cincinnati, Hamilton, and Dayton depot, corner of Fifth and Hoadly Streets, reached by the Third-street and by the Baymiller-street lines of horse-cars. Kentucky Central depot, corner of Eighth and Washington Streets, Covington, Ky., reached by Covington lines of horse-cars. Little Miami depot, corner of Front and Kilgour Streets, reached by the Elm-street line of horse-cars. Ohio and Mississippi depot, corner of Front and Mill Streets, reached by the Third-street line of horse-cars. Plum-street depot, corner of Plum and Pearl Streets, reached by Third-street line of horse-cars. Southern Railroad depot, corner McLean Avenue and Gest Street, reached by Eighth-street line of horse-cars. Cincinnati Northern, Court above Broadway, reached by the Avondale and Walnut-hills horse-cars. Grand Central, Central Avenue and Third Street, reached by Third-street line of horse-cars.

The following is the list of railroads entering Cincinnati, and the depots into which they enter: Atlantic and Great Western, Cincinnati, Hamilton, and Dayton depot; Cincinnati, Washington, and Baltimore, Plum-street; Bee Line (Cleveland, Columbus, Cincinnati, and Indianapolis), Grand Central; Cincinnati and Eastern (Batavia Narrow Gauge), Little Miami; Cincinnati and Muskingum Valley, Little Miami; Cincinnati and Portsmouth, Little Miami; Cincinnati and Westwood (Narrow Gauge), Cincinnati, Hamilton, and Dayton; Cincinnati, Hamilton, and Dayton, Cincinnati, Hamilton, and Dayton; Cincinnati, Hamilton, and Indianapolis, Cincinnati, Hamilton, and Dayton; Cincinnati, Richmond, and Chicago, Cincinnati, Hamilton, and Dayton; Cincinnati Southern, Southern Railroad; Cleve-

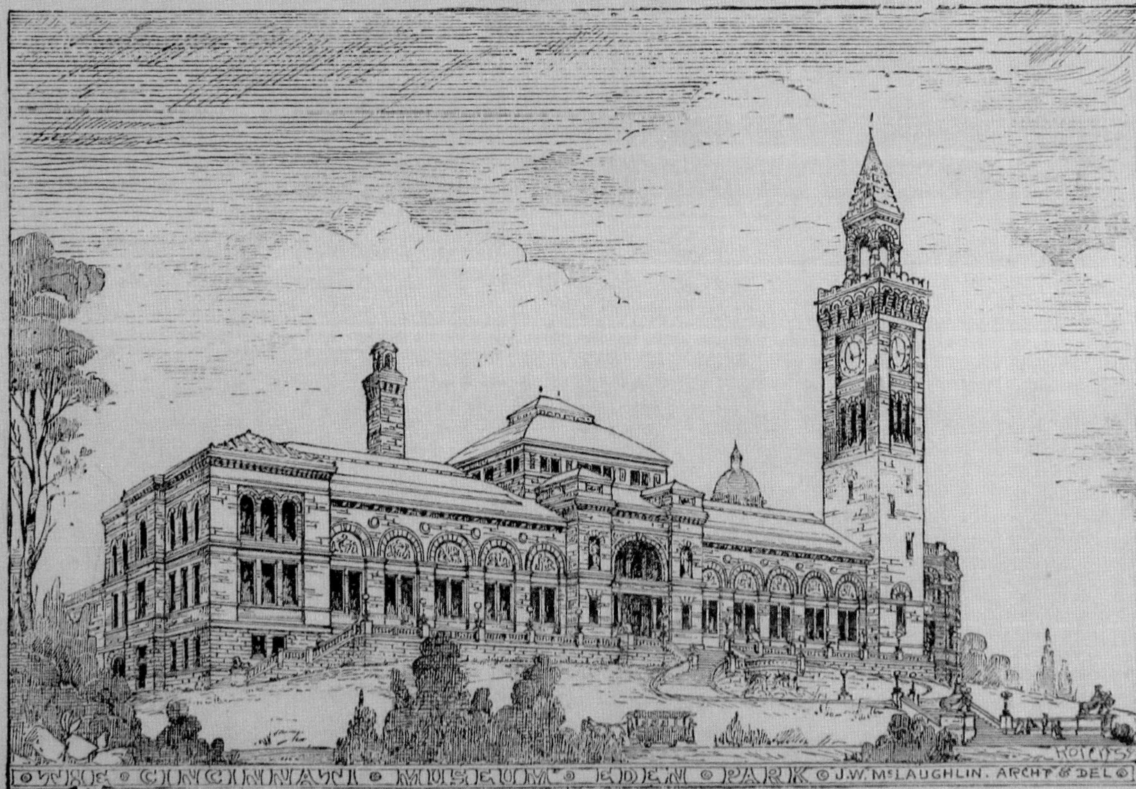
THE CINCINNATI MUSEUM EDEN PARK
J.W. McLAUGHLIN. ARCHT & DEL

land, Mount Vernon, and Columbus, Little Miami; College Hill (Narrow Gauge), Cincinnati, Hamilton, and Dayton; Dayton Short-line, Grand Central; Fort Wayne, Muncie, and Cincinnati, Grand Central; Grand Rapids and Indiana, Cincinnati, Hamilton, and Dayton; Indianapolis, Cincinnati, and Lafayette, Grand Central; Kentucky Central, Kentucky Central; Little Miami (Pan-handle), Little Miami; Louisville Short-line, Little Miami; Ohio and Mississippi, Ohio and Mississippi; Pittsburg, Cincinnati, and St. Louis, Little Miami; Whitewater Valley, Grand Central; Cincinnati Northern, Cincinnati Northern; Georgetown and Portsmouth, Little Miami; Chesapeake and Ohio, Kentucky Central.

Dexter Hall. — See Music-hall and Exposition Building.

Dinner Sets. — Nothing lends an air of refinement to the family dining-room more readily than exquisite table-linens. The John Shillito Company now exhibit many new and beautiful designs in double satin damask table-cloths, with napkins to match. The patterns are the most artistic ever woven, and include arabesque, Moresque, Egyptian, Greek, Alhambra, and many other curious designs. All the choicest productions of the most celebrated Irish, Scotch, English, French, and German looms are shown by this firm.

Dispensaries. — See Miami Medical College Dispensary, Ohio Medical College Dispensary, Homœopathic Free Dispensary, Women's Dispensary Association, City Physicians, and Ohio College of Dental Surgery.

Distilleries, as well as the breweries, are among the most interesting objects in Cincinnati. The amount of distilled and rectified liquors manufactured in 1881 in this city reached 23,556,093 gallons, valued at the almost incomprehensible sum of $28,267,314.60. Engaged in the business, there are 85 distilleries and rectifying-houses, with an invested capital of $4,180,000, giving employment to 900 hands, and paying last year a revenue tax of $10,349,065.80. The largest of these distilleries, and second largest in the world, is that of James W. Gaff & Co., situated in the lower end of the city, between the tracks of the Ohio and Mississippi, the Indianapolis, Cincinnati, and Lafayette, the Cincinnati, Washington, and Baltimore, the Dayton Short-line, and the Cincinnati, Hamilton, and Dayton Railroads, and about 100 feet from the Ohio River. The area of the distillery property, including the stock-pens and adjuncts, is 16 acres; and it has a frontage of 500 feet. The distillery has a capacity of 16,000 gallons a day, the pens for 4,000 head of cattle and 10,000 head of hogs; and the four-story bonded warehouse has storage-room for 30,000 barrels. When running at the full capacity, the distillery employs nearly 100 hands. At 876 West Sixth Street is the large rectifying-house, where the same firm rectify and compound every grade of liquors. Visitors will be admitted, but only upon permits obtained at the office of J. W. Gaff & Co., room 22, Pike's Opera House.

Drives. — The beautiful suburbs and excellent macadamized roads which abound both within and without the city limits, east, west, and north in Ohio, and southwardly in Kentucky, make it eminently delightful for recreation by carriage or horseback. Perhaps the finest drive in the city, where only one can be taken, is that which leads *viâ* Hunt Street, through Avondale, past the Zoölogical Gardens, through the Burnet-woods Park and Clifton, to Spring-grove Cemetery, returning by Spring-grove Avenue, through Cumminsville, to Fountain Square. This drive will occupy about three hours, and is replete with magnificent scenery and elegant private residences throughout its whole course. To those so inclined, a drive through Spring-grove Cemetery, which is reached by the Avenue, is very attractive. The drive may be continued on to College Hill, and a return made by way of Clifton, Avondale, Walnut Hills, and Mount Auburn, returning to the city by Sycamore Street. Another beautiful drive is by the Harrison Pike, through Fairmount, to Cheviot and Westwood. The Price's-hill drive is also delightful. The top of the hill is reached by way of Eighth or Gest Streets, thence west to Warsaw through a remarkably picturesque region, returning by the Lick-Run Pike, through the villages of Lick Run and Fairmount. There is a beautiful drive through Eden Park, *viâ* Gilbert Avenue. Continued, this drive will lead through East Walnut Hills and Woodburn; and a return can be made through Mount Auburn. The Carthage Pike leads through Mount St. Bernard, past Longview Asylum to Carthage; and a return can be made by Chester Driving Park, Spring-grove Cemetery, and Cumminsville, by the Avenue. The finest drive in Kentucky is by the Lexington Pike to Latonia Springs, five miles south of Covington. These are only a few of the many drives, and either will well repay its cost to citizen or stranger. Carriage-hire varies in price, the average price being $1.50 per hour for a hack carrying four persons; but the stranger would do well to make his bargain beforehand, to avoid imposition and trouble. The

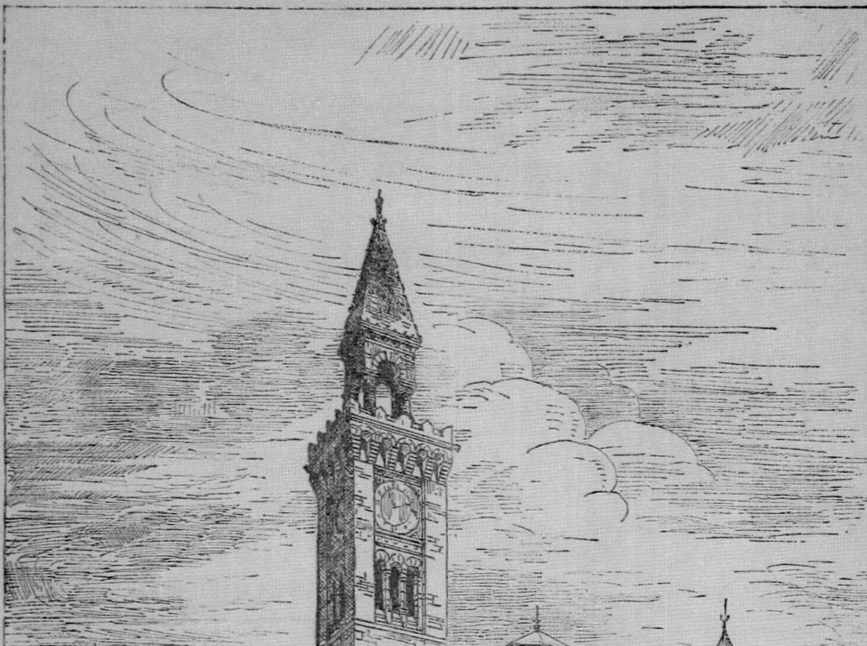

THE CINCINNATI MUSEUM J.W. McLAUGHLIN ARCH & DEL.

principal hack-stand is at the Custom House, one square from the Esplanade, on Vine Street. The livery-stables charge for buggies $4 a day, but on Sundays and holidays $5.

Druids, a mutual-benefit secret order, paying weekly benefits to its sick members. There are about 500 members in the city. Their assemblies are called "groves." Their principal hall is at No. 36 West Court Street, where four of the six Cincinnati groves hold their meetings semi-monthly.

Duhme & Co.'s jewelry establishment is one of the mercantile places in the city where anybody can profitably spend hours in seeing elaborate and costly works of art. Bronzes, statuary, gold and silver goods, precious stones, and ornaments, displaying the most exquisite skill and ingenuity, are here to be seen in an endless variety. The firm was established in 1836, and is to-day probably the most extensive manufacturers and dealers in their line in the West, and surely one of the most trustworthy establishments in the United States. Their stores are on the south-west corner of Fourth and Walnut Streets.

East-End Garden, situated on the river-bank, at the eastern extremity of Pendleton, near the depot of the Columbia and Mount Lookout dummy Railroad, contains about 12 acres of ground, divided by gravelled walks into lawns, flower-beds, poplar-groves, and an orchard. It has been known by several different names. The public house attached was for many years called Sportsman's Hall, and the garden had the same name. Later it was Ohmer's Garden, named after its proprietor, who converted it into a miniature zoölogical garden. For several years past it has been known as the East-End Garden. It was for many years a favorite place for picnics and pleasure-parties, for which purposes it is still frequently used. It is now known as Woodland Park.

Eclectic Medical Institute, organized in 1843, and chartered in 1845, has its building on the north-west corner of Plum and Court Streets. The course of medical instruction is on the eclectic plan. Students have the privilege of attending clinics at the Cincinnati Hospital on payment of $5.

Economy in Time.—Our new cash system. Modern business transactions have assumed such magnitude that it has become important that there be as little waste of time as possible upon each detail. Of no business is this more true than of a large wholesale and retail dry-goods house such as ours. The system just adopted reduces the time required to procure change, to a minimum, say forty seconds, to any part of our large salesrooms, enabling us to wait on customers with greater promptness than has been possible heretofore.

Eden Park, the largest of the city parks, contains 206 acres, all improved except 25 acres. In the park are located the large reservoirs of the water-works. The Eden-park and Walnut-hills line of horse-cars run through the park, and afford a pleasant ride and a number of the finest views of the surrounding country. In the Shelter House is a well-appointed restaurant, where the sale of intoxicating liquors is prohibited. Eden Park was first improved in 1872, and has already cost $450,000. It is situated a mile east of Fountain Square, and is reached both by the Gilbert-avenue route of horse-cars, and the Mount-Adams and Eden-park Inclined Plane, with its connections. Open at all times, free.

Education, the Board of, has exclusive control of the public schools, and is composed of one member from each of the twenty-five wards of the city, and twelve members at large. It meets every alternate Monday night in the Council Chamber, City Buildings. Howard Douglass is president, and Robert G. Stevenson, clerk. The office of the board is in the Public Library Building. Following are the names of the present members: 1st ward, H. J. Buntin; 2d ward, H. P. Boyden; 3d ward, James O'Kane; 4th ward, Daniel Finn; 5th ward, Thomas McLaughlin; 6th ward, Jno. F. McCarthy; 7th ward, John Keck; 8th ward, David A. Alexander; 9th ward, F. S. Spiegel; 10th ward, Gustav R. Wahle; 11th ward, J. H. Charles Smith; 12th ward, George Emig; 13th ward, George Kreh; 14th ward, Philip Kiehborth; 15th ward, John H. Walker; 16th ward, John B. Callahan; 17th ward, Louis Kramer; 18th ward, James Brown; 19th ward, Anton Weber; 20th ward, W. H. Adams; 21st ward, Wooster B. Morrow; 22d ward, H. M. Merrell; 23d ward, Henry Behrens; 24th ward, Jacob E. Cormany; 25th ward, Charles A. Miller. Members at large: Thomas E. Matthews, William S. Thornton, Frank Ratterman, A. S. Babbitt, Howard Douglass, Francis Ferry, Harry D. Crane, George Twachtman, J. F. McCarthy, Joseph Moses, Thomas Lee, W. A. Hopkins.

Eighth-street Parks are simply two open improved squares, extending on Eighth Street from Vine to Elm Streets, and cover a site originally intended for a market-place.

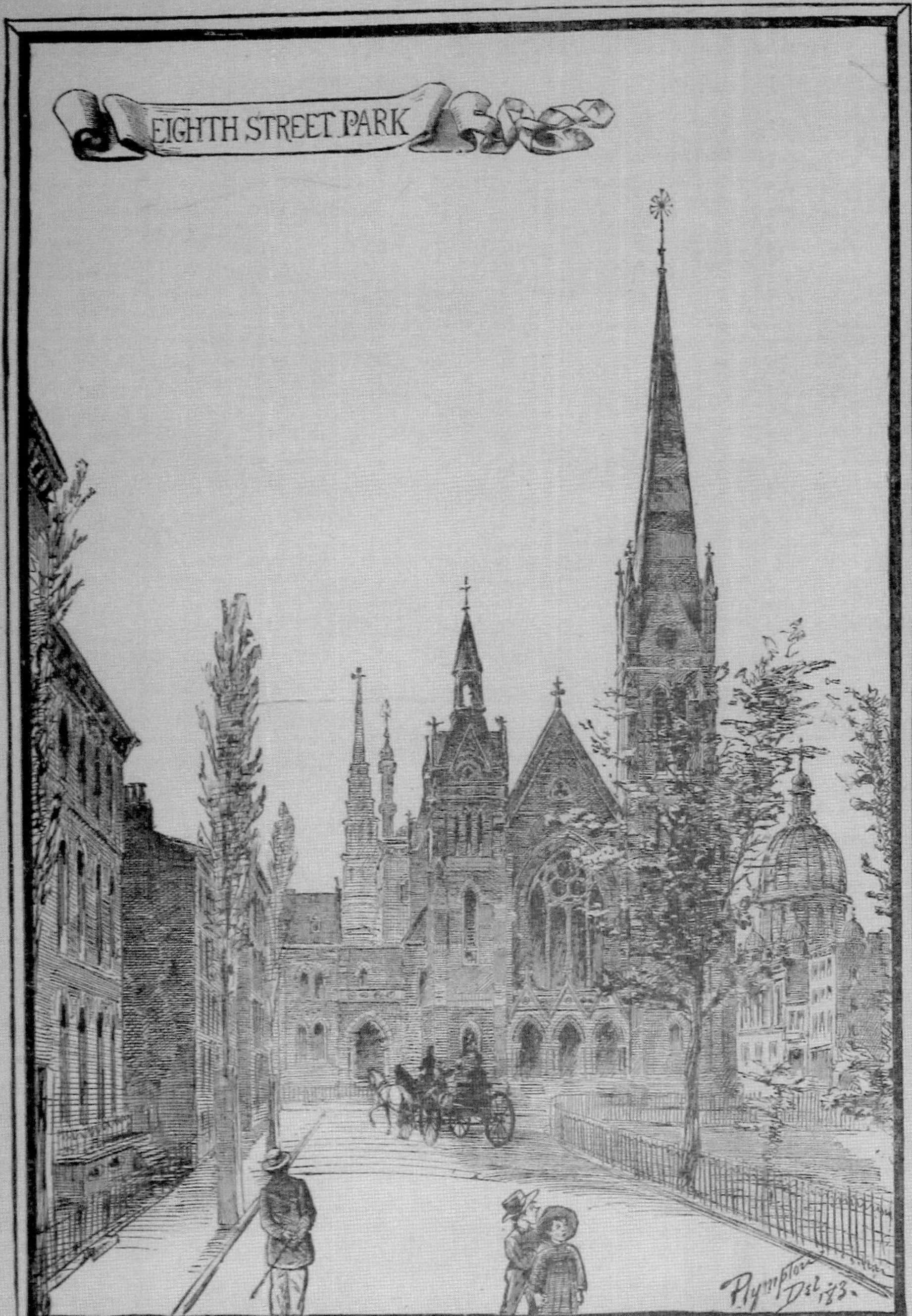
EIGHTH STREET PARK
Plympton Del '83.

Elections. — Under the laws of Ohio, two general elections are held each year: one, the first Monday in April, at which municipal officers are chosen; the other, the second Tuesday in October, at which the officers of the county, of the State, and of the United States, are elected.

Elm-street Club, the. — Organized by George Moerlein, and originally composed of brewers and men connected with brewing interests. Its growing influence in politics attracted many local politicians of both parties to the club, and it is now as much a political machine as it is a social club. There are about 250 members. The initiation-fee is $5, and the dues $6 a year. The club has suitable rooms at 672 Elm Street.

Embroideries. — We have throughout the Old Testament constant mention of embroidery. The curtains wrought with needlework, in Exodus, the virtuous woman clothed in tapestry, of the Proverbs, and the king's daughter in raiment of needlework, in the Psalms, plainly show how much the art was appreciated by the Jews. The ancient Greeks highly esteemed it. Minerva, goddess of wisdom, took it under her special patronage. Cut-work came into universal use in the sixteenth century, and from this was derived the origin of lace. The linen grave-cloths of St. Cuthbert, as described by an eye-witness to his disinterment in the twelfth century, were ornamented in this manner. Elegant patterns can be procured from The John Shillito Company.

Emery Arcade, one of the largest in the world, extends from Vine to Race Streets, between Fourth and Fifth. It is a passage 400 feet long, protected from the weather by a glass roof. Along the sides are shops of all kinds, and the Hotel Emery; and at the Vine-street entrance is the Arcade Bookstore.

Enterprise Fire and Marine Insurance Company of Cincinnati has its office in its own building, 82 West Third Street. The building, in the late Norman-Gothic style, is one of the finest business structures in the city, and is four stories in height above the basement. It contains twenty-two large rooms, many of them being very choice offices; and the upper floors are reached by two staircases and an hydraulic passenger-elevator. The Enterprise Insurance Company was organized in 1865; and from that time the management has been characterized by a degree of liberality and skill that has won it friends everywhere. Jan. 1, 1882, the paid-up capital was

$200,000; the total assets, $271,301; the liabilities, including the reserve for re-insurance, $110,151; and the net assets, $161,150. The president, John W. Hartwell, has been in the insurance business in this city longer than any other person now engaged in it, and has been president of this company since 1869. The secretary is James W. McCord.

Equalization, the Boards of, are for hearing complaints, and equalizing the valuation of all real and personal property; but they cannot reduce the value of real property below the aggregate value as returned by the assessors. There are seven of these boards: viz., *The Annual County Board*, having jurisdiction over the property in each county outside of cities of the first and second class, and composed of the county commissioners and county auditor. *The Annual City Board*, having jurisdiction over property of cities of the first and second class, and composed of the county auditor and six citizens. This board meets at the auditor's office on the fourth Monday of May. *Annual State Board for Banks*, composed of the State auditor, treasurer, and attorney-general, who equalize the shares of incorporated banks, and meet on the third Tuesday of June. *Annual State Board for Railroads* constituted as above for equalizing the valuation of property of railroad companies. *Decennial County Board*, composed of the county auditor, surveyor, and commissioners; who meet on the Tuesday after the first Monday of September, 1880, and every tenth year thereafter. They have power to equalize the valuation of property, outside of cities of the first and second class, as returned by the district assessors. *Decennial City Board*, composed of the county auditor and six citizens, who have the same powers in cities of the first and second class as the county board have in their jurisdiction. *Decennial State Board* meet on the first Tuesday of December, 1880, and every tenth year thereafter, and consist of as many members as compose the State senate. They are elected by the electors of each senatorial district, and have power to reduce or increase the value of property as returned by the county auditors, provided such increase or reduction shall not exceed twelve and a half per cent.

Ernst Station, also called Brighton Station, and Fairmount, is in the twenty-fourth ward, where the Harrison-avenue Bridge crosses Mill Creek. There is a small depot near the bridge. The Cincinnati, Hamilton, and Dayton, the Cincinnati, Washington, and Balti-

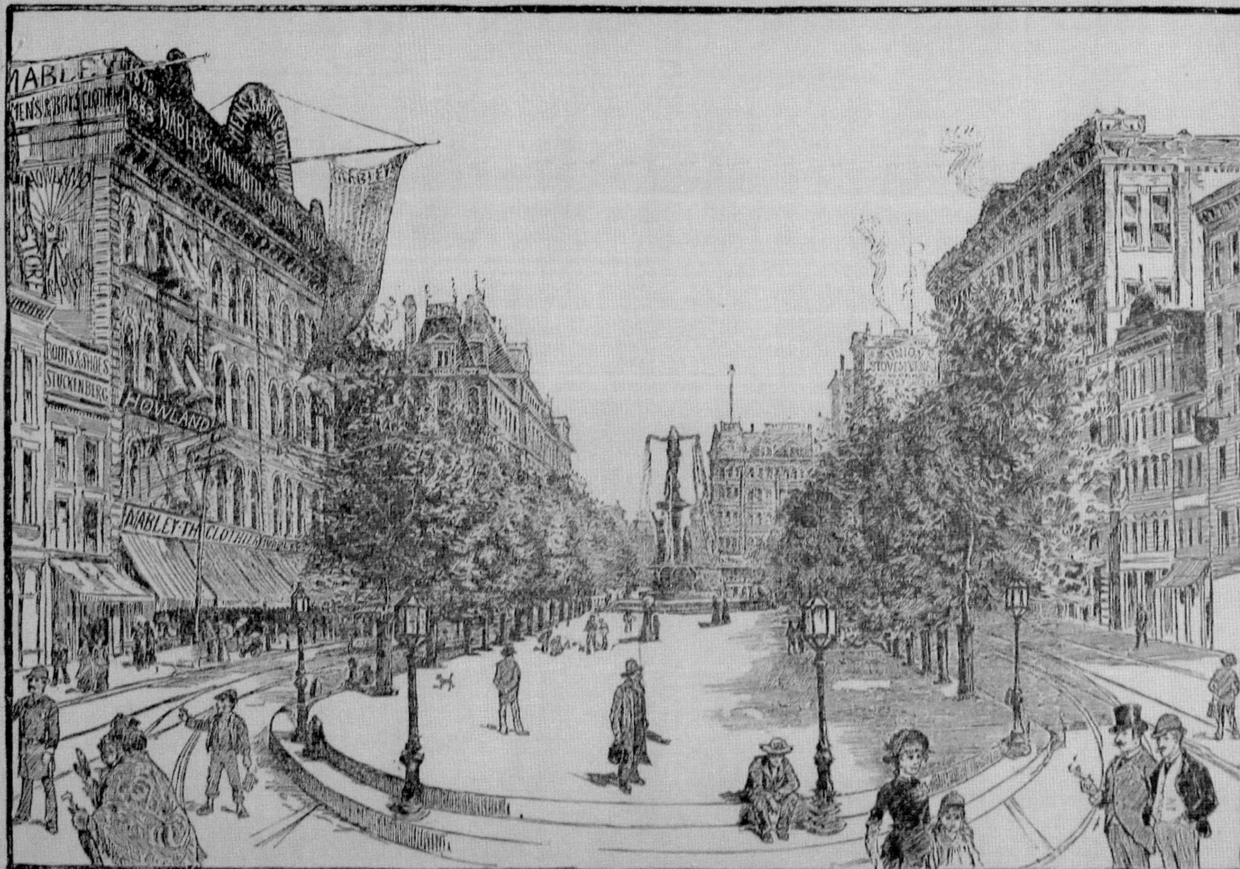

Esplanade and Fountain.

more, the Westwood Narrow-gauge, and the Dayton Short-line roads all stop their accommodation-trains at this station.

Esplanade, the, is situated in the centre of Fountain Square. The Tyler-Davidson Fountain springs from the centre of it. The Esplanade is a raised structure 28 inches above the crown of the street. It is oval in form, extending the entire length of the square, 400 feet, and is 60 feet in width. The outer rim, and the steps approaching it, are made of hewn Quincy granite. The floor is made of Buena Vista sandstone, smooth dressed, and laid in diamond and circular designs. Within the granite rim, at distances of 20 feet, is a row of thrifty young sycamore-trees. Between the trees, around the entire structure, are ornamented bronze gas posts and lamps, which are lighted every night. The cost of the Esplanade was $75,000. Unless otherwise stated, the distances given in this book are calculated from this point. All the horse-cars pass by or close to it.

Etching Club, formed March, 1879, Dr. Daniel S. Young, president, meets every second Saturday, at four P.M., at the studio of H. F. Farney, Room 62, Pike's Opera-House Building. Dues nominal. Members use the press in the studio for taking impressions of their etched plates.

Exposition, the Cincinnati Industrial, is an annual exhibition of arts, manufactures, agriculture, mining products, and other industries, foreign and domestic. These annual expositions are public institutions, guaranteed by subscriptions, and are in no sense a private speculation. They are managed by a board of fifteen commissioners appointed by the Chamber of Commerce, the Board of Trade, and the Ohio Mechanics' Institute; and the officers for 1883 are W. W. Peabody, president; Hugh McCollum, vice-president; Benjamin E. Hopkins, treasurer; and W. H. Stewart, secretary. The first six expositions of the present series were held in a building erected for the National Saengerfest in 1870, on the site of the present Music-hall and Exposition Building. The first exposition was held in 1870, and followed a successful textile-fabric exhibition held in 1869. The textile-fabric exposition was originated and managed by James H. Laws, and was the first of its kind in this country. From 1870 to 1875 inclusive, the expositions were held in the same building; but in the latter year the old building was thought unsafe, and consequently abandoned. At this time Reuben R. Springer came forward with his munificent plan for a combined Music-hall and Exposition

Building. An interval of four years elapsed before the completion of the new buildings; but delay had only increased the enthusiasm for their resumption, and the seventh exposition and subsequent ones were held in the largest and most beautiful and suitable permanent buildings of this kind in the United States. The average attendance on the first six expositions was, in round numbers, 500,000 persons. The expositions are self-supporting, and are secured by a guaranty fund of $100,000 each year. There are eight acres of exhibiting-space in the building. Very liberal premiums are offered in all departments open to competition. Special excursion-trains make frequent trips on the railroads entering the city, carrying passengers at half rates, and often at round-trip rates much less. The expositions open as nearly as possible on the 10th of September each year, and last one month. Admission, 25 cents. Elm-street cars pass the doors, Vine-street and John-street cars close by. (See Music Hall.)

Express Companies, the chief, are: the Adams, 57 West Fourth; the American, 118 West Fourth; the Baltimore and Ohio, 59 West Fourth; Cincinnati, Washington, and Baltimore, 59 West Fourth; the Ohio and Mississippi, 59 West Fourth; the United-States, 122 West Fourth.

Expressmen's Aid Society, organized in 1874, is a co-operative life-assurance association; H. B. Plant, St. Louis, president.

Fairmount, formerly a suburban village, but now within the corporation, forming a part of the 24th ward, is on the west bank of Mill Creek, opposite Ernst Station. The Harrison Pike and Lick-run Pike pass through the village. It is surrounded by high hills, on the summit of one of which is the old Baptist College, now transformed into a German club-house, and called the "Schützenplatz," from which a charming view of the city and surrounding country in all directions can be had. The Westwood Narrow-gauge Railroad has a terminus here.

Farmers' College originated in Pleasant-hill Academy, founded, and conducted for twelve years, by F. G. Cary, as a private enterprise. It was opened in 1833, with four pupils, in the residence of Mr. Cary. It prospered constantly, and during the first twelve years almost 1,200 young men were educated there. In the winter of 1846–47 the academy was incorporated as the "Farmers' College;" and a substantial building, 120 feet front by 48 feet deep, was erected on a tract of four acres on College Hill. Mr. Cary was elected presi-

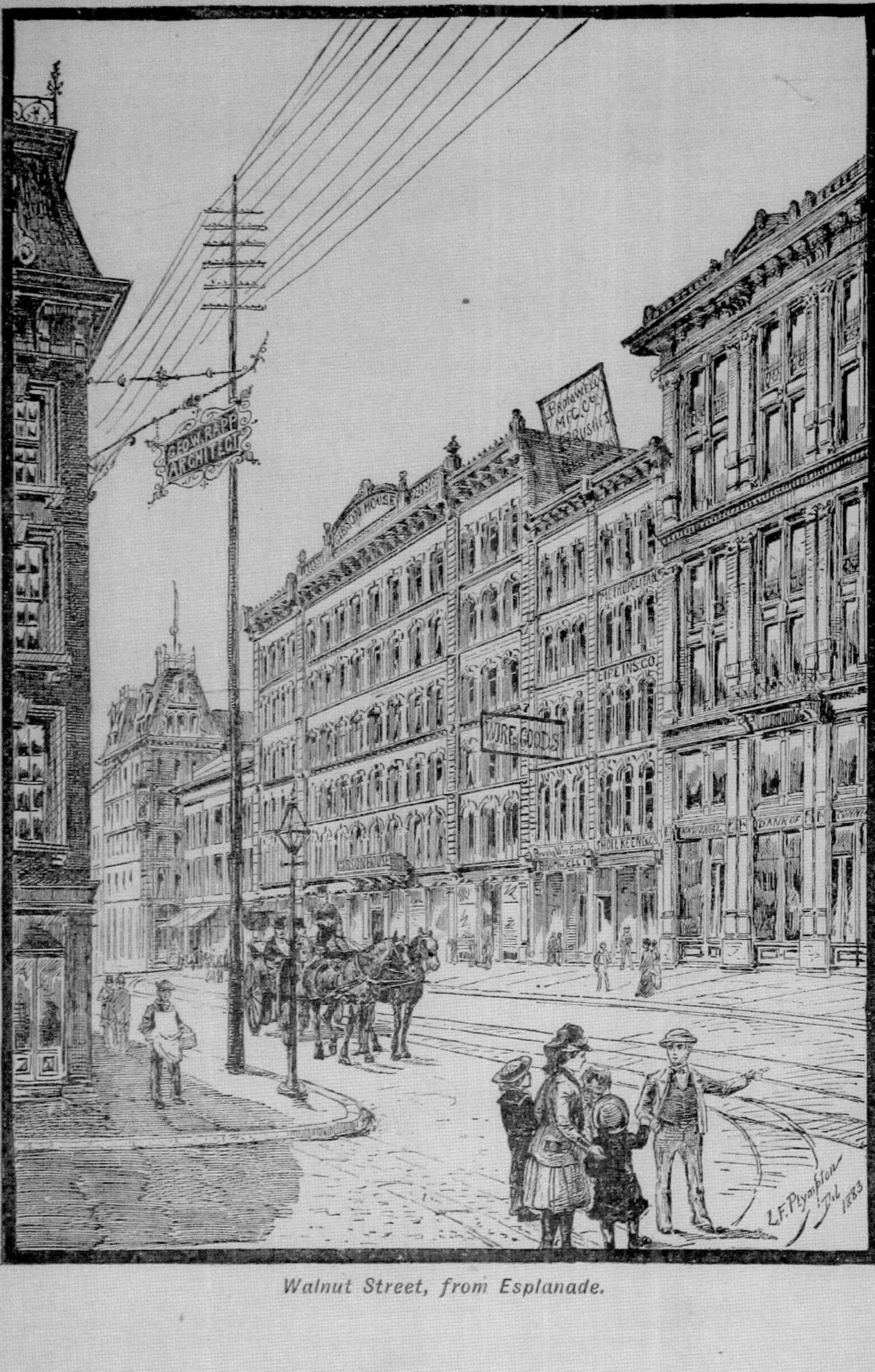

Walnut Street, from Esplanade.

dent. The institution is now divided into two departments, — the college department, comprising the following courses: the classical of four years, the philosophical of four years, the scientific of three years, the ladies' classical of three years, and the teachers' course of one year; and the preparatory department, fitting boys and girls for the college department. The college is a Protestant institution, but is not at all sectarian. There are two terms, of twenty weeks each, beginning Sept. 3. In the year 1881–82 there were in the whole college 97 students. Lowe Emerson is president of the college, and Miss Abby A. Judson principal of the preparatory department.

Ferries. — Since the completion of three bridges over the Ohio, the ferries have lost most of their former business. The usual fare for pedestrians is two cents; but the ferries make half-hourly trips between midnight and daylight, during which time the fare is five cents. There are now four lines, as follows: *Anderson's Ferry*, six miles down the river, and used principally by Kentucky farmers bringing their produce to market; *Covington Ferry*, with its Cincinnati landing at the foot of Central Avenue; *Ludlow Ferry*, starting from the foot of Fifth Street, and landing at the eastern limit of Ludlow, Ky.; and the *Newport Ferry*, with its landing in this city at the foot of Lawrence Street. Skiffs and small craft carrying passengers at reasonable rates are available at all places on the river from Columbia to Riverside.

Fertilizer Company, the Cincinnati, has its sheds on the Ohio and Mississippi and Cincinnati, Indianapolis, St. Louis, and Chicago Railroads, six miles west of the city, on the river-bank. By a contract with the city this company gathers and consumes all the garbage, offal, and dead animals found within the city limits. These are manufactured into a fertilizer, soap-grease, bone-dust, etc., and shipped to the South, East, and to Europe. The enterprise is quite profitable, both to the city and the Fertilizer Company.

Fire-Department, the, of Cincinnati, is acknowledged to be one of the best equipped and most efficient in the world. It was the first paid steam fire-department in this country, and was organized in 1853. It consists of 18 steam-engines, 1 hand-engine, 1 chemical-engine, 5 hook-and-ladder companies, all in use, beside 2 steam-engines in reserve, 40 hose-reels, 34,250 feet of hose, 95 horses, and a total of 154 men. During the year 1882 there were 435 alarms, with losses aggregating only $734,074, and insurance of $449,392. It is managed by a board of five commissioners, appointed by the mayor, and confirmed by the Common Council. The fire-marshal is Joseph Bunker, who has been connected with the fire-department since 1854. The headquarters are on the south side of Sixth, between Vine and Race Streets. (See Cisterns.)

Firemen's Insurance Company of Cincinnati, incorporated in 1832, has always maintained a leading position among the local insurance companies. The corporation was formed by a subscription of stock by the fire-engine companies of the city. The first president of the company was George W. Neff, who managed its affairs until his death in 1850. He was succeeded by Josiah Lawrence, at whose death in 1852 Henry E. Spencer, who had been mayor of the city four consecutive terms, from 1843 to 1851, was elected, and continued president until his death, a period of over 27 years. George McLaughlin is now president, having succeeded Mr. Spencer after many years service as secretary. Its dividends in the last 25 years have averaged 18 per cent per annum; and in one year (1863) the cash dividends paid the stockholders amounted to 41 per cent.

First Congregational (Unitarian) Church was incorporated in 1830. The society has been administered to, and has had its pulpit occupied at various times, by many distinguished persons, among whom were Revs. John Pierpont, William H. Channing (during whose stay the congregation was spoken of as "the Church of the Christian Brethren"), James H. Perkins, Horace Mann, James Freeman Clarke, Henry W. Bellows, Theodore Parker, Ralph Waldo Emerson, Abiel A. Livermore, Moncure D. Conway, C. G. Ames, John Weiss, Samuel Longfellow, Robert Collyer, Thomas Vickers, and C. H. Wendte. The society prospered harmoniously until 1859, when the preaching of Mr. Conway created a decided opposition to him. The opponents formed "the Church of the Redeemer," and bought the Universalist Church, corner of Mound and Sixth Streets. The First Society worshipped in various places until, in Mr. Vickers's ministration, the church was built on the north-east corner Plum and Eighth Streets. In 1875 a re-union of the two congregations took place under the pastor, C. H. Wendte; and since then the building has been modernized and the membership increased.

First Presbyterian Church. — The history of this church runs parallel with that of the city, or rather is inseparably interwoven with it. The three pioneer settlers of this vicinity were all members of

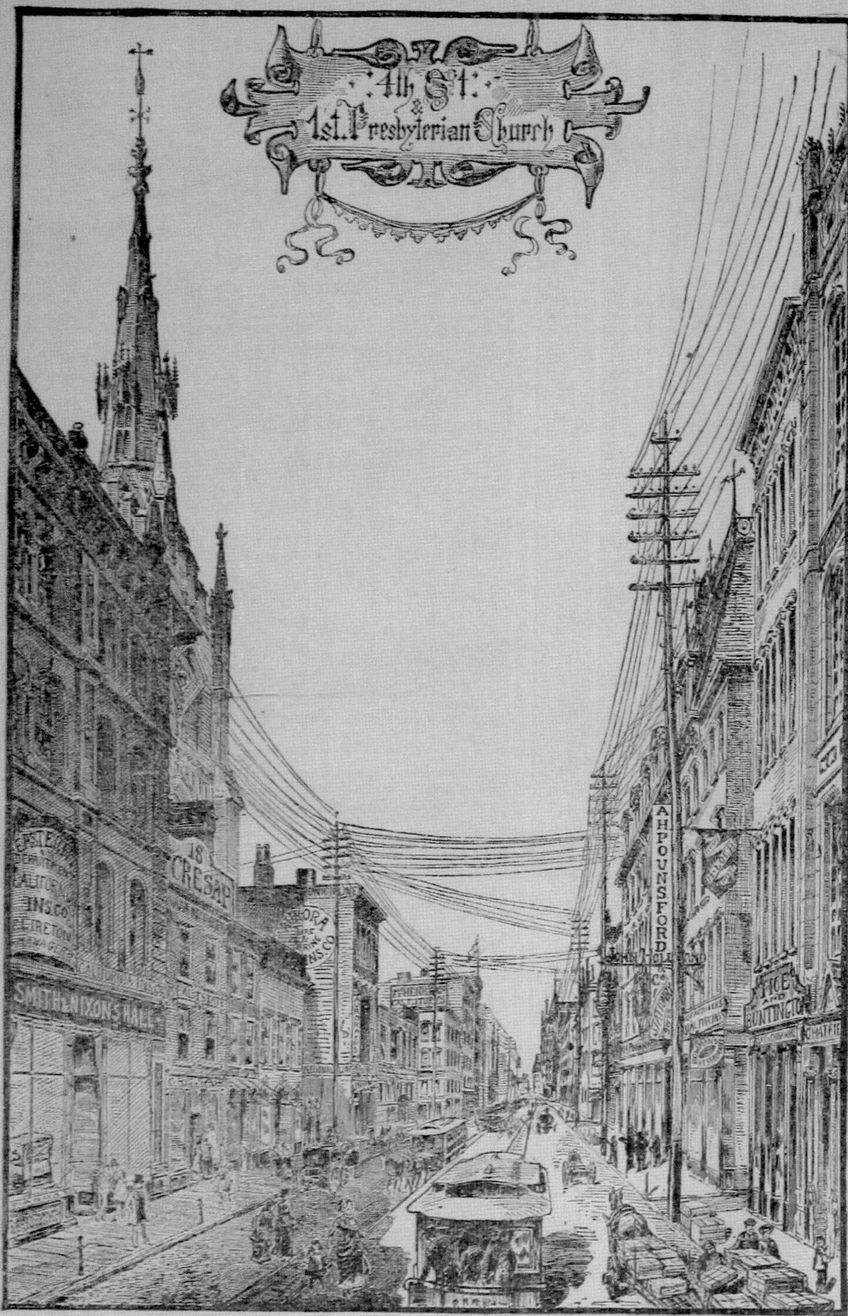
4th St. & 1st. Presbyterian Church
SMITH & NIXON'S HALL
A H POUNSFORD & Co.
CRESAP
CALIFORNIA INS. CO

the Presbyterian Church, and, in laying out the plan of their future city, did not forget its claims. They set aside for its use a plat of ground occupying the south half of the square bounded by Main and Walnut and Fourth and Fifth Streets, on part of which the present church is built. Until 1793 the congregation worshipped on this ground, "with no dome but the canopy of heaven, no aisles but the majestic trees of the ancient forest, and no carpet but the green-sward." In this year, through the exertions of James Kemper, their first regular minister, a meeting-house was erected, "a substantial frame building, about 40 feet by 30, enclosed with clapboards, but neither lathed, plastered, nor ceiled. In that humble edifice the pioneers and their families assembled for public worship, and during the continuance of the war they always attended with loaded rifles by their side." About a quarter of a century after, this structure was removed, and a brick church built in its place; and this in turn was replaced in 1851 by the beautiful edifice that now stands on the old site. It is said to have the highest steeple in the country; viz., 285 feet. Very little of the spacious grounds it once owned has been retained by the church; and little by little the land, including the burial-ground, has been sold, until now the church is surrounded by business blocks. The membership is between 200 and 250; F. C. Monfort is pastor.

Flower-Mission. — Formed by ladies of the city and suburbs to supply the sick poor with flowers, sent, chiefly by ladies residing outside the city proper, to the Young Men's Christian Association Building, where they are arranged, and afterwards distributed to the patients in the hospitals, by ladies who meet weekly for this purpose. This is one of the most unostentatious yet useful of the many local charities.

Foresters, Independent Order of, is an organization having weekly sick-benefits and an insurance feature; $1,000 being paid to the family of a deceased member, and $5 per week during sickness. The lodges are called "courts," of which Cincinnati has seven; each having an average of 50 members. Annual dues, $3; each death assessment, $1.

Fort Washington, a block-house and large enclosure of pickets, was erected about 1790 for the early settlers of Losanteville (now Cincinnati), and dignified by the name of Fort Washington. It was intended for a protection against the savages, and was large enough to contain the entire population, with provisions to stand a siege. It was directly opposite the mouth of the Licking River, on high ground, the village then lying on the plateau toward the river. The fort stood, according to the testimony of the oldest inhabitants, on Third Street, between Broadway and Ludlow Street, extending southward almost to Columbia or Second Street. After standing a few years it was dismantled, and the site soon afterward covered with buildings, the ground having been subdivided by the government, and sold.

Fountains. — See Tyler-Davidson Fountain.

Fountain Square. — The square between Walnut and Vine, on Fifth Street, the site of the old Fifth-street Market-house, and the present site of the Esplanade and Tyler-Davidson Fountain. The street in this square, and the one adjoining it on the east, which is occupied by the government buildings now in course of erection, is sixty feet wider than the remainder of Fifth Street, having been designed for, and for fifty years or more occupied by, a market-house, which was in the middle of the street. Both sides of the square are lined with handsome business-houses. Every line of horse-cars passes by or within one block of this square. Its location in the heart of the business portion of the city, and its general accessibility, have led the publisher to adopt it as the point from which most of the distances mentioned in this work are computed.

Friends. — There are two churches, one known as the Hicksite Congregation, Fifth, between Central Avenue and John; and the other as the Orthodox Congregation, Eighth and Mound.

Fry's Carving-School is over William Wiswell's art-store, No. 70 West Fourth Street. It is conducted by Henry L. Fry, assisted by his son William H. Fry, and granddaughter Laura Ann Fry. Some of the most exquisite wood-carving ever executed in this country is that by the parties just named. The three generations are masters in their line of work; and the last generation promises best of all, for Miss Fry has already shown extraordinary skill and taste in wood-carving, drawing, and modelling. The Frys did a large part of the elaborate carving in Henry Probasco's residence in Clifton, and of the casement of the great organ in Music Hall. Instruction is given daily from ten A.M. to four P.M.; terms, $10 per month for lessons two days each week. Art-furniture of all kinds is also made to order, and many specimens of the handiwork of this family are to be found in various parts of the United States.

Fulton. — That portion of the city on the river-front lying south-east of Eden Park at the foot of the hills, commencing at the Little Miami Railroad depot, and extending north-east to Pendleton. It comprises a portion of the 4th ward. The Elm-street horse-cars and the Little Miami Railroad traverse the district. Fulton is built on both sides of East Front Street, which, after crossing Washington Street, is known as Eastern Avenue.

Furniture Exchange. — Established in the interest of manufacturers of furniture throughout the United States, and of persons engaged in kindred branches of industry. It occupies room No. 16, Johnston Building.

Garden of Eden. — This was the name of a portion of the ground now occupied by Eden Park when it was the property of the late Nicholas Longworth, and it is still so called by many old residents. Much of the ground was formerly used as a vineyard, and a large proportion of the grapes used in the wine manufactured by Mr. Longworth was cultivated on its sunny hillsides.

Gas. — The Cincinnati Gas-light and Coke Company is the name of a joint-stock corporation having a monoply in supplying the city with illuminating gas. It was established in 1841, and, by contract with the city, was granted the exclusive right to lay gas-mains in the streets for a period of twenty-five years. At the expiration of that period the city had the privilege of buying the works at a fair valuation, but preferred to extend the original privileges to the company for ten years, the price of gas to consumers being largely reduced by the terms of the extension. Gas is now furnished to citizens at $1.60 per thousand cubic feet. It is made of the best quality of second-pool Youghiogheny, or Pittsburg bituminous coal, and is of seventeen-candle power. The office of the company is in an elegant five-story freestone building, south-west corner of Fourth and Plum Streets. The works are on the river-front, between Smith and Mill Streets. Two hundred miles of street-mains are in use; the longest main extending eight miles to Carthage, from which a branch reservoir is supplied to light that village. The streets of the city are lighted by 6,000 street-lamps, under control of the company. The amount of gas manufactured yearly is 500,000,000 cubic feet. Of this, thirteen and a half per cent is lost by leakage and other waste. The invested capital of the company is $4,250,000. Value of the works and appurtenances estimated at $6,000,000. Gen. Andrew Hickenlooper is president.

German Protestant Orphan Asylum has its building in Mount Auburn, on Highland Avenue, opposite the Widows' Home. It was established in 1849, and is under control of a board of trustees chosen from the various German Protestant denominations, and is supported chiefly by an endowment-fund, contributions, and by subscriptions from nearly 1,000 members. The building is a red brick of three stories and a basement, and is quite commodious. The grounds contain seven acres, well cultivated. Separate from the main building, there is also a large dining-hall used every spring and autumn for a festival which is sometimes attended by 20,000 people, each of whom is expected to donate something. The receipts at one of these festivals have amounted to $10,000. The provisions used at the festivals are donated and prepared by ladies. Children having one parent living are admitted if the father is or was a member in good standing. The average number of inmates is about 100. At a proper age, children are placed in families, or to learn a trade; and a boy or a girl at eighteen years of age receives $100. There are branches of the society in Covington and Newport.

Germania Fire and Marine Insurance Company of Cincinnati was organized in 1864. Its cash capital is $100,000, and assets $150,676. Up to 1879 it had paid cash dividends of $108,000, being an average of twelve per cent a year. The president is Peter A. White; the secretary is D. B. Meyer, who has been assistant secretary or secretary since its organization; and the assistant secretary is Charles A. Farnham. Office, 27 West Third Street. The Germania is one of the few local companies doing an agency business, and has now about thirty agencies in Ohio and Michigan.

Gibson House, on the north-west corner of Fourth and Walnut Streets, for many years has been, and is to-day, one of the most popular of the hotels in Cincinnati. In size it is the largest in the city, and for cleanliness in every department it cannot be surpassed by any in this country. The hotel has 300 well-furnished rooms, and has accommodated 880 persons at one time. In 1873 the whole exterior and interior were remodelled; and now the Gibson House is one of the most imposing blocks in Cincinnati. In 1879 the hotel was re-frescoed and refitted, and is now in excellent condition throughout. It is probably the most conveniently situated of the large hotels, and all lines of horse-cars pass either by or close to the house. The terms are $2.50 and $3 a day, the hotel being kept on the American plan.

Globe Insurance Company of Cincinnati was organized, under the general insurance laws of Ohio, in 1865. The cash capital paid in was $52,700. Up to July 1, 1879, the Globe had paid $297,138 for fire-losses; $194,572 for cargo-losses; $77,683 for hull-losses; and $2,778 for flatboat-cargo losses; making a total payment of $572,171 for losses. The balance of its capital stock of $100,000 and its surplus of $26,944 have been earned by the company; and, in addition to this, $159,000, free of taxes, had been paid to the stockholders for dividends; making the total earnings amount to $214,844. S. F. Covington, the president, has been connected with the Globe since its organization, and was its first secretary. The present secretary is B. F. Clemons. Solomon Levi and Samuel J. Hale have been directors of the company from the beginning. The Globe bought its office building, No. 68 West Third Street, in 1865.

Good Fellows, Ancient Order of. — There are fifteen lodges of this order within the limits of Cincinnati and suburbs; the membership being mostly composed of Germans, or citizens of German descent. The lodges will average about seventy members each. Sick members receive benefits of $5 per week.

Good Samaritan Hospital is a noble charity. The building is delightfully situated on the south-east corner of Sixth and Lock Streets, on the Mount-Adams slope. It was built by the United-States Government for a marine hospital, but was never used for that purpose. During the late war it was a soldiers' hospital; and after the close of the war the property, which is said to have cost the government about $500,000, was bought by Lewis Worthington and Joseph C. Butler for $75,000, and given to the Sisters of Charity, one branch of the Sisters of St. Vincent de Paul. There are accommodations for 175 resident patients. Diseases of all kinds are treated. The donors stipulated that one-half of the beds should be open to the poor if calls were made for them; and now from 300 to 500 charity patients are cared for each year in the hospital. Sister Anthony, who has lived in Cincinnati for forty-three years, and has been connected with the hospital for twenty-two consecutive years, says that she feels compelled to receive any one who comes there, — a resident or stranger, with or without money, and of any religious belief. A number of parties have given $3,000 or more, with which sum a "free bed" is founded. It is hoped ultimately to make the hospital free; but at the present time there are various charges for the different kinds of accommodations afforded. There is a free dispensary connected with the hospital. Visitors are admitted at any hour of the day. Horse-cars, Baymiller-street line.

Government Building, the United-States, now in course of erection on the north side of Fifth Street, between Main and Walnut, will contain the post-office with its auxiliary departments, the custom-house, the United-States courts, the assistant treasurer's office, and other government offices. It is a massive structure in the Renaissance style, of five superimposed orders, and built of granite from Maine and Missouri. Its dimensions are 354 feet by 164 feet, four stories and mansard roof above the sidewalk, and basement and sub-basement below. The ground cost $700,000, and the structure will cost over $5,000,000. The superintendent of the construction is S. Hannaford.

Government of the City is vested in the mayor, common council, board of public works, board of sinking-fund commissioners, board of fire-commissioners, board of education, and police-court. All other departments are subordinate to these, and these to each other. The mayor, comptroller, city solicitor, city treasurer, and city infirmary directors, members of common council, members of board of public works, members of board of education, police-court judge and clerk are elected by the people. The other officers are appointed as follows: The sinking-fund commissioners, by the courts; the fire-commissioners, superintendent of police, and rank and file of police, by the mayor; the city engineer and subordinates, the superintendent of water-works and subordinates, and superintendent of street cleaning and repairs, by the board of public works; the members of board of health, wharfmaster and register, city weigher, and city clerk, by the common council. The city-infirmary directors have charge of and appoint overseers of poor; the board of health appoints district physicians, sanitary police, and market-masters. The board of education has entire charge of the public schools and the Public Library. The fire-commissioners have exclusive control of the fire-department, and appoint the officers and members thereof. The police-court has final jurisdiction of all offences against the laws and ordinances, the punishment for which is not confinement in the penitentiary. In the latter cases it is merely an examining court. The Cincinnati Hospital is managed by a board of seven trustees, appointed by the courts, of which board the mayor is *ex officio* a member. The House of

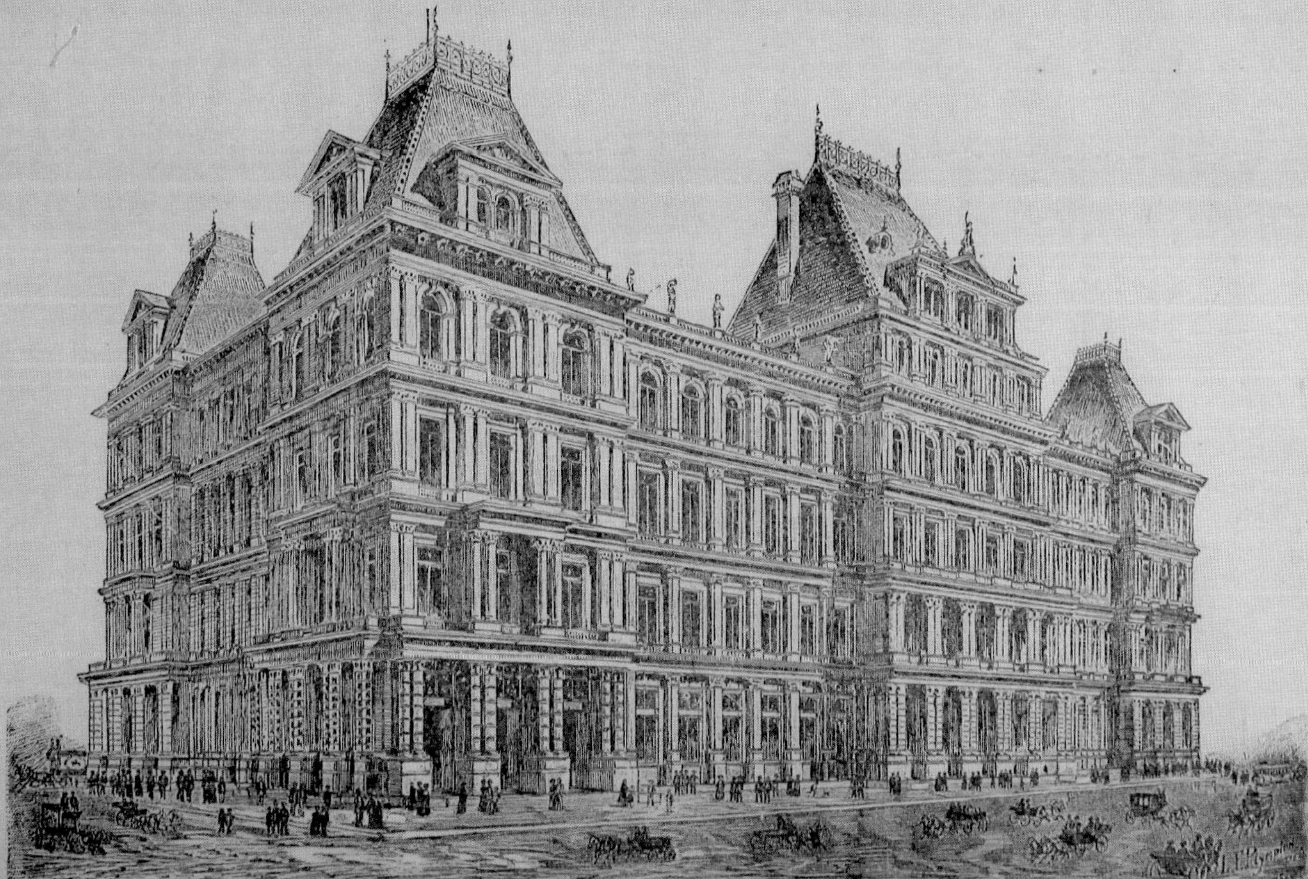

New Government Building.

Refuge is managed in the same manner. The workhouse is in charge of a board of five directors, one of whom is appointed each year by the mayor, and confirmed by the common council, to serve five years. The University board consists of eighteen members, who serve six years, three being elected each year. The common council is simply a legislative body, and appoints none but its own officers.

Grand Hotel, the Cincinnati, is one of the finest hotels in this country, and one of the grandest buildings in this city. It was built by a joint-stock company, whose prime object was to provide Cincinnati with a hotel strictly first-class in every respect. The building, six stories above the sidewalk, is of Ohio freestone, and contains 300 guest-rooms. It fronts 175 feet on Fourth Street, and 200 feet on Central Avenue; but a part extends through to Third Street, a distance of 400 feet. The rotundas and corridors are among the grandest in this country: the main rotunda, 100 feet square, is probably the largest in any hotel in the world. Throughout the building the furniture and appointments are of the choicest and most expensive kind. Every requisite of a first-class modern hotel is found at the Grand. The whole property is valued at $1,000,000. The hotel was opened in 1874, and has ever since been conducted by the lessees and proprietors, Gilmour & Sons, who had previously been the proprietors of the Eutaw and St. Clair Hotels at Baltimore. The Grand is conveniently situated, and is on the American plan; the terms being $3 and $4 a day.

Grand Opera-House, north-west corner of Longworth and Vine Streets, main entrance on Vine, gallery entrance on Longworth Street. The auditorium is on the ground-floor; seating capacity, 2,300. There are six proscenium boxes, a gallery, balcony, dress-circle, and parquette. The means of egress are the most perfect of any theatre in the city: besides the regular modes of exit, there are six large windows on each side of the auditorium, reaching down to the floor, which can easily be pushed open outward, on the one side into Longworth Street, and on the other into an alley between the theatre and the Ohio Mechanics' Institute. The Opera-House is devoted to opera and the drama, Robert E. J. Miles being the lessee and manager. Only first-class performances are given. The regular dramatic season begins in September, and closes in April. Admission to dress-circle, 75 cents; parquette, $1.00; balcony, 50 cents; gallery, 25 cents; reserved seats, 25 cents extra. The Opera-House is half a minute's walk from Fountain Square.

Greenwood Hall, in the third story of the Ohio Mechanics' Institute building, south-west corner of Sixth and Vine Streets, and named in honor of Miles Greenwood, who superintended the construction of the building, and was for several years president of the Institute, is a commodious hall, with side-room conveniences, and is largely used for balls, concerts, and travelling entertainments.

Grocers' Exchange is an association of wholesale grocers, who meet at the call of the president to discuss matters of interest to the trade. Its monthly meetings are held in the rooms of the Board of Trade and Transportation. Dues, $25 a year. Bradford Shinkle is president.

Gymnasiums. — See Cincinnati Gymnasium, and see Turnverein.

Hacks. — *Stands:* No. 1, on the west side of Broadway, between Front and Second Streets; No. 2, on the south side of Fifth, between Main and Sycamore; No. 3, on the east side of Walnut, between Gano and Seventh; No. 4, in the centre of Fifth, between Main and Walnut; No. 5, on the west side of Vine, between Fourth and Baker; No. 6, on the west side of Vine, between Third and Pearl, southwardly from Pearl 100 feet; No. 7, on the south side of Sixth Street, between Plum and Elm Streets. *Ordinances:* Section 7. — *Driver to exhibit Card.* — The driver shall hand to each adult passenger in his coach, before a bargain for his services is made, a card whereon shall be printed in a clear, legible manner, the number of his coach, the name of the owner and driver, and the rates of fare. Sect. 8. — *Rates of Fare.* — The rates of fare for carrying a single passenger shall not exceed the following rates: where no bargain is made, it shall not be more than 50 cents; in all cases, children over ten years of age half-price; under that age, free. Each passenger may have a trunk conveyed without additional charge, but must pay for every additional trunk 25 cents, and for all other articles occupying a seat, weighing over thirty pounds, 25 cents each.

Halls, Public. — Scattered throughout the city, there are more than a hundred public halls used for general purposes. Among the most important are Greenwood Hall, Sixth and Vine; Melodeon Hall, Fourth and Walnut; College Hall, Walnut, between Fourth and Fifth; Apollo Hall, Sixth and Walnut; Eureka Hall, Ninth and Walnut; Geyer's Assembly Rooms, Court Street, between Main and Walnut; Mozart Hall, Vine and Longworth; Women's Christian Temperance Union Hall, 115 West Sixth; Young Men's Christian Association Hall, Sixth and Elm.

Hamilton County, of which Cincinnati is the county-seat, exclusive of the town-lots, contains 213,000 acres. It has fifteen townships; viz., Anderson, Cincinnati, Colerain, Columbia, Crosby, Delhi, Green, Harrison, Miami, Millcreek, Spencer, Springfield, Sycamore, Symmes, Whitewater. The villages in the county are Camp Dennison, Montgomery, Loveland, Reading, Sharon, Runyan, Evendale, Lockland, Carthage, Wyoming, Scott, Harrison, Cleves, North Bend, Warsaw, Delhi, Cheviot, Avondale, Clifton, Ludlow Grove, Oakland, Winton Place, College Hill, Sharpsburg, St. Bernard, Linwood, Madisonville, Pleasant Ridge, Crance, Plainville, Mount Carmel, Newtown, California, Mount Washington, Riverside, Mount Airy, Hartwell, Glendale, Home City. Hamilton County is in the southwest corner of Ohio, between the Great and Little Miami Rivers. In round numbers there are over 50,000 voters in the county, showing a population of over 350,000.

Harrison Pike connects with Harrison Avenue at the bridge over Mill Creek, at Ernst Station. It passes north through Fairmount, winding around one of the high hills in gaining the summit, and then takes a westerly course, passing through a lovely country, where almost every sunny slope is a vineyard, to Cheviot, and thence west to the village of Harrison, from which the pike takes its name. The road is well macadamized, and furnishes one of the many delightful drives out of the city.

Hartwell is an incorporated village, about ten miles north of Fountain Square. It is named after John W. Hartwell, who was vice-president of the Cincinnati, Hamilton, and Dayton Railroad at the time the station was located. It is a neat village, with a population of about four hundred, having a Methodist church and a graded school, and is the home chiefly of Cincinnati business-men. The Cleveland, Columbus, Cincinnati, and Indianapolis, and the Cincinnati, Hamilton, and Dayton Railroads have depots in the village.

Harvard is a word familiarly used to signify Harvard College or Harvard University. Although the University is situated in Cambridge, Mass., about a thousand miles from Cincinnati, still, as there are many of its graduates and undergraduates here, the name Harvard has become quite familiar. The college has for several years held examinations for admission simultaneously at Cambridge and Cincinnati, so that persons not desiring to go East can try the examinations in this city. The alumni have formed a club, known as the

Harvard Club, with the purpose of retaining the community of feeling shared while in college, and of working unitedly whenever any interest of the college is to be advanced. There are about a hundred graduates of the university in this city, and they hold many important professional and business positions; about a third being lawyers, and a fourth being physicians. The club gives an annual dinner.

Health of Cincinnati, the, judged by the death-rate in proportion to population, as compared with other large cities where accurate records are kept, is a theme for congratulation. Estimating the population of the city at 280,000, — the basis on which such calculations have been made for a number of years past, — the mortality of 1878 was in the proportion of 17.23 per thousand, or one in every 58.05 inhabitants. This places Cincinnati in the foremost rank of the healthful populous centres of the United States.

Hebrew Relief Association elects annually a board of directors, who meet every Sunday morning at the south-west corner of Fifth Street and Central Avenue to give weekly pensions to the poor, especially widows and people unfit for work, and also to aid transient poor from other cities. About $9,000 a year are donated for these purposes. The association is composed of Israelites, and Joe Zeiler is president.

Hebrew Union College. — Founded in 1875 by the union of American Hebrew congregations, governed by a board of governors; B. Bettmann of Cincinnati being its presiding officer. It has two departments, — 1, preparatory; 2, collegiate, — each of four years. Students in the preparatory must simultaneously attend the classical course of the high school, and those in the collegiate department must attend the academical course at the University of Cincinnati, if they enter for the degree of rabbi. The subjects taught are the Jewish literature, theology, and history, Semitic philology, preparing for the Jewish pulpit, and professorships in Semitic philology. The semesters open annually the first Monday in September and February. Tuition free, books free, no religious or other test. The first collegiate class opened Sept. 1, 1879, the other classes to be added year after year: the preparatory is complete. In the year 1878–79 there were twenty-three regular students and twelve extra hearers. The sessions for regular students are held daily at four P.M.; for students in Semitic languages, daily at five P.M. The college is on

Sixth Street, west of Cutter. A number of students receive stipends from $150 to $400 a year, provided by the collections of Hebrew ladies' societies throughout the country. The president is M. Loth.

Heuck's Opera-House. — On the north-west corner of Vine and Thirteenth Streets, the best of the "Over-the-Rhine" amusements, under the management of its proprietor, after whom the building is named. A dramatic company is kept, and the performances are principally of the comedy and variety order. The seating capacity of the auditorium, which contains a parquette, dress-circle, and gallery, is 1,500. There are entrances on Thirteenth Street, and through the beer-saloon on Vine Street. Beer, wine, liquors, and cigars are allowed; and each chair is fitted with a little bracket on which to rest the glasses. Admission ranges from 15 to 50 cents. The Vine-street cars pass the door.

Hibernia Hall. — South-east corner of Ninth and Plum Streets, second story. The A. O. U. W. Hall is on the floor above. It is the meeting-place of the various Irish societies, notably the Ancient Order of Hibernians and the Friendly Sons of St. Patrick. It is also rented for balls, assemblies, lectures, and political meetings.

Hibernians, Ancient Order of. — A mutual-benefit secret order of Irishmen, governed by a central division, to which subordinate divisions send delegates. The executive officers of each local division form the executive council of the central division, by which all benefits are dispensed. There are four local divisions in the city, three of which, as well as the central body, meet at Hibernia Hall.

Highland House and Belvedere, the newest and by far the most fashionable of the unique hill-top resorts, is situated on Mount Adams. The attractions at this delightful place are unsurpassed, and never fail to draw forth the most enthusiastic admiration of visitors. The halls, restaurant, bowling-saloon, billiard-room, ladies' reception-room, and parlor are decorated and furnished in a costly manner. The views from all parts of the house and grounds, and especially from the esplanade, belvedere, and balconies, are as grand as any in this locality. The Ohio River, spanned by three magnificent bridges, the romantic beauty of the Kentucky hills, the picturesque scenery of the Licking valley, the charming landscape of Eden Park, together with a full view of Cincinnati, Covington, and Newport, form a panorama of the grandest and most varied character. Connected with the Highland House is a ladies' riding-school and pony-track.

In the belvedere and on the grounds various entertainments take place; and on Tuesday and Friday evenings, until Oct. 1, the Theodore Thomas orchestra concerts are given here. At the concerts the admission is twenty-five cents, but at other times free, unless otherwise advertised. The Highland-house property is owned by a stock-company, of which G. B. Kerper is president. *Horse-cars.* — Sixth and Baymiller Streets run direct; and on all other lines of the Consolidated Street-railroad Company, tickets to the Highland House are sold, and the passengers transferred at Walnut Street.

Hilltops, the. — A name given generally to the elevated ground forming the boundary of three sides of the city, before its encroachments on adjacent territory. They form a semicircle about the lower levels, the east-and-west diameter of which is three miles, and the north-and-south radius a mile and a half. They have an average elevation above the Ohio River of four hundred feet; reaching higher at many points, but seldom lower than that figure. They are broken only by Deer Creek and Mill Creek on the north, and Lick Run on the west. They are now covered with elegant private residences, public institutions, and places of public resort. The summit is reached in all directions by the four inclined-plane railways.

Historical and Philosophical Society of Ohio, College Building. Library of 7,500 volumes and 30,000 pamphlets. Museum of historical curiosities. It has 83 members. Terms, $10 a year, $100 for life; corresponding and honorary members not charged. Meetings, first Saturday evening of each month. Open from ten A.M. to one P.M., except Sundays. Visitors welcome.

Home of the Friendless. — An institution having for its object the reclamation of abandoned women. It is managed by ladies connected with the various Protestant denominations of the city The building is on the south side of Court Street, between Central Avenue and John Street, is four stories in height, and can accommodate about 150 inmates. Commitments of young and incorrigible girls, who are on the road to ruin, are sometimes made from the police-court, when they are too old to enter the House of Refuge These are kindly cared for, although the Home has no authority to detain them. An average of 500 women and abandoned infants find temporary quarters in the Home each year.

Homœopathic Free Dispensary, the Cincinnati, corner Seventh and Mound Streets. All kinds of cases treated free. There are three departments, — the medical, the surgery and diseases of women, and the eye and ear. Consultation, nine to eleven A.M.; dispensary open from two to four P.M. daily.

Hopkins Park is named in honor of a former dry-goods merchant, L. C. Hopkins, who gave the city the three-fourths of an acre that the park contains. It is situated on the brow of Mount Auburn, at the head of Sycamore Street, and south end of Auburn Avenue.

Horse-Cars. — Fountain Square is the horse-car centre of Cincinnati; the cars of all the lines below the hills passing it in their route, with the exception of the Third-street and Eighth-street lines, which pass within a square's distance. On almost all lines a single fare is five cents: tickets in packages of six, four cents each; or twenty-five for a dollar. On route 9, single fare is four cents; twenty-five tickets for ninety cents. Route 9 tickets are not taken on the other lines: all other tickets are good on either line. Transfer tickets are given, without extra charge, on all West-End lines, to persons desiring to go as far west as Spring-grove Avenue or Brighton Station, a change of cars being made at Coleman Street. Through tickets, including two Bottom lines, one Inclined-plane and one Hill line, are sold on the cars for ten cents. Single fare on the inclined planes, five cents. The following is a list of the various lines, with their routes; the most popular name of the route being given.

Avenue line. — See Cumminsville and Spring-grove line.

Avondale line. — Starting from Fourth and Walnut Streets, thence north on Walnut to Fifth Streets, east to Broadway, north to Hunt Street, north-eastwardly to Montgomery Road, following same to Reading Road, and thence to Clinton-springs Avenue in Avondale; returning by same route to Fourth Street and Broadway, thence west to starting point.

Baymiller-street line start from the corner of McLean and Harrison Avenues, south on McLean to Western Avenue, south-east to Liberty, east to Baymiller, south to Sixth, east to Vine, south to Fifth, east to Lock, south to Third, west to Lawrence, north to Fourth, west to Elm, north to Sixth, thence west and north by double track to place of beginning.

Clifton line start from top of Clifton Inclined Plane, north to Calhoun, east to Vine, north to Hammond, east to Carthage Pike, north to Zoölogical Gardens, Burnet Woods, and Clifton.

Covington lines. — There are two lines to Covington, all starting from the Vine-street end of Fountain Square, south on Vine to Front, east to suspension-bridge, which they all cross.

Cumminsville and Spring-grove Avenue line start from stables Harrison and McLean Avenues, thence south on McLean Avenue to Western Avenue, thence south-east to Liberty Street, east to Freeman Avenue, south to Clark, east to Central Avenue, south to Twelfth Street, east to Walnut, south to Fourth Street, west to Vine Street, north to Twelfth Street, thence returning by double track to Spring-grove Avenue, and northwardly on said avenue to Cumminsville, connecting at Knowlton's Corner with cars running direct to the gate of Spring-grove Cemetery; returning by double track to the place of starting.

Eden-park and Walnut-hills line start from Fourth and Vine Streets, north on Vine to Fifth, east to Mount-Adams Inclined Plane, northwardly through Eden Park over a trestle-bridge 454 feet long and by Gilbert Avenue to Curtis Street, east to Kemper Lane, north to McMillan, east to Park Avenue, north to Chestnut; returning by same routes.

Eighth-street line start from west end of Eighth Street, east on Eighth to Central Avenue, south to Fourth, east to Main, north to Sixth, west to Elm, north to Eighth, west to place of beginning.

Elm-street line start from East-end Garden in Pendleton, west on Eastern Avenue to Washington and Third, thence on Third to Martin, thence to Pearl, west to Broadway, north to Fourth, west to Elm, north to McMicken Avenue; returning on Elm to Fifth, east to Broadway, south to Pearl, east to Front, and continuing by Front and Eastern Avenue to place of beginning. Connection is made at the East-end Garden with the Columbia and Mount-Lookout steam dummies.

Freeman-street line. — Same as Seventh-street line.

Gilbert-avenue line. — Same as Walnut-hills line.

John-street line start from Fourth and Main, west on Fourth to John, north to Findlay, west to Baymiller, north to Bank, west to Coleman, north to Central Avenue; returning east and south on Central Avenue to Fifth, east to Main, and south to Fourth.

Liberty-street line. — Starting from Fourth and Main Streets, west on Fourth to Elm Street, north to Liberty Street, west to Freeman Avenue, north to Central Avenue, west to Colerain Avenue, thence northwardly to Centre Street in Camp Washington; returning by same route to Freeman Avenue and York Street, thence east on York Street to Linn Street, south to Liberty Street, east to Elm Street, south to Twelfth Street, east to Vine Street, south to Fifth Street, east to Main Street, and south to Fourth Street.

Main-street line start at Fifth and Main, north on Main to Inclined Plane, from the summit of which north on Locust to Mason, east on Mason to Auburn, and north on Auburn and Washington Streets to Zoölogical Gardens; returning by same route to Main and Court, west on Court to Walnut, south to Fifth, and east to Main.

Newport line start from the Walnut-street end of Fountain Square, east on Fifth to Broadway, south to Pearl, east to the Louisville Short-line Railroad Bridge, thence across the bridge to Newport, making connection with the Bellevue and Dayton steam dummy.

Riverside and Sedamsville line start from Eighth-street and Walker mill Road, south on the latter to Lower River Road, and west to Riverside; return by same route.

Seventh-street line cars start from Fourth and Vine, north on Vine to Seventh, west to Freeman, north to Bank, west to Coleman, north to Central Avenue, east to Freeman; returning, south on Freeman to York, east to Linn, south to Ninth, east to Walnut, south to Fourth, west to Vine.

Sixth-street line. — Same as Baymiller-street line.

Third-street line start from Third and Lawrence, north on Lawrence to Fourth, west to Smith, north to Fifth, west to Freeman, north to Sixth, west to Mill-Creek Bridge; returning by the same route to Fifth and Wood, south on Wood to Third, and east to Lawrence.

Vine-street, or Route 9, start from Vine-street end of Fountain Square, north on Vine to McMicken Avenue, thence north-west to Mohawk Bridge, connecting with cars on Brown Street; thence northwardly to Cliff Street; returning by same route.

Walnut-hills line start from Fourth and Walnut, north to Fifth east to Broadway, north to Hunt, east *viâ* Effluent-pipe Street to Gilbert Avenue, north to Walnut Hills; returning by Gilbert Avenue to Broadway, south to Fourth, and west to Walnut Street.

Horticultural Society, the Cincinnati, has been established about thirty-six years. At its rooms, 180 Main Street, meetings are held every Saturday, when topics of interest to horticulturists and agriculturists are discussed, and specimens of fruit exhibited. The membership is about six hundred.

Hospital for Contagious Diseases (popularly known as the "Pest House)." A branch of the Cincinnati Hospital, located in an isolated tract of ground in Lick-Run Valley, in the vicinity of the Potter's Field, or pauper burying-ground. The house is new and commodious, and has accommodations for about a hundred patients. It is designed for the treatment of small-pox and other contagious diseases. A physician and corps of nurses are employed, the former at a salary of $50 per month.

Hospitals. — See Cincinnati Hospital, Good-Samaritan Hospital, St. Mary's Hospital, Jewish Hospital, Hospital for Contagious Diseases.

Hotels. — The principal hotels are the Burnet House, Third and Vine Streets; Crawford House, Sixth and Walnut Streets; Gibson House, Fourth and Walnut Streets; Grand Hotel, Fourth Street and Central Avenue; Hotel Emery, Vine, between Fourth and Fifth; Hunt's Hotel and Dining-Rooms, Vine, between Fourth and Fifth; St. James, Fourth and Hammond Streets, St. Nicholas, Fourth and Race; Walnut-street House, Walnut, between Sixth and Seventh; Palace Hotel, Sixth and Vine.

Hotel Emery is on Vine Street, between Fourth and Fifth Streets, but has its entrance in the Emery Arcade. It was opened in November, 1877, and has 175 guest-rooms, all well furnished. It is one of the newest, largest, and best-kept hotels in the city, and is conducted on both the European and American plans. On the European plan the prices of rooms range from $1 to $2.50 per day, and meals are served in the hotel restaurant at moderate prices. On the American plan the terms are $3 and $4 per day.

House Decorations and Upholstery. — Interest in home beautifying has lately grown in importance, until the family that has not all or part of the house decorated to some degree, in conformity with the demands of modern æstheticism, is considered poorly off indeed. Different varieties and degrees of taste are manifest in these attempts, and the effect is more or less complete as the parties possess a greater or less degree of culture or refinement. That this should be so is natural, the more so when we consider that no matter what degree of taste the person may have, not having made a study of the subject in its most minute details, the general effect must be incomplete and

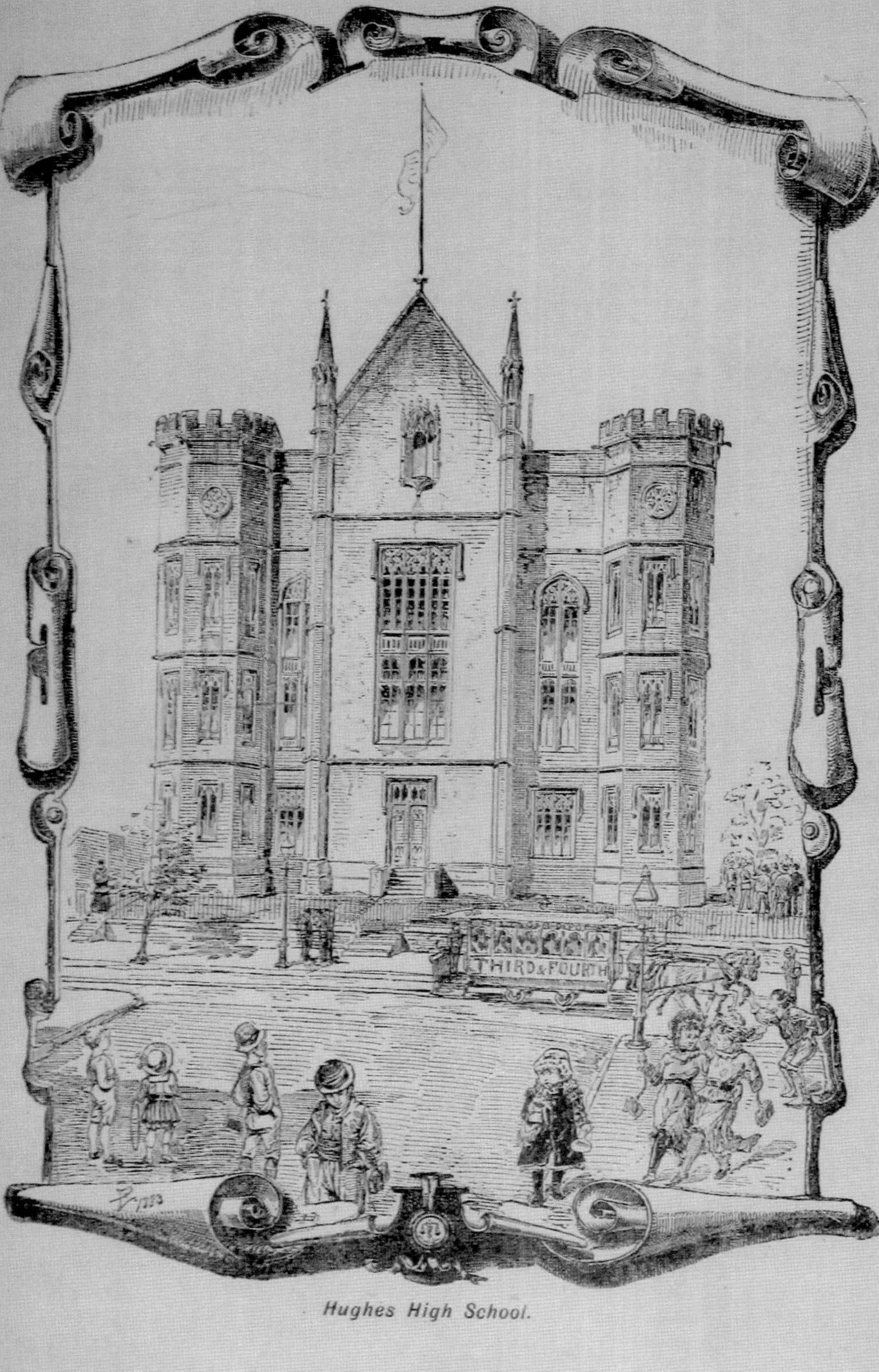

Hughes High School.

unsatisfactory. The irresistible conclusion, then, is that in house decorations, one should go to that person or firm best qualified to accomplish the desired end in the most pleasing and artistic manner; and to such persons desiring a reliable house, none can be more conscientiously recommended than The John Shillito Company, where will be found a competent corps of artists in this branch, whose taste and experience can be relied upon to produce the most gratifying results.

House of Refuge. — A house of correction for incorrigible and criminal youth of both sexes, between the ages of eight and sixteen years. The building is situated in Camp Washington, on the Colerain Pike, three miles and a half from Fountain Square. The buildings are of blue native limestone, with window-caps and cornices of white limestone. It is four stories in height, besides the basement, and has a frontage of 227 feet. There are now about 500 inmates, four-fifths of whom are boys. They are given the rudiments of a general education, including music, and are taught useful trades. Incorrigible children are committed from the police-court. The term of confinement lasts during the minority of the child. The annual cost to the city, by which the Refuge is maintained, is about $50,000.

Hughes High School. — Named in honor of its benefactor, Thomas Hughes, who left the bulk of his fortune by will to the city, for the purpose of founding a high school. The building is situated on Fifth Street, opposite the beginning of Mound Street, and was built in 1853, at a cost of $25,000. It is a massive building, and in architectural beauty is worthy of the city. The average attendance of pupils is about 500. Pupils must reside in the district west of Central Avenue and south of Clark Street.

Hunt's Hotel and Dining-Rooms, on the east side of Vine Street, between Fourth and Fifth, is one of the most widely known places of its kind in this city. The restaurant is exceedingly popular, and is one of the most commodious in the West. The prices are low, and the *cuisine* is good. This restaurant, in the oyster-season, has the largest oyster-trade in the city. The hotel has a hundred rooms, and is conducted on the European plan; the prices of rooms ranging from 50 cents to $1 a day. The proprietors are C. B. Hunt & Co.

Imports. — The imports from foreign countries, through this and other ports, show a very marked increase over preceding years. The total value of goods imported in 1882 aggregated $1,966,361 in comparison with $1,497,262 in 1881; $1,092,366 in 1880; and $964,614 in 1879; being an increase of more than 31 per cent above those of 1881, 80 per cent above 1880, and 103 per cent above 1879. A glance at these figures shows a healthy and most gratifying condition of business, and indicates that Cincinnati is making rapid strides towards the front rank among ports of entry, and that her merchants are more largely and generally than ever before making their purchases and imports direct from markets abroad. These facilities guarantee lower prices, and larger varieties of goods in this market. Jobbers and retailers can now make their purchases virtually at their doors, saving the expense and fatigue incident to long journeys to distant markets, at one time necessary to obtain supplies of goods.

Inclined Planes. — There are four of these popular and useful elevators in the city, — one in the western, one in the eastern, and two in the northern parts. All land their passengers on the heights about four hundred feet above the level of the river. *Clifton Inclined Plane* is at the intersection of McMicken Avenue and Elm Street. The Elm-street and the Vine-street horse-cars lead directly to it; and at the top is the Bellevue House, where connection is made with horse-cars for Mount Auburn, Corryville, Zoölogical Gardens, Burnet-woods Park, and Clifton. *Mount-Adams and Eden-park Inclined Plane* is on Lock Street, about a hundred feet south of Fifth Street. The Baymiller-street line of horse-cars pass the foot of the plane; and when special attractions are offered at the Highland House, which is situated at the head of the plane, cars from various parts of the city are run direct to the Inclined Plane. At the Highland House connection is made with the Eden-park, Walnut-hills, and Avondale lines of horse-cars. *Mount-Auburn Inclined Plane* is at the head of Main Street, and is reached by the Main-street line of horse-cars. The Lookout House is at the top of the plane, and horse-car connection is there made with the Mount-Auburn line for the Zoölogical Gardens. *Price's-hill Inclined Plane* begins at the foot of Eighth Street, where it intersects the State Avenue. This is the only one of the inclined railways that has a double track and double set of machinery, — one for pedestrians, and the other for horses and vehicles. The Eighth-street horse-cars stop at the foot of the plane.

India Shawls, or, as they are known by the trade, Valley-Cashmere shawls, can be seen in large variety in the salesrooms of The John Shillito Company. Cashmere is a province of Northern India, separated from the kingdom of Thibet by the Himalaya Mountains, and was formerly included in the Sikh Dominion, a part of the Lahore Monarchy. In 1846 it was erected by Great Britain into a separate state, and placed under a native ruler. Among other curious manufactures of Cashmere is that of *shawls;* and the delicate wool of which the finest are made is the produce of a species of goat of the adjoining country of Thibet. These shawls, for fineness of fibre and depth of coloring, have attained a world-wide reputation.

Insane Asylum. — See Longview Insane Asylum, and see Sanitarium.

Insurance Companies.

FIRE AND MARINE INSURANCE COMPANIES IN OHIO AND OTHER STATES HAVING AGENCIES IN CINCINNATI.

Incorp'd.	Name	Home Office	Gross Assets.	Agent.	Office.
1819	Ætna	Hartford, Conn.	$9,054,610	Chapman Johnson	171 Vine Street.
1877	Allen County Mutual	Lima, O.	420,000	A. R. Witham	57 West Third St.
1818	American	Boston, Mass.	580,267	A. A. Long & Co.	35 West Third St.
	American	Newark, N.J.	1,600,730	Adam Gray & Co.	55 West Third St.
1853	American Central	St. Louis, Mo.	1,150,000	Simon Sturm	76 West Third St.
1857	American Fire	New York, N.Y.	1,110,065	Charles Bonsall & Sons,	17 West Third St.
1851	Ashland Mutual	Ashland	558,024	A. R. Witham	57 West Third St.
1872	Boston Underwriters	Boston, Mass.	2,129,154	Adam Gray & Co.	55 West Third St.
1872	Boylston Mutual	Boston, Mass.	980,720	A. A. Long & Co.	35 West Third St.
1874	Buckeye Mutual	Shelby, O.	538,000	A. R. Witham	57 West Third St.
1867	Buffalo German	Buffalo, N.Y.	936,940	— — —	37 West Third St.
1863	California	San Francisco, Cal.	920,503	J. M. Sears	24 West Fourth St.
1877	Canton Mutual	Canton, O.	250,000	T. A. Patterson	30 West Fourth St.
1877	Capital City Mutual	Columbus, O.	240,000	T. A. Patterson	30 West Fourth St.
1836	Citizens'	New York, N.Y.	1,033,998	Miller, Dickerson, & Co.	7 West Third St.
1837	Citizens'	St. Louis, Mo.	400,000	S. F. Covington	68 West Third St.
1870	City of Pittsburgh	Pittsburgh, Penn.	197,984	George W. Neff & Co.	21 West Third St.
1850	Clinton	New York, N.Y.	501,752	John Kennett & Son	11 West Third St.
1882	Columbia	Dayton, O.	229,304	William Young	37 West Third St.
	Columbus Mutual	Columbus, O.	—	— — —	72 West Third St.
1859	Commerce	Albany, N.Y.	421,277	J. Kennett & Son	11 West Third St.
1850	Commercial	New York, N.Y.	506 622	J. H. Beattie	260 Vine Street.
1850	Connecticut	Hartford, Conn.	1,781,626	Adam Gray & Co.	55 West Third St.
1852	Continental	New York, N.Y.	4,450,535	Charles Bonsall & Sons,	17 West Third St.
1867	Cooper	Dayton, O.	282,460	Miller, Dickerson & Co. and William Young	7 West Third St. 37 West Third St.
1876	Corn City Mutual	Toledo, O.	400,000	T. A. Patterson	30 West Fourth St.
1851	Dayton	Dayton, O.	1,000,000	Simon Sturm	76 West Third St.
1876	Delaware Mutual	Delaware, O.	275,000	A. R. Witham	57 West Third St.
1835	Delaware Mutual Safety	Philadelphia, Penn.	2,005,493	Charles Bonsall & Sons,	17 West Third St.
1866	Detroit	Detroit, Mich.	669,236	Charles Bonsall & Sons,	17 West Third St.

Fire and Marine Insurance Companies in Ohio and other States having Agencies in Cincinnati. — Continued.

Incorp'd.	Name.	Home Office	Gross Assets	Agent.	Office
	Dwelling House	Boston, Mass.	–	– – –	13 West Third St.
1872	Farragut	New York, N. Y.	$530,252	M. G. Dodds & Co.	68 West Third St.
1820	Fire Association	Philadelphia, Penn.	4,404,646	John H. Law & Co.	Third and Walnut.
1863	Fireman's Fund	San Francisco, Cal.	1,322,425	William B. Cassilly	53 West Third St.
	Firemen's	Baltimore, Md.	–	– – –	8 West Third St.
1835	Firemen's	Dayton, O.	436,111	Adam Gray & Co.	55 West Third St.
1855	Firemen's	Newark, N. J.	1,309,583	Charles Bonsall & Sons,	17 West Third St.
	Franklin	Boston, Mass.	–	– – –	24 West Fourth St.
1829	Franklin	Philadelphia, Penn.	3,086,637	Law & Gansel	62 West Third St.
1862	German	Pittsburgh, Penn.	413,493	Law & Gansel	62 West Third St.
1872	German American	New York, N.Y.	3,704,275	Fred Rauh	32 West Third St.
1859	Germania	New York, N. Y.	2,566,658	A. A. Long & Co.	35 West Third St.
1853	Girard	Philadelphia, Penn.	1,200,000	Simon Sturm	76 West Third St.
1849	Glen's Falls	Glen's Falls, N.Y.	1,212,330	Charles Bonsall & Sons,	17 West Third St.
1850	Hanover	New York, N.Y.	2,560,000	Law & Gansel	62 West Third St.
1810	Hartford	Hartford, Conn.	4,337,280	Adam Gray & Co.	55 West Third St.
	Home	Columbus, O.	–	– – –	8 West Third St.
1853	Home	New York, N. Y.	7,208,489	William B. Cassilly	53 West Third St.
1825	Howard	New York, N.Y.	827,976	Francis H. Cloud	Race and George Sts.
1876	Illinois Mutual	Alton, Ill.	260,000	T. A. Patterson	30 West Fourth St.
1794	Insurance Company of N. America,	Philadelphia, Penn.	8,881,053	Miller, Dickerson, & Co.	7 & 9 West Third St.
1794	Insurance Company of the State of Pennsylvania	Philadelphia, Penn.	716,226	George W. Neff & Co.	21 West Third St.
1867	Kenton	Covington, Ky.	318,716	George W. Neare	4 Public Landing.
1871	Lorillard Fire Insurance Company,	New York, N.Y.	397,094	H. C. Schell & Son	64 West Third St.
1879	Louisville Underwriters'	Louisville, Ky.	716,761	G. W. Neare	4 Public Landing.
1873	Manufacturers'	Boston, Mass.	972,917	– –	
1882	Manufacturers' and Merchants' Mutual	Rockford, Ill.	150,000	T. A. Patterson	30 West Fourth St.
1853	Mechanics' and Traders'	New York, N.Y.	503,910	Miller, Dickerson, & Co.	7 West Third St.
1882	Mechanics' Mutual	New York, N.Y.	500,000	T. A. Patterson	30 West Fourth St.
1871	Mercantile	Cleveland, O.	384,974	Charles Bonsall & Sons,	17 West Third St.

Fire and Marine Insurance Companies in Ohio and other States having Agencies in Cincinnati — Continued.

Incorp'd.	Name.	Home Office.	Gross Assets.	Agent.	Office.
1823	Mercantile Marine	Boston, Mass.	$717,260	J. H. Beattie	260 Vine Street.
1855	Merchants'	Newark, N.J.	1,164,171	John Kennett & Son	11 West Third St.
1876	Merchants' and Manufacturers' Mutual	Mansfield, O.	525,000	A. R. Witham	57 West Third St.
	Miami Valley	Dayton, O.	–	– – –	31 West Third St.
1852	Milwaukee Mechanics'	Milwaukee, Wis.	914,066	William Young	37 West Third St.
1881	Monitor Fire Association	Canton, O.	100,000	T. A. Patterson	30 West Fourth St.
1882	Mutual	New York, N.Y.	230,000	T. A. Patterson	30 West Fourth St.
1871	National	Hartford, Conn.	1,733,281	W. B. Cassilly	53 West Third St.
1838	National	New York, N.Y.	387,182	S. F. Covington	68 West Third St.
1810	Newark Fire	Newark, N.J.	726,441	John Kennett & Son	11 West Third St.
	New-England Underwriters	Providence, R.I.	923,549	J. H. Beattie	260 Vine Street.
1869	New Hampshire	Manchester, N.H.	915,132	Law & Gansel	62 West Third St.
1805	New-Orleans Fire-Insurance Co.	New Orleans, La.	1,861,351	J. Kennett & Son	11 West Third St.
	New York Alliance	New York, N.Y.	–	– – –	13 & 32 West Third.
1864	New-York Underwriters' Agency	New York, N.Y.	5,000,000	John S. Perkins	31 West Third St.
1850	Niagara	New York, N.Y.	1,776,836	Fred Rauh	32 West Third St.
1869	North-western National	Milwaukee, Wis.	1,127,312	J. Burnet, jun.	81 West Third St.
1865	Ohio	Dayton, O.	278,247	George W. Neff & Co.	21 West Third St.
1848	Ohio Farmers'	Le Roy, O.	1,118,000	H. S. Collier	63 West Fifth St.
1877	Ohio Mutual	Salem, O.	750,000	A. R. Witham	57 West Third St.
1867	Orient	Hartford, Conn.	1,395,404	Miller, Dickerson, & Co.	7 West Third St.
	Orient Mutual	New York, N.Y.	–	– – –	260 Vine Street.
1825	Pennsylvania	Philadelphia, Penn.	2,301,946	Miller, Dickerson, & Co.	Third and Main Sts.
1854	Pennsylvania Fire-Insurance Co.	Pittsburgh, Penn.	299,238	Law & Gansel	62 West Third St.
1876	People's	Ravenna, O.	200,000	A. R. Witham	57 West Third St.
1851	People's	New York, N.Y.	253,239	John P. Whiteman	12 West Third St.
	Philadelphia Underwriters	Philadelphia, Penn.	–	– – –	Third and Main Sts.
1853	Phoenix	Brooklyn, N.Y.	3,295,327	– – –	37 West Third St.
1854	Phoenix	Hartford, Conn.	4,446,209	Francis H. Cloud	Race and George Sts.
1872	Prescott	Boston, Mass.	382,029	J. M. Sears	24 West Fourth St.
1799	Providence-Washington	Providence, R.I.	1,007,364	John Kennett & Son	11 West Third St.

Fire and Marine Insurance Companies in Ohio and other States having Agencies in Cincinnati. — Concluded.

Incorp'd.	Name.	Home Office.	Gross Assets.	Agent.	Office.
1841	Reliance Fire-Insurance Company,	Philadelphia, Penn.	753,906	Law & Gansel	62 West Third St.
1851	Rhode Island	Providence, R.I.	900,000	Simon Sturm	76 West Third St.
1851	Richland Mutual	Mansfield, O.	1,538,144	A. R. Witham	57 West Third St.
1865	St. Paul	St. Paul, Minn.	1,048,673	Miller, Dickerson, & Co.	7 West Third St
1872	Shoe and Leather	Boston, Mass.	976,373	J. M. Sears	24 West Fourth St.
1849	Springfield of Massachusetts	Springfield, Mass.	2,395,288	Adam Gray & Co.	55 West Third St.
1859	Standard	New York, N.Y.	405,882	Charles Bonsall & Sons,	17 West Third St.
1864	Star	New York, N.Y.	759,141	Charles Bonsall & Sons,	17 West Third St.
1864	Sterling	New York, N.Y.	421,922	S. F. Covington	68 West Third St.
1848	Toledo	Toledo, O.	215,093	Miller, Dickerson, & Co.	7 West Third St.
1865	Traders'	Chicago, Ill.	1,057,217	William Young	37 West Third St.
	Tradesmen's	New York, N.Y.	–	– – –	32 West Third St.
1874	Union	Buffalo, N.Y.	132,301	John Kennett & Son	11 West Third St.
1865	Union	California	1,098,513	F. Rauh	32 West Third St.
1804	Union	Philadelphia, Penn.	884,299	J. M. Sears	24 West Fourth St.
1824	United States	New York, N.Y.	526,561	M. G. Dodds & Co.	68 West Third St.
1876	Van Wert Mutual	Van Wert, O.	545,635	A. R. Witham	57 West Third St.
	Watertown	Watertown, N.Y.	–	– – –	31 West Third St.
1837	Westchester	New York, N.Y.	924,010	Adam Gray & Co.	55 West Third St.
1882	Western Manufacturers' Mutual	Chicago, Ill.	500,000	T. A. Patterson	30 West Fourth St.
1846	Western Mutual	Urbana, O.	401,667	A. R. Witham	57 West Third St.
1853	Williamsburgh	Brooklyn, N.Y.	1,068,647	Adam Gray & Co.	55 West Third St.

HOME FIRE AND FIRE-AND-MARINE INSURANCE COMPANIES.

Incorp'd.	Name.	Office.	Gross Assets.	President.	Secretary.
1871	Amazon	260 Vine	$574,705	Gozzam Gano	J. H. Beattie.
	Aurora	6 West Fourth			
1829	Cincinnati	81 West Third	235,015	J. Burnet, jun.	L. L. Townley, *Assistant Secretary.*
1826	Cincinnati Equitable	60 West Third	348,478	– – –	T. S. Goodman.
1851	Citizens'	79 West Third	149,993	Lewis Glenn	John B. Abernathy.
1838	Commercial	67 West Third	236,583	J. A. Townley	J. W. Johnson.
1850	Eagle	73 West Third	169,923	Henry Kessler	Samuel P. Post.
1865	Enterprise	82 West Third	271,301		
1864	Eureka	23 West Third	256,742	John Kyle	E. E. Townley.
1866	Farmers'	19 West Third	120,461	Joseph F. Larkin	H. F. Finke.
1832	Firemen's	29 West Third	180,467	George McLaughlin	T. C. Champlin.
	German Mutual	Walnut and Twelfth.			
1864	Germania	27 West Third	150,676	Peter A. White	D. B. Meyer.
1865	Globe	68 West Third	130,361	S. F. Covington	B. T. Cleman.
1876	Manufacturers' Mutual	21 West Fourth	152,788	J. H. Brunsman.	
1838	Merchants' and Manufacturers'	15 West Third	290,699	William H. Calvert.	
	Merchants' Mutual	Third and Main.			
1837	Miami Valley	33 West Third	137,782	George W. Jones.	
1874	Mutual	183 Walnut	178,849	R. W. Keys	S. A. McCune.
1851	National	69 West Third	196,374	H. C. Urner	G. W. Pohlman.
	Phoenix Mutual	Third and Main.			
1881	Security	23 West Third	191,477	John Kyle	E. E. Townley.
	Sun Mutual	3 Gr'd Opera-house.			
1859	Union	66 West Third	127,000	Abraham C. Edwards	Joseph T. Blair.
1836	Washington	76 West Third	265,000	E. V. Brookfield	Charles Rule.
1836	Western	82 West Third	184,717	F. X. Reno	Charles F. Runck.

HOME LIFE-INSURANCE COMPANY.

Incorp'd.	Name.	Office.	Gross Assets.	President.	Secretary.
1867	Union Central	Fourth and C'l Ave.	$1,837,091	John Davis	E. P. Marshall.

FOREIGN FIRE-INSURANCE COMPANIES HAVING OFFICES IN CINCINNATI.

Incorp'd.	Name.	Home Office.	Gross Assets in U. S.	Agent.	Office.
1833	British-American Assurance Co.	Toronto, Can.	$827,980	Miller, Dickerson, & Co.	7 West Third St.
1881	City of London	London, Eng.	767,837	Fred Rauh	32 West Third St.
1861	Commercial Union Assurance	London, Eng.	2,160,258	Miller, Dickerson, & Co.	7 West Third St.
1880	Fire-Insurance Association	London, Eng.	5,349,944	Adam Gray & Co.	55 West Third St.
1821	Guardian Assurance Company	London, Eng.	1,096,914	Fred Rauh	32 West Third St.
1854	Hamburg Bremen	Germany	978,600	Fred Rauh	32 West Third St.
1810	Imperial	London, Eng.	13,164,200	John H. Law & Co.	Third and Walnut.
1852	Lancaster	Manchester, Eng.	1,106,317	Fred Rauh	32 West Third St.
1879	Lion of London	London, Eng.	1,000,000	Simon Sturm	76 West Third St.
1836	Liverpool and London and Globe	Liverpool, Eng.	33,320,106	J. M. DeCamp	Third and Main Sts.
1720	London Assurance Corporation	London, Eng.	16,283,465	Adam Gray & Co.	55 West Third St.
1861	London and Lancashire	Liverpool, Eng.	1,285,496	– – –	Third & Walnut, and 62 & 64 West Third.
1861	London and Lancashire Fire	Liverpool, Eng.	8,459,976	John H. Law & Co.	Third and Walnut.
	North British and Mercantile	Edinburgh, Scot.	–	– – –	19 West Third St.
1809	North British and Mercantile	London, Eng.	3,250,000	William B. Cassilly	53 West Third St.
1836	Northern of London	London, Eng.	14,286,000	John H. Law & Co.	Third and Walnut.
1797	Norwich Fire-Insurance Society	England	1,000,000	Simon Sturm	76 West Third St.

FOREIGN FIRE-INSURANCE COMPANIES HAVING OFFICES IN CINCINNATI. — Concluded.

Incorp'd.	Name.	Home Office.	Gross Assets in U. S.	Agent.	Office.
1782	Phoenix Assurance Company	London, Eng.	$5,610,595	Adam Gray & Co.	55 West Third St.
1858	Queen of Liverpool and London	Liverpool, Eng.	1,752,208	Law & Gansel	62 West Third St.
	Rhenish-Westphalian-Lloyd	Germany	–	– – –	13 West Third St.
1845	Royal	Liverpool, Eng.	32,000,000	John H. Law & Co.	Third and Walnut.
1824	Scottish Union and National	England	1,000,000	Simon Sturm	76 West Third St.
	Standard	London, Eng.	–	– – –	76 West Third St.
1710	Sun	London, Eng.	1,252,754	William Young	37 West Third St.
1872	Trans-Atlantic	Germany	369,752	Fred Rauh	32 West Third St.
1851	Western Assurance Company	Toronto, Can.	900,000	George W. Neff & Co.	21 West Third St.

LIFE-INSURANCE COMPANIES IN OHIO AND OTHER STATES DOING BUSINESS IN CINCINNATI.

Incorp'd.	Name.	Home Office.	Gross Assets.	Agent.	Office.
	Ætna	Hartford, Conn.	–	– – –	Fourth and Race Sts.
	Charter Oak	Hartford, Conn.	–	– – –	Wiggins Block.
	Columbus Mutual-Relief Association	Columbus, O.	–	– – –	216 West Ninth St.
1846	Connecticut Mutual	Hartford, Conn.	$51,602,423	Robert H. Kellogg	1 Johnston Build'g.
1862	Continental	Hartford, Conn.	2,734,418	W. E. Bonfrey	24 Johnston Build'g.
1859	Equitable Life-Assurance Society	New York, N.Y.	48,025,751	George P. Bassett	5 Johnston Build'g.
	Fidelity Mutual-Aid Association	Philadelphia, Penn.	–	– – –	10 Glenn Building.
1860	Germania	New York, N.Y.	10,000,000	George Bauer	4 Johnston Building.

LIFE-INSURANCE COMPANIES IN OHIO AND OTHER STATES DOING BUSINESS IN CINCINNATI. — Concluded.

Incorp'd.	Name.	Home Office.	Gross Assets.	Agent.	Office.
1866	Hartford Life and Annuity	Hartford, Conn.	$1,114,304	W. W. Mosher	47 West Second St.
1860	Home	New York, N.Y.	5,191,683	R. W. Bruehl & Son	82 West Third St.
1850	Manhattan	New York, N.Y.	10,662,477	Robert L. Douglass	3 Johnston Build'g.
1851	Massachusetts Mutual	Springfield, Mass.	7,332,797	E. H. Jones	28 Johnston Build'g.
1866	Metropolitan	New York, N.Y.	2,013,201	John Wilson	183 Walnut Street.
	Mutual	New York, N.Y.	–	– – –	259 West Fourth St.
1845	Mutual Benefit	Newark, N.J.	35,005,349	Robert Simpson	182 West Fourth St.
1874	Mutual Protection Association of Patrons of Husbandry	– – –	–	Col. William H. Hill	18 Gazette Building.
	New York	New York, N.Y.	–	– – –	76 West Third St.
1858	Northwestern Mutual	Milwaukee, Wis.	19,794,672	M. J. Mack	2 Hammond Build'g.
1847	Penn Mutual	Philadelphia, Penn.	8,483,808	F. G. Cross	5 Wiggins Block.
1851	Phoenix Mutual	Hartford, Conn.	10,625,451	Paul Feinknopf	57 West Third St.
	Provident Life and Trust Company,	Philadelphia, Penn.	–	– – –	134 West Fourth St.
	Southern Ohio Mutual Relief Association	– – –	–	– – –	27 Emery Arcade.
1864	Travelers' Life and Accident	Hartford, Conn.	6,667,394	James J. Morcom	162 Vine and 249 West Fourth Sts.
	Union Mutual	Maine	–	– – –	10 Johnston Build'g.
1860	Washington	New York, N.Y.	6,574,020	James B. Day	27 Johnston Build'g.
1873	Western Mutual Protection	Bellefontaine, O.	Assessment Plan	Alvah Parker	57 West Third St.

Furniture Department.

In connection with our upholstery department we show a large variety of fine furniture, embracing

Suits,

in the

Different Styles and Woods,

also

Large Assortment of Odd or Single Pieces

in numerous styles.

Vienna Bent Wood, Rattan,

and

Reed Furniture,

in the various colorings, always in stock, at the lowest prices.

Re-covering and Re-upholstering a Specialty.

We are prepared to furnish private residences throughout,—

Carpets, Draperies, Furniture, etc.

Designs and estimates furnished when requested.

Competent Workmen execute all Orders with Despatch.

The John Shillito Company.

Inwood Park. — A name given to the old Shoenberger homestead, on Vine Street, about half way up the Vine-street Hill. The grounds contain fourteen acres, and are used for picnics, balls, and pleasure-parties. The surface is diversified with hills and ravines. It has all the necessary appurtenances for dancing, swinging, and athletic exercises, besides a wine and beer house and restaurant. The most convenient way of reaching the park is by the Mount-Auburn Inclined Plane. A bridge 1,100 feet in length spans the principal ravine between the Lookout House and Inwood Park.

Jewish Congregations. — *Brotherly Love*, purely Germans, occupies a brick building, dedicated by Rabbi I. M. Wise in 1867. It is situated on the corner of John and Melanchthon Streets, and its seating capacity is 400. Membership, 60 families. *Children of Israel*, Reformed; founded in 1830. The present building, south-east corner of Eighth and Mound Streets, known as the Mount-street Temple, is in a modified Gothic style. It was finished in 1868, at a cost, it is said, of $150,000. Seating capacity, 1,200; membership, 200 families; rabbi, Raphael Benjamin. *Children of Yeshurum*, Reformed, founded in 1844. The present building, south-east corner of Eighth and Plum Streets, known as the Plum-street Temple, completed in 1866, is one of the most unique and costly church structures in the city. It is in the pure Moorish style, elegantly furnished and decorated, and without the ground is said to have cost $275,000. Seating capacity, 1,540; membership, 240 families; rabbi, Isaac M. Wise. *K. K. Adath Israel*, Polish, corner of Walnut and Seventh Streets; membership, 60 families; rabbi, Henry Kuttner. *Orthodox Polish*, of an old creed; worship in a small room on the south-west corner of Eighth Street and Central Avenue. *Sherith Israel*, founded in 1856; worship on Lodge Street, between Sixth and Seventh. Membership, 80 families; rabbi, S. H. Epstein.

Jewish Hospital, the, founded in 1847 for the benefit of sick Israelites only, was originally located on Betts Street and Central Avenue. It was removed to the present building, corner of Third and Baum Streets, in 1863. It contains two wards, one for male and one for female patients, besides a dozen rooms for pay-patients. The wards will accommodate about thirty persons.

Kindergartens. — Since Friedrich Froebel began to successfully teach infants by means of a class of schools named kindergartens, there have sprung up, throughout Europe and America, many schools based upon the same methods and adopting the same name. In many American cities, such as New York, Boston, St. Louis, and Philadelphia, kindergartens have been made an important branch of the public-school system; while in many other cities kindergartens have been established by individuals and educational institutions. In Cincinnati there are no kindergartens connected with the public schools; but there are five of them in a flourishing condition, one conducted by Miss Helene Goodman, another by the Cincinnati Wesleyan College, a third by Miss Lizzie Beaman, a fourth by Miss Katherine Dodd, and a fifth by the Cincinnati Orphan Asylum. Miss Goodman's kindergarten is the best known, and occupies part of the first floor of Miss Nourse's school-building, 166 West Seventh Street, where the rooms are lofty, well ventilated, neatly furnished, and so arranged that the little children are made quite comfortable while being amused and taught their first lessons. Miss Goodman was a pupil of Madame Krauss of New-York City, and established her kindergarten in this city in 1875. Since that time she has enthusiastically devoted herself to her work, and in so doing has had the hearty support of influential citizens.

Knights of Pythias. — A secret benevolent order, similar in character to the Masons and Odd Fellows. The members are uniformed, and make a handsome display on parade. There are fifteen lodges and one division in Cincinnati. Their principal armories are at the north-west corner of Sixth and Walnut, and the south-west corner of Eighth Street and Central Avenue. Total membership estimated at 1,500.

La Belle Rivière is the name given by the French to the Ohio River.

Landmarks and Historical Places. — The pioneers built log houses for defence and shelter, but they were only of a temporary character. A few small-windowed two-storied houses yet remain of those built in the second period of houses in this city; all without special interest, except one on the south side of old Congress Street, east of Lawrence, and known as Rose Cottage. Here lived Judge Daniel Symmes, and after him Nicholas Longworth. While living at Rose Cottage, Judge Symmes built in 1812, on the south side of Congress Street, near Lawrence, a stone house, which after Judge Symmes's death was occupied by Peyton S. Symmes, and was for a long time the centre of social interest in the city. The walls are built of limestone taken from the bed of the river; and the roof is a high gable, slanting toward the street, with an attic-room in the peak, and without a dormer window. The hall is on the west side; and it is deep and broad, with a handsome staircase in the rear. The ornamentation on the woodwork is quite elaborate and interesting. Doubtless in its day it was one of the finest houses in this region; although it is by no means the oldest now standing, nor has it the most historical interest. The St. Clair House, shut in from the streets by later buildings, stands in the block bounded by Seventh, Eighth, and Main Streets, and St. Clair Alley. The date of its erection is unknown, and there is a doubt whether it was built by Gen. St. Clair or by his son. From the records of real-estate transfers, it seems to have been built in 1806, and tradition says by the general. The walls are of brick brought from Pittsburg; and the door-step is a huge block of sandstone, said to be the first piece of this kind of stone used for that purpose in the city. The house has a hall through the centre, with doors in front and rear, and a series of rooms built on each side, forming a semi-court at the back. The staircase is wide, and the stairs of easy ascent. The old house, hidden from sight and almost forgotten, is still in good condition, and the walls complete; and it is one of the points of great local interest. The "Bazaar" is the most curious, and, architecturally speaking, the oddest old landmark, in the city. It stands on the south side of Third Street, just east of Broadway. In 1829 Mrs. Frances Trollope thought to revolutionize the trade and society of the growing town, so she built a house where pleasure and business should be combined. Her efforts were without effect, and the old structure looks as if it had been dropped from some other country among uncongenial mates. The design of the façade is nondescript. There are three high windows, reaching over two stories; and the windows have a half Gothic, half Moorish effect, which is not altogether displeasing. There is an iron balcony running across the front below the cornice. Here were held the Fourth-of-July celebrations and the annual balls of the early times.

The element of the population that held Virginia traditions built, between 1825–30, several fine houses in the semi-classical style; the oldest being the Key's House, where Charles McMicken lived, and a part of which may yet be seen in front of the University of Cincinnati building. It is on a side hill overlooking the Hamilton Road once the great thoroughfare between the North and South. In much the same style is the house now owned and occupied by David Sinton, on the east side of Pike Street, almost opposite the east end of Fourth. The house was begun by Martin Baum, and finished by Nicholas Longworth, who died there. It is a one-story house, very wide and deep, with a broad hall through the centre, resting on a half-story or basement. The place has always been known as the gathering spot for the culture and refinement of the city. In the square on Bank Street, occupied by the Sisters of the Good Shepherd, is another of those grand old houses. It was the home of Major Daniel Gano. Another of the same class was built by Thomas Carneal, and still stands in Ludlow, Ky. On the north-east corner of Orchard and Main Streets is a plain brick house, having long porches in the rear, which was the home of William Woodward, the founder of Woodward College. When Third was the fashionable street, there were many fine houses on both sides of it, built mostly with Greek-temple façades. Here lived Samuel Foote and Griffin Taylor. Of this class of houses only one remains, — that of George T. Williamson, between Plum and Elm Streets. Major William Barr built two now old and noted houses. The first, or at least part of it, can be seen on the north-west corner of Smith and Sixth Streets; and the second is standing on Barr Street, near Mound. Major Clarkson's house, on Bank Street, is a relic of the time when the north-west section of the city below the hills was only farm-land. There were many other dwellings of note; but the old public buildings have been destroyed. The court-house was twice burned, and the early churches and mills have disappeared. Near a century's life has left in the city but little that is either quaint or charming. — *Pitts H. Burt.*

(See Burnet Residence and Lytle House.)

Lane Theological Seminary was chartered and first opened for academic instruction in 1829. The theological department went into operation in 1832, under the presidency of Rev. Lyman Beecher, D.D.; and since that time about 700 students have received theological training. In 1835 the academic department was discontinued. At present there are six instructors, and accommodations for 50 students. The grounds comprise about five acres; and the buildings include a dormitory, boarding-hall, library-hall, chapel, and several dwellings for the professors. Besides these, there is now being erected a recitation-hall, which will be a beautiful structure, and also a valuable adjunct to the seminary property. The building is to be of blue limestone, three stories in height, with mansard roof. It will contain recitation-rooms for all the seminary classes, chapel for daily prayers, gymnasium, etc. The library now contains 13,000 volumes of standard theological, rare, valuable, and miscellaneous works. Lane Seminary is under control of the Presbyterian Church; but all students, whatever may be their denominational connection, are welcomed. It has had a prosperous career, and has a promising future. It is situated on Gilbert Avenue, Walnut Hills, and can be visited at any time during the day. *Horse-cars,* — Eden-park, Walnut-hills, and Avondale line, and the Gilbert-avenue line.

Latonia Springs. — A beautiful suburb in Kentucky, six miles from Fountain Square, on the Lexington Pike. It was once a noted watering-place, and favorite resort of Kentuckians. There is a fine hotel, ample grounds, spring-houses, and other convenient buildings. The waters possess no medicinal virtues, and as a watering-place Latonia Springs is a thing of the past. It is a beautiful drive, however, the route being picturesque throughout its length.

Law-Courts. — *Common Pleas Court for Hamilton County* is composed of seven judges, elected by the people for a term of five years. This is the court of general, civil, and criminal jurisdiction, and throughout the State is the court established for this purpose by the constitution. It has appellate jurisdiction, as well as jurisdiction in proceedings in error, from justices of the peace in civil actions for any amount, and original jurisdiction in all civil cases for amounts of $100 and upwards. It has also appellate and error jurisdiction from the probate court. Sessions held in the Court House. *Probate Court for Hamilton County* has one judge, elected by the people for a term of three years. It has original and exclusive jurisdiction in all matter of wills, administrations of estate, and guardianship; and concurrent jurisdiction with the common pleas in habeas corpus and in condemnation of lands for public uses. This court was established by statute, and has no appellate jurisdiction. Sessions held in the Court House. *Superior Court of Cincinnati* has three judges, elected for a term of five years, by the people. Its jurisdiction is limited to the city, and therein is concurrent with the common pleas in all civil cases of $100 and upwards. It has no criminal or appellate jurisdiction, but is a special court established by statute. *District Court for*

RAILROAD SUPPLIES.

WE ARE PREPARED TO FURNISH

Plushes, Terries, Raw Silk,

AND OTHER DRAPERIES,

Shades, Burlaps, Fringes,

Furniture Gimps, Carpets, Oil Cloths,

and Linoleums

For railroad uses, and can supply the above articles at short notice, as we keep them constantly in stock.

Import orders for large quantities taken upon a commission basis.

Railroad Purchasing Agents

SHOULD OBTAIN OUR PRICES BEFORE BUYING.

THE JOHN SHILLITO COMPANY.

First Judicial District, that is, for Hamilton County, is composed of any three judges of the court of common pleas, whose term is fixed by such rules as the court of common pleas may make. This court has original jurisdiction in mandamus and *quo warranto* cases, and appellate jurisdiction from common pleas in all cases where the constitutional right of trial by jury is not granted. On appeal, all cases are tried *de novo*. It has jurisdiction in error in all civil cases from the common pleas and superior courts. Error in criminal cases lies to supreme court direct. This court also was established by statute. Sessions held in the Court House. *Police Court of Cincinnati* consists of one judge, elected by the people for two years. It has jurisdiction over all offences against the city ordinances, and of any misdemeanors within four miles of the city. In all felonies it has jurisdiction to hear and bind over to the grand jury. Sessions held in the City Building. *Justices of the Peace* are elected by the people for three years. They have original jurisdiction in all civil cases for money only under $100, and concurrent jurisdiction in cases up to $300. In cases of all crimes and misdemeanors, including bastardy, they have power to hear and bind over to the grand jury. There are ten justices, who have their offices or court-rooms in different parts of the city. *United-States Circuit and District Courts* for the Southern District of Ohio are held in Cincinnati in the Post-Office and Custom-House Building.

Law-Library, the Cincinnati. — As early as 1834 a special charter was obtained from the General Assembly for the incorporation of the "Cincinnati Law-Library;" but no organization took place under this charter, and nothing effective was done until 1846, when a committee was appointed to obtain subscriptions. Rooms were then provided, and the library started on a modest scale. It has steadily increased, both in number of books and members, until now it contains ten thousand volumes, and is one of the most conveniently arranged and most complete law-libraries in the country. The rooms are in the Court House, and are open to members, introduced strangers, and to the senior class of the Cincinnati Law-School.

Law-School, the Cincinnati, a department of the Cincinnati College, occupies rooms in the third story of College Building. The school is divided into two classes, junior and senior, each having a separate course of study and text-books. The term begins on the Thursday next following the second Tuesday of October, and continues until the second Wednesday of the ensuing May. The students enjoy the use of a library of 1,600 volumes belonging to the school, and seniors also have access to the Cincinnati Law-Library. During the school-year 1881–82 there were 127 students attending the lectures. Jacob D. Cox, the dean; Rufus King, George Hoadly, Henry A. Morrill, Manning F. Force, and Ex-Gov. John W. Stevenson compose the faculty.

Law's Insurance Agency is the oldest in the city, and the leading agency in the State of Ohio. It is conducted by John H. Law, who represents several of the largest and strongest companies in the world; and among them are the Royal of Liverpool, with assets of $32,000,000; the Imperial and Northern of London, $37,495,000; the London and Lancashire of Liverpool, $8,460,000; the Fire Association of Philadelphia, $4,400,000; the Phenix of New York, $3,300,000; the United Firemen's of Philadelphia, $650,000; and the Metropolitan Plate Glass of New York, $146,000. The agency employs a score of men, and occupies elegant and commodious quarters on the south-east corner of Third and Walnut Streets.

Libraries. — The most important public libraries are the Public Library, the Mercantile Library, the Cincinnati Law Library, the libraries of the Historical and Philosophical Society, the St. Xavier College, the Sisters of Notre Dame Academy, the Lane Theological Seminary, Mount St. Mary's Seminary, and the Cincinnati Hospital. There are numerous valuable private libraries, many of which are rich in specialties. Some of the noteworthy private libraries are those of A. T. Goshorn, most of which was presented to him by the citizens of Philadelphia, in recognition of his services as director-general of the Exposition in 1876, the room itself being exquisitely fitted up by a committee sent here for the purpose; Robert Clarke, containing bibliography and literary history, science, and rare and numerous works in Scottish history and poetry; Henry Probasco, a costly collection of ancient, rare, and exquisitely bound books, well arranged, classified, and catalogued; E. T. Carson, having probably the most complete Masonic collection in the world, besides a fine Shakspearian collection; J. B. Stallo, a large library with a specialty of philosophical works; Stanley Matthews, abounding in law, scientific, and theological works; George McLaughlin, containing standard historical works, and a great variety of books on art, as well as many curious books; M. F. Force, a fine collection of books relating to

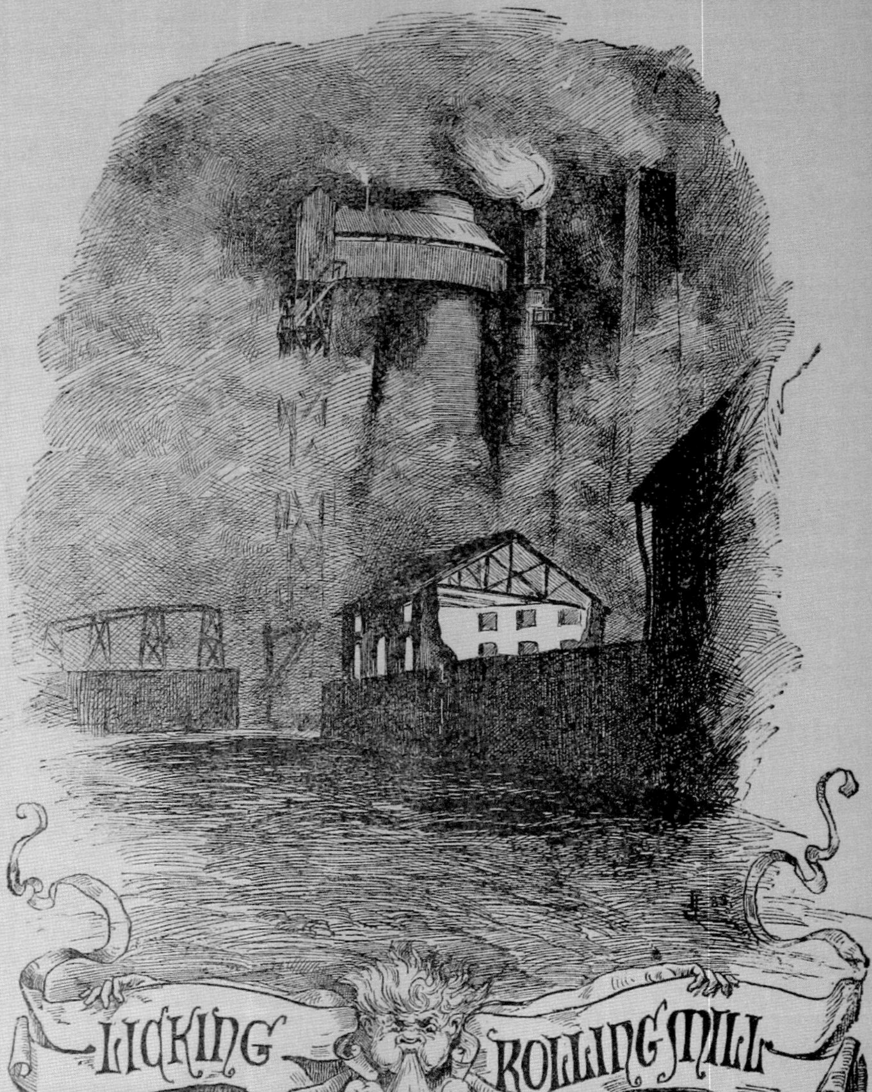
LICKING ROLLING MILL

American Indians; T. D. Lincoln, one of the most extensive and useful collections of law-books in the world.

Licking River has its source in Floyd County, Ky., 180 miles from its mouth. It empties into the Ohio, between the cities of Newport and Covington, opposite the foot of Broadway, Cincinnati. It is navigable for steamers as far as the falls at Cole's Garden, four miles from its mouth. Above that point, in dry summers, it has but little water; but in winter and spring flatboats descend it for 70 or 80 miles. An effort was once made to improve the channel by means of dams and locks, but the enterprise was abandoned.

Lick Run. — This name applies to a village, a creek, and a turnpike. The village is a short distance west of Fairmount, and is part of the 24th ward of the city. Lick-run Creek rises in Green township, and flows almost due east to Mill Creek, emptying into that turbid stream at Fairmount. The Lick-run Pike adheres closely to the bed of the stream, and terminates at Fairmount, where it joins the Harrison Pike.

Lincoln Club. — A Republican club, organized in 1879, and similar in its organization and objects to the Union League of New York. Its club-house, on the south-west corner of Eighth and Race Streets, was until recently the residence of Dr. George Mendenhall. It is elegantly furnished and well located. None but Republicans are eligible for membership, which now numbers four hundred. Each member holds one share of stock, valued at $25, and pays $10 a year for dues. Visitors may be introduced by members, and Republicans from other places are cordially welcomed.

Lincoln Park, situated in the West End, covers ten acres. There is a lake and an island; the lake being used in winter for skating, and in summer for boating. *Horse-cars,* Freeman-street line.

Linwood, a village incorporated in 1874, with a population of five hundred, is on the east border-line of Cincinnati. It is situated on the Little Miami Railroad, six miles and a half from the Court-House, and lies nestled among the hills, from the tops of which can be seen the farms lying in three counties. There is a graded school, Congregational, Baptist, and Methodist churches, a hame-factory, etc.; but the people are chiefly business-men of Cincinnati; and the town presents the appearance of a neat New-England village.

Literary Club. — Organized 1849. Meetings are held Saturday evenings from September to June. Membership is limited to one hundred, seven-eighths of all votes cast required to elect. Initiation-fee, $10; annual dues, $20. The rooms at 24 West Fourth Street are adorned with numerous fine engravings, statuettes, busts, sketches, and paintings. Visitors are admitted, but only at the invitation of members. The president is Charles B. Wilby. Ex-President Hayes has been a member since 1849.

Longview Insane Asylum, the largest institution of its kind in the West, is supported by Hamilton County alone, although two directors are appointed by the governor of Ohio. It costs about $100,000 annually to run it. The noble edifice is located half a mile south-east of Carthage, on rising ground. It is of brick, is 612 feet long, five stories in height, and is thought fire-proof. The stairways are built of iron. The building contains 650 rooms. The yearly average of patients treated is about 1,000; the average of resident patients being 750. It was completed in 1860, and cost $500,000. Any one can visit the institution and examine the grounds on Thursdays.

Lookout House is on Jackson Hill, at the head of the Mount-Auburn Inclined-plane Railway. The structure is oblong in shape, eighty by two hundred feet, including the south balcony, which extends its entire length. The grounds, which contain about six acres, are handsomely divided into lawns and flower-beds, the lawns being furnished with refreshment-tables. It is the oldest, and was for several years the only, place of the kind in the city. Five thousand guests can easily be entertained. Admission free. *Horse-cars*, — Main-street line.

Lookout Opera-House. — A large octagonal building surmounted by a dome, in the grounds adjoining the Lookout House. It contains a stage for dramatic performances. The auditorium is arranged in the form of an amphitheatre. The house can also be used for a circus, the ring being cast in the parquette. Admission is usually twenty-five cents. *Horse-cars*, Main-street line.

Ludlow. — A Kentucky suburb, opposite the mouth of Mill Creek. Distance from Fountain Square, two miles. The population is about 1,500, composed chiefly of Cincinnati business and working men. The Fifth-street ferry lands at the eastern end of the village. The Third-street horse-cars connect with the ferry.

Lytle House, the, No. 66 Lawrence Street, was built in 1814; and although one of the oldest buildings now standing, it is yet in an excellent state of preservation. It was built for Gen. William Lytle, and has always been occupied by his family and descendants. His grandson was Gen. W. H. Lytle, who fell at the battle of Chickamauga. One of the men who worked on the house at the time of its erection was Joseph Jones, now in his ninety-fourth year, one of the oldest living residents of the city. In 1837 Andrew Jackson visited Cincinnati, and during his stay remained at this house.

Männerchor, A. P. A. — A singing-club connected with the German branch of the American Protestant Association. The chorus numbers about fifty voices. Weekly meetings are held.

Männerchor, Cincinnati, a German singing society, having male and female voices, under the direction of Otto Singer. The society has about 120 active and 200 contributing members. Meetings for practice were held weekly in Männerchor Hall, corner Vine and Mercer Streets. The building was destroyed by fire on the 4th of August, 1879, and the valuable musical library belonging to the society burned. Weekly meetings are now held in Eureka Hall.

Männerchor, Germania, was organized in the year 1872, by seceders from the Cincinnati Männerchor. From a small beginning the society has increased its numbers to 250, most of whom are contributing members. The active members do not exceed forty.

Männerchor, St. Cecilia. — Originally composed of the members of the choir of St. Mary's Catholic Church. It now has about forty active members, belonging mostly to the German Catholic choirs of the city. The society was organized in May, 1867.

Manufactures. — Cincinnati occupies a leading position among the manufacturing cities of the United States, and an eminent one among those of the world. She is singularly well situated for procuring raw material, and for distributing manufactured goods. The business centre of a great iron region, convenient to lumber of all kinds, grain, cotton, cattle, sheep, hogs, wool, stone, and other raw materials in great abundance, with a community of manufacturers distinguished for their economical administration, pecuniary ability, scientific attainments, mechanical skill, and artistic taste, the future development of her industries will only be measured by the ambition and activity of her citizens. A distinguishing feature of the city is the scope of her products and the large number of individual manufacturers. To her manufacturers the year has been one of singular activity. In nearly all departments there has been increased production, as in the case of buggies and carriages, the production of which, in late years, has shown most remarkable development, the increase having been of a very pronounced character. Her manufactured products, in 1881, according to the figures of J. F. Blackburn, secretary of the Board of Trade and Transportation of Cincinnati, aggregated $163,351,497. The cash capital invested to produce this value was $67,651,552; the value of the real estate occupied, $40,096,458; the number of establishments engaged, 5,450; and the number of hands employed, 80,839. These figures are easily made on paper: their magnitude is likely to pass without attracting the attention they deserve. But when one remembers that the number of men, women, and children now employed in production is greater than was the entire population of the city little more than 30 years ago, and that the production itself has increased tenfold in 40 years, the growth and extent of our industrial forces become more apparent. With whatever drawbacks there may be, there never was more to encourage our manufacturers than now. The desirableness of removing all unnecessary expense to production is so apparent, that this will speedily come; the attention from thoughtful and active citizens, which local transportation is receiving, being one of the promises of such a consummation. The only true standard for the measurement of the relation of the work of different years is the quantities of various commodities which change hands. Thus, the aggregate value of our manufactures, which last year reached $163,351,497, represents material which, at the close of the war, would have immensely exceeded these figures; while the sales of dry-goods and clothing, which in the past year aggregated $41,808,234, represent in packages, pieces, yards, etc., a very much larger quantity than the same sum would have purchased when the prices for standard fabrics were from six to eight times greater than those now prevailing. From the detailed table it will be seen that the aggregate value of specific commodities in the past year was $179,712,718, an increase of $11,799,816 over 1879. In these figures are not embraced dry-goods, clothing, books, hats and caps, silks, millinery goods, paper, musical instruments, silverware, jewelry, etc. If the approximate value of these were added, it would swell the aggregate to $274,651,218, an increase over 1879 of $18,513,316. Of the whole production in 1881, the manufactures of metals aggregated $24,847,286; wood, $14,204,244; food, $20,668,153; liquors, $26,647,000; clothing, $18,695,844; leather, $11,338,735; soap, candles, and oils, $8,317,682; drugs, chemicals, etc., $4,425,522; paper, $4,416,326; tobacco, $5,339,024; printing and publishing, $4,401,735; carriages, cars, etc., $6,548,690; stone and earth, $2,559,510; cotton, wool, hemp, etc., $1,592,013; bookbinding and blank-books, $341,700; fine-arts, $826,827; miscellaneous, $8,181,206. The manufactures of either food, metals, or liquors were larger in 1881 than the entire manufactures of Cincinnati in 1840. Many products of this city, too, are as wide in their distribution as the whole is varied in its nature. They go, not only throughout this country, but to all the nations of Europe, China, Japan, Australia, South America, British Columbia, Sandwich Islands, etc. They carry the good name of the Cincinnati producers with them, and are steadily laying the foundations for a trade, both at home and abroad, of which the present is but a feeble promise.

Markets. — One by one the old-fashioned markets are disappearing. The Pearl-street Market, on Pearl, between Plum and Central Avenue, was the first to disappear; and its place was taken by the Plum-street Depot. The Fifth-street Market, which was regarded the finest in the city, gave way to the Esplanade and Tyler-Davidson Fountain; although the Esplanade is occasionally used as a flower-market, an ornamental stand being placed thereon for the purpose, to fill the letter of the law, inasmuch as the site was deeded sixty years ago for market purposes only. The markets now in active operation are: Lower Market, on Pearl Street, between Sycamore and Broadway; Sixth-street Market, on Sixth, between Plum and Central Avenue; Court-street Market, on Court, between Walnut and Vine; Findlay Market, on Findlay, between Elm and Plum; and Wade-street Market, on Wade, between Central Avenue and John Street. During market-days, hucksters and farmers are allowed to occupy the streets for a number of squares at each end of the market-houses. It is surmised that all the market-houses will soon be abolished.

Masonic Temple. — This is a massive freestone building, in the Byzantine style, situated on the north-east corner of Third and Walnut Streets. It is five stories high, 195 by 100 feet, with unfinished spire, and cost about $200,000. The basement and ground-floor are occupied by banks and other business offices. The second floor is chiefly occupied by lawyers' offices. The upper stories are devoted to the uses of the Masonic order, and are the meeting-places of most of the city lodges. There are separate halls for the entered apprentice, fellow-craft, and master-masons' lodges, the royal arch chapter, commandery, and consistory. The Temple contains also a large banquet-hall. It is under the control of Nova Cesarea Harmony Lodge, No. 2. In an architectural point of view, it is one of the chief ornaments of the city; and the interior, which can be visited any week-day at ten A.M., is well worth being seen.

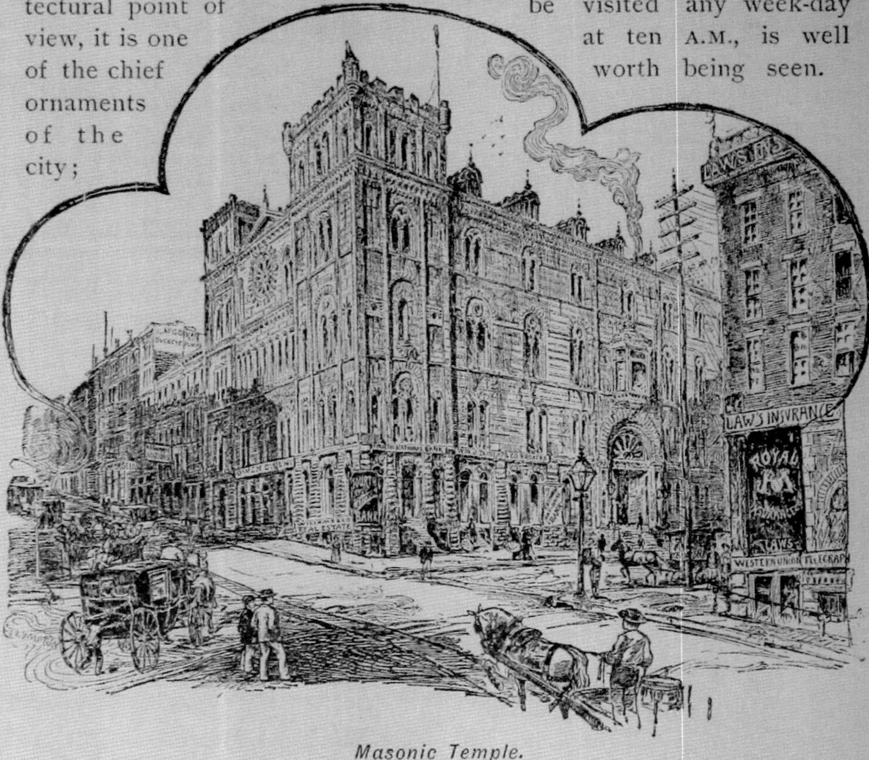

Masonic Temple.

Masons, Free and Accepted. — In this city there are sixteen lodges of Master Masons, including three colored lodges. Of these, nine lodges meet monthly in Masonic Temple: viz., N. C. Harmony, No. 2; Miami, No. 46; Lafayette, No. 81; Cincinnati, No. 133; McMillan, No. 141; Cynthia, No. 155; Hanselmann (German), No. 208; Kilwinning, No. 356; and Excelsior, No. 369. Vattier Lodge, No. 386, meets on the north side of Sixth Street, between Central Avenue and John Street; Hoffner Lodge, No. 253, meets in Cumminsville; Walnut-hills Lodge, No. 483, meets at north-west corner of Gilbert Avenue and McMillan Street; Yeatman Lodge, No. 162, meets at 1079 Eastern Avenue. Of the higher Masonic bodies, the following meet in Masonic Temple: Cincinnati, No. 2, McMillan, No. 19, and Willis, No. 131, Chapters of Royal Arch Masons; Cincinnati Council, No. 1, Royal and Select Masters; Cincinnati, No. 3, and Hanselmann, No. 16, Commanderies of Knights Templar; and the Ancient and Accepted Scottish Rite, consisting of Ohio Consistory S. P. R. S., 32°; Cincinnati Chapter of Rose Croix, 18°; Dalcho Council, P. of J., 16°; and Gibulum Lodge of Perfection, 14°. Kilwinning Chapter of Royal Arch Masons, No. 96, and Kilwinning Council of Royal and Select Masters, No. 52, meet on the north side of Sixth Street, between Central Avenue and John Street. Three colored lodges meet at the north-west corner of Sixth and Main: viz., Corinthian, No. 1; True American, No. 2; St. John, No. 3. Prince White Chapter, R. A. M., No. 1, and Zerubbabel Commandery, Knights Templar, No. 1, meet at the same place. The number of Masons in Cincinnati is estimated at three thousand.

Medical Colleges. — See Miami Medical College, Medical College of Ohio, College of Medicine and Surgery, Eclectic Medical Institute, Pulte Medical College, and Physio-Medical Institute.

Medical College of Ohio. — The oldest medical college in the West, having been founded in 1819. The college edifice is on the south side of Sixth Street, between Vine and Race Streets. Two sessions per annum are held: the regular session, beginning in October, and ending in March following; the spring session, beginning in March, and lasting until June. Fees for the course, $75; matriculation, dissecting, hospital, and practical chemistry, each $5; graduation, $25. There are ten professorships. Professor W. W. Seely is dean of the faculty. Daily clinics are held at the Good Samaritan Hospital, of which the college faculty have charge. Students also have the privilege of the clinics at the Cincinnati Hospital.

Medical Society, the Cincinnati. — A society of physicians of the regular school, for the reading of papers and the discussion of topics of interest to the medical profession. It originated in 1874 by a secession from the Academy of Medicine, caused by an unsatisfactory solution of a problem of medical ethics. During the autumn, winter, and spring months, the society holds weekly meetings at 203 West Seventh Street. Membership fee, $3; annual dues, $2. Dr. T. T. Goodman is president, and Dr. Reynolds secretary.

Melodeon Hall. — North-west corner of Fourth and Walnut

Streets, in the third story. It is one of the large public halls in the city, and is used for first-class entertainments. It was for a term of years leased by the Allemania Club. It is now the property of Peter Gibson, owner of the Gibson House adjoining. He purposes tearing the building down, and extending the hotel to Fourth Street.

Memphis and Ohio-river Packet Company, located, and its boats owned, in Cincinnati. Three boats a week will run between Cincinnati and Memphis, requiring four first-class steamers to meet the service; viz., the "Andy Baum," "J. W. Gaff," "Vint Shinkle," "Cons. Millar." Passenger and freight rates fluctuate, according to the season and stage of water. Wharf-boat at foot of Sycamore Street. Office, 11 and 12 Public Landing. Robert W. Wise is superintendent, and James D. Parker secretary and treasurer. J. W. Gaff, President.

Mercantile Library. — See Young Men's Mercantile Library Association.

Merchants' and Manufacturers' Insurance Company of Cincinnati is one of the oldest and largest of the local companies. Its charter, granted in 1838, is perpetual. Its cash capital is $150,000, and assets $286,493. In the forty years of its existence it not only has paid $866,146 for losses, but also has declared dividends that will average over twelve per cent a year; for 1879 the dividend being ten per cent. A general fire and cargo business is done, and the company's office is at 15 West Third Street. The record of the time of service of its officers is noteworthy. B. B. Whiteman was secretary of the Cincinnati Insurance Company from 1832 to 1850; and then became connected with the Merchants' and Manufacturers', which he served as secretary and president from 1850 to 1879. He was succeeded as president by William H. Calvert, who had been the secretary of the Cincinnati Insurance Company for eleven years.

Merchants' Exchange. — See Chamber of Commerce.

Meteorological data for 1882. — Highest barometer, 30.739, on Dec. 7; lowest barometer, 29.478, April 19; mean barometer for the year, 30.088; highest temperature, 95.5, June 25; minimum, 1°, Dec. 8; mean yearly temperature, 56.9; thermometric range of temperature, 94.5. Total number of miles of wind during year, 49,626; greatest number miles during any month, 6,176 in March; least number, 2,961 in October; greatest hourly velocity of the wind, 29 miles from the west on July 18. Total amount of rainfall, 52.12 inches; greatest monthly rainfall, 8.47, May; least, 1.57, November; greatest amount in any 24 consecutive hours, 2.54, on March 20; annual mean of cloudiness (in tenths), 5.77; greatest, 7.87, January; least, 4.30, October; annual mean relative humidity, 68.7; greatest, 74.2, December; least, 59.8, March. At the observations taken at 6.30 A.M., 2.30 P.M., 10.30 P.M., the wind blew from the north 133 times, from the north-east 97 times, from the east 123 times, from south-east 166 times, from south 136, from south-west 132, from west 139, from north-west 135; number of calms, 34. There were 83 clear, 158 fair, and 124 cloudy days; rain, other than sprinkles, fell on 152 days. Highest daily temperature below 32° on 8 days; lowest temperature below 32° on 44 days; highest temperature above 90° on 6 days (all in June). Highest stage of river, 58–7, on Feb. 21, which is the highest since 1847. On April 16 there was a very brilliant aurora borealis, and several others during the month; also one on Nov. 19. Last frost of spring, May 23; first frost of autumn, Oct. 20; last snow of spring, April 10; first snow of autumn, Nov. 18; number of thunder-storms, 41; number of auroras, 4. Solar and lunar halos were quite numerous. — *B. B. Watkins, Observer, Signal-Corps, U. S. A.*

Miami Canal. — See Canals.

Miami Medical College, established in 1852, owns and occupies the building on Twelfth Street, nearly opposite the Cincinnati Hospital, where daily clinics are held during the college sessions. The faculty consists of seventeen well-known physicians, of which Dr. John A. Murphy is the dean, and Dr. W. H. Taylor the secretary. The college museum is one of the most extensive in the country. Two sessions are annually held. The preliminary term of the regular winter course begins in September, and lasts one month, when the regular winter session begins, which lasts until March. The spring course of lectures begins in March, and ends in June. Fees for the entire course of lectures, $75; matriculation, demonstrator, and hospital tickets, $5 each; graduation, $25. Connected with the college is the Miami Medical College Dispensary, which is open to students.

Miami Medical College Dispensary. — A noble charity, in the buildings of the Miami Medical College. All sick persons who apply are treated and furnished medicines free of charge. The morning session, between eight and nine o'clock, is devoted to diseases of the eye and ear; the afternoon, between three and four, to all other complaints. The dispensary is open all the year round. During the lecture-season, students of the college are admitted to the clinics, making it an important part of their medical education. The attending physicians are the faculty of the college. The annual number of patients treated is nearly eight thousand.

Miami Stock-yards, on Eggleston Avenue, Cleveland and Court Streets, are in complete order, with accommodations for ten thousand hogs, sheep, and cattle. The Little Miami and the Louisville Short-line Railroads enter the yards, and the Cincinnati and Eastern and the Miami-valley Narrow-gauge Railroads make their terminal points near these yards. The cattle-yards are covered, and every pen floored, and are provided with every convenience for watering and feeding. The yards occupy three acres, and were opened in 1876. The company has a capital of $100,000. The president and treasurer is Benjamin Eggleston, and the superintendent is H. A. Bowman. The receipts for the year were over a hundred thousand hogs.

Military. — See Army.

Mill Creek has its source in Butler County, about thirty-five miles from its mouth. As it passes through the city, its waters are exceedingly filthy, having received the noxious discharges of paper-mills, starch-factories, breweries, and distilleries, for a distance of twelve miles. The Great-Liberty-street and McLean-avenue sewers add to its filthiness between Ernst Station and the Ohio. Until 1870 Mill Creek was the west corporation line of the city. The corporation line is now two miles west of the creek. The Mill-creek Bottoms are subject to annual overflow by back-water from the Ohio. As a consequence they are exceedingly fertile; and all available places not used for manufacturing purposes, stock-yards, and brick-kilns, are devoted to market-gardening. In the lowest grounds the clay deposit of the annual inundations is used for making brick. This deposit is very smooth, and in some places is made to a depth of four inches. It is removed when of the consistence of potter's clay, and needs but little manipulation to be pressed into bricks.

Monuments. — The McCook Monument is in Washington Park, and was erected in 1876, in honor of Col. R. L. McCook, by the Ninth Ohio Regiment, which, during the late war, he commanded until he lost his life. The base, die, shaft, and capital are of Quincy granite; and the bust is of heroic size, representing Col. McCock in uniform. The Woodward Monument is placed in the school-yard of Franklin Street, between Sycamore Street and Broadway. It consists of a bronze statue of William Woodward, representing him draped in a cloak, and standing on a granite pedestal. It was erected by the alumni of the Woodward college and high-school, of which Mr. Woodward was the founder and benefactor.

Mount Auburn, formerly one of the most beautiful suburbs, but now the second precinct of the 2d ward, lies on the hill at the head of Main Street, and is easiest reached by the Mount Auburn Inclined-plane Railway. Avondale adjoins it on the north, the corporation line dividing them. It abounds with elegant private residences and public institutions.

Mount Harrison. — The western highlands immediately north of Price's Hill. It was named Mount Harrison because this elevation was the home of ex-President Harrison, who, in the early history of the city, built a dwelling on the slope facing Cincinnati. The dwelling was an old landmark until removed in 1876. On one part of this elevation Chief-Justice Chase, during the early period of his residence in this city, erected a dwelling which yet stands. The locality has comparatively few improvements, but some of these are of the best character; and the whole district, with its delightful elevations, its graceful slopes and groves, is one of surpassing natural beauty.

Mount Lookout is a subdivision of the 1st ward, about four miles direct from Fountain Square. It is one of the most attractive suburban districts in the city. The observatory of the University of Cincinnati is situated here. It also contains a large park, which is used for picnics, barbecues, etc. A steam dummy-railroad connects Mount Lookout with the Elm-street line of horse-cars. The distance by railroad is six miles. The car-fare is ten cents.

Mount Washington is one of the north-eastern suburbs of Cincinnati, its residents chiefly business-men from the city. It is noted for its beautiful rolling private grounds, perfect drainage, and consequent good health; also for its fine avenues of evergreens and deciduous trees, with probably the finest collection of hardy magnolias in the county. It has a town-hall, a fine graded public school, young ladies' seminary, and three churches. Five hundred feet above the Ohio-river level, the views are magnificent, reaching on some high points five miles each way river-ward. The Little Miami River flows at its base. Residences comfortable, and some very fine. Reached by Little Miami and Cincinnati, Georgetown, and Portsmouth Railways. Incorporated, with mayor, council, marshal, board of health, etc.; a thousand inhabitants, and a thick population of thousands around it, and depending on it for business purposes.

Mozart Hall. — In the third story of the Catholic Institute, corner of Vine and Longworth Streets. The Grand Opera-House is on the ground floor. The hall belongs to the institute, and is used for fairs, lectures, balls, church and other entertainments. It is quite accessible, being half a square north of Fountain Square.

Museums. — Although there are no public museums, there are many collections belonging to individuals and societies, which, if brought together, would form a nucleus for a museum that from its beginning would take a good rank among the public museums of this country. There is, as has been stated under Art, a project to build a grand art-museum; but it is quite probable that in the same building accommodations will be provided for various collections usually not classified under art-matters. The following list is only a part of the many collections in and around the city, and they can be seen by obtaining for this purpose an introduction to the persons owning or having charge of them. — *Art-Collections.* See heading Art. *Autographs and Manuscripts.* — An exceedingly valuable collection, by reason of its immense numbers, rare manuscripts, unique arrangement, and admirable classification, is owned by L. J. Cist, who has been engaged at this work for nearly forty-three years. Robert Clarke has a large collection of literary manuscripts, including some fine letters and poems of Robert Burns. The Historical and Philosophical Society and the libraries also have collections. *Birds and Fishes.* — See Cuvier Club, Natural History Society, and Zoölogical Society. Charles Dury of Avondale has an extensive collection of stuffed native birds. *Books.* — See Libraries. *Coins.* — The collection of Thomas Cleneay is said to be the most costly, most numerous, and most valuable in the United States. Joseph Tilton also has a large collection, on which considerable money and many years' time have been spent. *Fossils.* — The largest private collection in this country is that of Paul Mohr. The collection of C. B. Dyer is noteworthy for its variety, and that of S. A. Miller for its arrangement. A valuable collection was presented to the University of Cincinnati by Robert Clarke. *Indian Relics.* — See Stone, etc., below. *Insects.* — A most beautiful collection of butterflies, moths, and beetles is the property of Charles Dury of Avondale, who has also a fine collection of other insects, and stuffed animals, birds, and fishes. V. T. Chambers of Covington is said to be one of the most scientific of American entomologists, and has a useful collection relating to entomology. *Medical Museums* can be seen at the various medical colleges and at the Cincinnati Hospital. *Natural History Specimens.* — See Natural History Society, Cuvier Club, and Zoölogical Society. *Paintings.* — See Art. *Shells.* — A beautiful and varied collection owned by Professor A. G. Wetherby of Avondale. *Statuary.* — See Art, Mercantile Library, and St. Peter's Cathedral. *Stone and Flint Implements, Ornaments, etc.* — Two of the most valuable and largest private collections of this class in the West are owned in this city by Thomas Cleneay and H. H. Hill. Another collection belongs to Florien Giauque of Glendale.

Musical Club, the. — Composed of leading local musicians, professional and amateur, and a number of gentlemen prominent as patrons of music. It was organized in 1876, and has about seventy-five members. The purpose of the club is the cultivation of classical and modern chamber-music, and the promotion of good feeling and harmony among musicians. The club meets weekly in the rooms of the Literary Club.

Musical Societies are almost innumerable, and it would be impracticable to mention all of them. Those, however, that have a regular place of meeting, and hold regular meetings, may be noticed here: viz., Alert Singing Club, A. P. A. Männerchor, Odd Fellows' Männerchor, Herwegh (Polish) Männerchor, Cincinnati Männerchor, St. Cecilia Männerchor, Germania Männerchor, Schweizer Männerchor, Cincinnati Music Club, the Orpheus, Druiden Sängerchor, Apollo Club, Harugari Männerchor, Oneida Singing Club, Turner Männerchor, and the College Choir. Most of these societies are noticed under their appropriate heads elsewhere.

Music-hall and Exposition Building is one of the chief ornaments of the city, and one in which the citizens have reason to take the greatest pride. It occupies most of the block bounded by Elm, Fourteenth, Plum, and Grant Streets, and faces Washington Park. The building is of brick, in the modernized Gothic style. The whole front on Elm Street is 402 feet; 95 feet being given to each of the Exposition buildings, and 178 feet 4 inches to the Music Hall. The widest part of the building is 316 feet. The highest point is the pinnacle of the front gable, — 150 feet above the sidewalk. The buildings are so arranged that they can be used separately or together, and the upper stories so that they can be connected by bridges. In these buildings is the grand Music Hall, 112 feet wide and 192 feet long, having a stage 112 feet wide by 56 feet deep In the Music Hall there are 4,428 seats, and standing-room for 3,000 persons, beside which the stage will accommodate 1,500. In this hall is the great organ, described elsewhere. Over the vestibule is Dexter Hall, named in honor of Julius Dexter, the chairman of the building committee. This hall is 112 by 46 feet, 30 feet high. The wings are known as the Exposition Buildings; but they are used for various purposes when the exposition season is over, and part of them will probably be used by the Women's Art Museum Association. The whole cost of the building will be about $500,000; of which sum Reuben R. Springer has given $235,000, — and by reason of this munificence the building is often called Springer Music Hall, — and citizens have contributed the balance. The whole property is managed by the Music-hall Association referred to below. *Horse-cars*, — Elm-street line passes the building, and the Vine-street line within two squares.

Music-hall Association, the Cincinnati, was organized in December, 1875, to build and control the Music Hall described above. Reuben R. Springer in May of that year had offered $125,000 towards the building of a music-hall, provided the citizens would contribute an equal sum, and the city would permit the hall to be erected on public ground. These conditions were fulfilled, and the association organized as follows: The whole subscribers to the fund selected fifty of their number to form a joint-stock company, and to hold one share of stock of the par value of $20. A shareholder cannot sell his share to anybody not first approved by the trustees; and at his death the share reverts to the association, to be at once put into the hands of a suitable person. The shareholders can hold only one share each; and they elect seven trustees, — one being elected every year to serve seven years. The Music Hall and the Exposition Buildings which have since been added must be rented as low as will keep them in repair. No profit can be made, and no trustee is permitted to receive any compensation. The president of the association is Joseph Longworth, and the secretary J. F. Blackburn.

Narrow-gauge Railroads. — Five narrow-gauge railroads enter Cincinnati. *Cincinnati and Eastern* cars start from the Little Miami Depot. *College-hill Narrow-gauge* begins at Winton Place, and runs through College Hill to Mount Pleasant. Passengers take cars at the Cincinnati, Hamilton, and Dayton Depot. *Westwood Narrow-gauge* begins at Ernst Station, where it has a depot; but down-town passengers take the cars at the Cincinnati, Hamilton, and Dayton Depot, and change at Ernst. The road runs eight miles west to Westwood, or Cheviot. *Cincinnati Northern*, four hundred miles long, enters at Court and Broadway, connects with St. Louis, Toledo, and all points north and east. Cincinnati, Portsmouth, and Georgetown starts from Columbia; passengers can reach depot either by horse-cars or Little Miami Railroad.

National Banks. — See Banks.

National Insurance Company of Cincinnati was chartered in 1851. It has a cash capital of $100,000, and assets of $162,864. Its premium receipts up to 1879 have amounted to $1,311,118; its losses, to $831,309. The business includes fire, marine, and inland insurance. Ths office, which is probably the most neatly furnished of those of the local insurance companies, is at 69 West Third Street. Henry Urner, president.

National Lafayette and Bank of Commerce was organized under the present name in 1879. It is virtually a consolidation of the National Bank of Commerce, established in 1876, and the Lafayette Bank, established in 1832. The capital paid in is $400,000, and the deposits are over $2,000,000. The bank is situated at No. 20 West Third Street, and part of its rooms are occupied by the Safe Deposit Company. William A. Goodman is president, Henry Peachey vice-president, William J. Dunlap cashier, and Charles J. Stedman assistant cashier. The directors are John Shillito, A. D. Bullock, A. H. Andrews, R. A. Holden, S. H. Burton, H. Peachey, and William A. Goodman.

National Theatre was the oldest and one of the largest theatres in the city. Many years it was the only theatre Cincinnati had, and on its boards have trod the greatest actors that ever visited this section. It was situated on the east side of Sycamore Street, between Third and Fourth, and its inconvenient location has caused its disuse for several years past. The building has lately been purchased by a tobacco firm, who propose to use it as a manufactory and storage warehouse.

Natural History, the Cincinnati Society of, comprising about two hundred gentlemen of scientific attainments, has an endowment of $50,000. The museum of the society is filled with rare and interesting objects, fossils, skeletons, minerals, shells, and other natural-history and geological specimens. The building is owned by the society, and situated at No. 108 Broadway. It is open free to the public on Saturdays, between the hours of ten o'clock A.M. and four P.M.; but strangers introduced by members can see the collections at other times.

New-Jerusalem Church. — South-west corner of Fourth and John Streets. The church has recently been remodelled, and has some claims to architectural beauty. The religious principles enunciated by Emmanuel Swedenborg are taught. The congregation numbers about four hundred. The church has a fine library of the works of Swedenborg and other writers on the dogmas of the church, which is open to the public.

Newport is south-east of Cincinnati, and connected with it by the Louisville Short-line Bridge across the Ohio, and is connected with Covington by a bridge across the Licking River. It is virtually a suburb of Cincinnati, although a city of Kentucky. The population is about twenty thousand. It is built on an elevated plain, commanding a fine view, and has numerous shade-trees. It is said to have an admirable water-works system, and excellent water. It is sought mainly by business-men of Cincinnati as a dwelling-place by reason of its pure air and pleasant surroundings. Horse-cars run to and from Newport to Fountain Square, fare ten cents.

Newsboys' Home. — A branch of the Union Bethel, where homeless bootblacks and newsboys are furnished free lodgings, baths, and cheap meals; ten cents being the full price.

Newspapers (daily). — The English morning papers of Cincinnati are the "Commercial Gazette," "Enquirer," "News," and "Journal." "The Gazette" was established in 1793, and was the first newspaper published in the North-west Territory. A bound volume of "The Centinel," as the forerunner of "The Gazette" was named, for the year 1793, is in possession of the Historical and

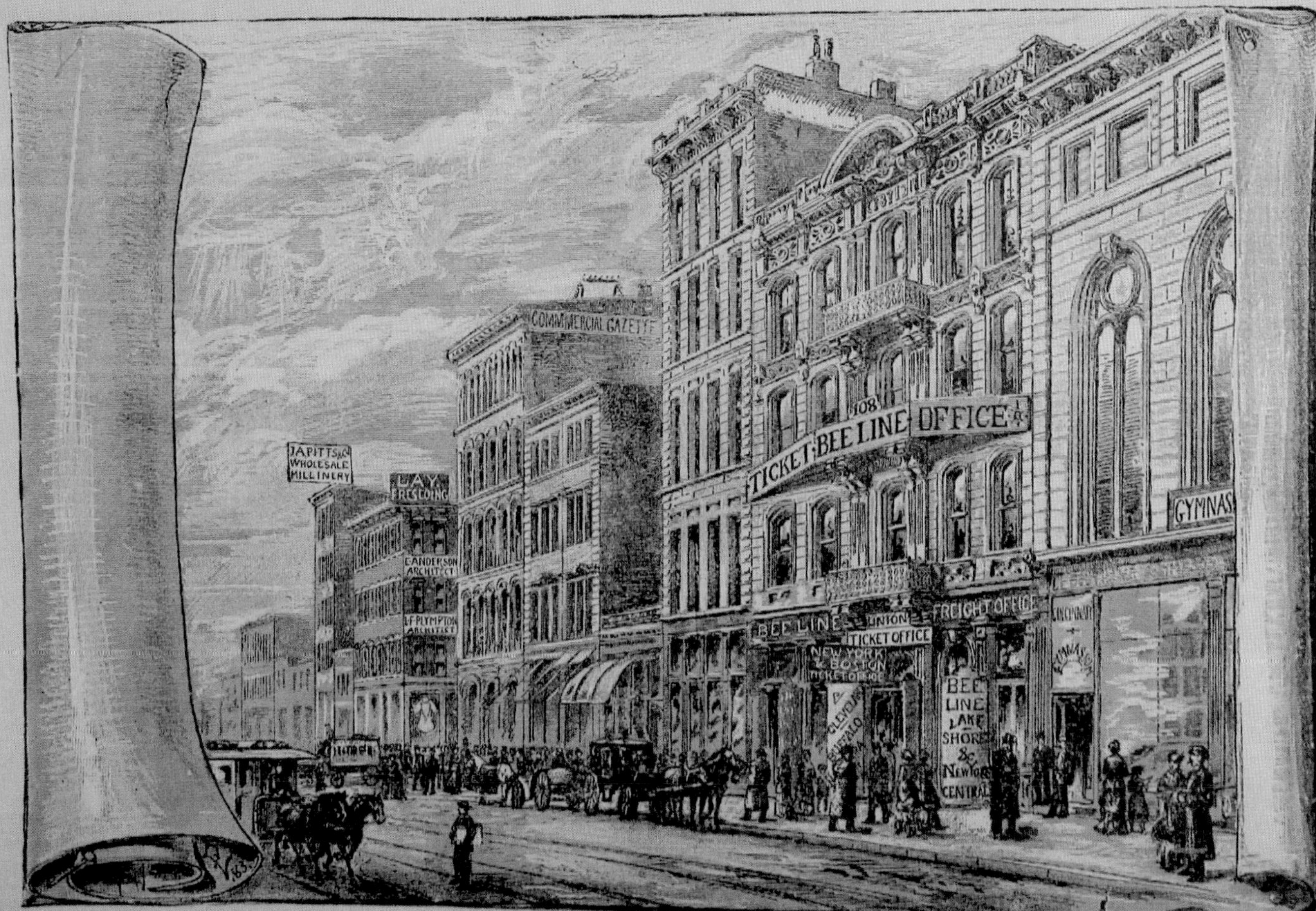

COMMERCIAL GAZETTE
J.A. PITTS & CO. WHOLESALE MILLINERY
LAY FRESCOING
E. ANDERSON ARCHITECT
L.F. PLYMPTON ARCHITECT
108
TICKET · BEE LINE OFFICE
GYMNAS
BEE LINE
UNION TICKET OFFICE
NEW YORK & BOSTON TICKET OFFICE
FREIGHT OFFICE
BEE LINE LAKE SHORE & NEW YORK CENTRAL
GYMNASIUM

Philosophical Society. Richard Smith is the chief editor. "The Commercial" was established in 1842, and has been a very successful paper. It is independent in its political views, but generally supports the Republican candidates. The principal editor and owner of "The Commercial" is Murat Halstead. Having in view the advancement of public polity and private interests, "The Gazette" and "Commercial" were on Jan. 1, 1883, consolidated under one management, and published as "The Commercial Gazette." The result of this movement has been a morning journal which stands without a peer in the West in all the elements that combine to produce a great newspaper. Its editorial corps embraces some of the most talented writers in the West, while its news department is unsurpassed in the collecting and arranging of the daily happenings of the world at large. Succeeding to the combined circulations of both "Commercial" and "Gazette," its list of subscribers is very large. Office, north-east corner of Fourth and Race Streets. "The Enquirer" has been in existence about forty years, and is a Democratic newspaper. It has made a great advance in popularity and influence by reason of its enterprise in gathering news from all parts of the world. "The Enquirer" publishes a weekly paper, having a large circulation. Office, 247 Vine Street. The chief editor is John R. McLean, who is also the proprietor. "The Morning Journal" is the outgrowth of the consolidation of "The Commercial" and "Gazette," and as such succeeds to the franchise of the Associated Press possessed by "The Gazette." It is Republican in politics, and was first published Jan. 7, 1883. It sells for one cent a copy. Being the only cheap paper in Cincinnati admitted to the Associated Press, it reaps all the benefits to be derived from so advantageous position. "The News" is a two-cent paper, Democratic in politics, established Dec. 1, 1882. Though not permitted to use the Associated-Press despatches, its facilities are such that it succeeds in getting the latest news, and gives promise of becoming a powerful organ of the Democracy of the West. The evening English dailies are "The Times Star" and "The Penny Post." "The Times Star" is an eight-page quarto sheet of forty-eight columns. It is printed from stereotype-plates, on the fast Bullock perfecting-press. It prints four editions daily; is independent in politics. Lewis A. Leonard, editor and business manager. The German dailies are the "Volksblatt," "Volksfreund," "Freie Presse," and "Abend Post." The "Volksblatt" has the largest circulation, and is independent in politics. It has improved machinery, and is printed from stereotype plates. It is owned by a joint-stock company. Frederick Hassaurek is the chief editor. Office, 269 Vine Street, between Sixth and Seventh. The "Volksfreund" is the German Democratic organ. It was established in 1850, and is owned and edited by Henry Haacke. The circulation of the daily, weekly, and Sunday editions is large. The office is 209 Vine Street. The "Freie Presse," daily and weekly, is a Republican paper of good circulation and considerable merit. It is the rival of the "Volksblatt" among German Republicans, and its influence is increasing. It is published at the north-east corner of Vine and Canal Streets. The "Freie Presse" also publishes an evening edition, called the "Tägliche Abend Presse." The "Abend Post" is an evening daily, Republican in politics, published at No. 342 Main Street, by Jeup & Raberg. It has been established about six years. Of the above dailies, the "Commercial Gazette," "Enquirer," "Morning Journal," "Times Star," "Volksblatt," and "Volksfreund" are members of the Associated Press, and use the despatches furnished by that organization. The "Times Star," "Freie Presse," and "Abend Post" use the National Associated Press despatches, which are furnished by the Atlantic and Pacific Telegraph Company. "The Cincinnati Law Bulletin" is a small daily devoted to the needs of the legal profession. It is published at No. 17 West Eighth Street.

Newspapers and Periodicals published in Cincinnati, according to the City Directory for 1882, exclusive of the dailies mentioned elsewhere, are as follows: 37 English weeklies, 12 German weeklies, 1 semi-weekly, 57 monthlies, 10 semi-monthlies, and 10 quarterlies. They are devoted to almost every conceivable interest, and are of all sizes and at all prices. Newspapers and periodicals can be obtained of J. R. Hawley, 164 Vine Street; Perry & Morton, 162 Vine Street; Alfred Warren, 219 Central Avenue; and the Cincinnati News Company, 181 Race Street.

Nourse, Miss Clara E. — For nineteen years Miss Nourse's family and day school has been recognized as one of the worthy educational institutions of Cincinnati. In 1879 its location was removed to 166 West Seventh Street, where it occupies the "Cochnower House," one of the finest residences in the central portion of the city. The school comprises an English department and a French department. It is conducted by Miss Nourse, assisted by fourteen competent teachers. The boarding-pupils are received into the family residence of Miss Nourse on Park Avenue, Walnut Hills, and are conveyed to and from the school in a private omnibus. Part of the first floor of the school-building is occupied by Miss Goodman's kindergarten.

Observatory, the Cincinnati, is situated on a four-acre lot on Mount Lookout, and is now a department of the University of Cincinnati. Here is placed the celebrated Mitchel telescope, one of the most perfect instruments in the world. The focal length is 16 feet; and the diameter of the object-glass is 11 inches, having magnifying powers varying from 100 to 1,400 times. A regular course of instruction in mathematics and astronomy is given, with practical applications of the principles studied. H. T. Eddy is the professor of astronomy and mathematics, and Ormond Stone the resident astronomer. The observatory may be reached by private conveyance, or by the Elm-street line of horse-cars connecting with the Mount Lookout steam dummy. (See Astronomical Society.)

Obstetrical Society, the Cincinnati, composed of prominent obstetricians, holds monthly meetings at the homes of members. The society is limited to twenty members. Dr. J. W. Underhill is president.

Odd Fellows, Independent Order of.—There are 32 lodges of this order in this city, composed of some 6,000 members. They have a revenue of over $60,000, and assets invested in government bonds and other property amounting to over $300,000. The beautiful Odd Fellows' Temple, on the corner of Fourth and Home Streets, cost over $90,000, besides which the order has in different parts of the city 14 lodge-rooms fitted up and furnished in handsome and appropriate style. Ohio Lodge No. 1, instituted in 1830, was the first lodge west of Pittsburg, and is the parent lodge in the State of Ohio, in which there are 647 lodges, and over 46,000 members. In addition to the lodges, there are 15 encampments, having over 1,600 members, with investments valued at over $50,000. The 32 lodges are: Ohio, 1; Washington, 2; Cincinnati, 3; Franklin, 4; William Penn, 56; Magnolia, 83; Eagle, 100; Fidelity, 71; Fulton, 112; Germania, 113; Metropolitan, 142; Woodward, 149; Mohawk, 150; American, 170; Palmetto, 175; Crystal Fount, 176; Teutonia, 177; Vulcan, 178; Hermann, 208; Queen City, 229; Mill-creek, 249; Humboldt, 274; North-western, 296; William Tell, 335; Losanteville, 336; Spencer,

347; Eclipse, 348; Nathan Stewart, 388; Kirkup, 401; Globe, 470; Moltke, 473; Fairmount, 480. The 15 encampments are: Wildey, 1; Washington, 9; Cincinnati, 22; Mahketewah, 32; Schiller, 42; Philadelphon, 53; Hermann, 66; Charter Oak, 77; Anderson, 85; William Tell, 109; Walnut Hills, 117; Covenant, 124; Mozart, 161; Ohio, 178; Pioneer, 37. In addition to the halls at Fourth and Home Streets, the 14 lodge-rooms are: Eagle Hall, south-west corner Eighth Street and Central Avenue; William Penn Hall, north-east corner Eighth Street and Central Avenue; Globe Hall, Ninth Street and Central Avenue; Magnolia Hall, Sixth and Walnut; Queen-city Hall, Eighth and Freeman Streets; Vulcan Hall, Martin Street; Fulton Hall, Eastern Avenue; Spencer Hall, Eastern Avenue; Germania Hall, Court Street; Kirkup Hall, corner Curtis and Gilbert Avenue; Moltke Hall, Freeman Street; Mill-creek Hall, Cumminsville; Nathan Stewart Hall, 21st Ward; Fidelity Hall, Clinton and Cutter Streets.

Ohio, one of the five States into which the North-west Territory was divided, and of which Cincinnati is the metropolis, contains 39,964 square miles, and in 1870 had a population of 2,665,260 persons. The first permanent settlement was made near the mouth of the Muskingum River by a party of 47 persons, mostly New-Englanders, under the leadership of Gen. Rufus Putnam, son of Israel Putnam of Revolutionary fame. They started on their long journey in the autumn of 1787, and reached their destination in the spring of the following year. The little town was named Marietta, in honor of Marie Antoinette, the unfortunate wife of Louis XVI. From this time the immigration, chiefly from the New-England States, was so constant, that in 1802 Ohio was admitted to the Union. Ohio is 210 miles from north to south, 200 miles from east to west, has a navigable frontier on the south, through the windings of the Ohio River, of 430 miles, has a lake shore on the north of 200 miles, and in 1875 ranked as the third State in population, wealth, and power. The word Ohio, which is of Indian origin, is said to mean "beautiful." It is also said to mean "bloody" and "white." The State is universally known as the Buckeye State.

Ohio College of Dental Surgery.—Established in 1845. The building is on the west side of College Street, between Sixth and Seventh Streets. The regular session each year commences in October, and ends in March. Fees: lectures, \$75; matriculation, \$5;

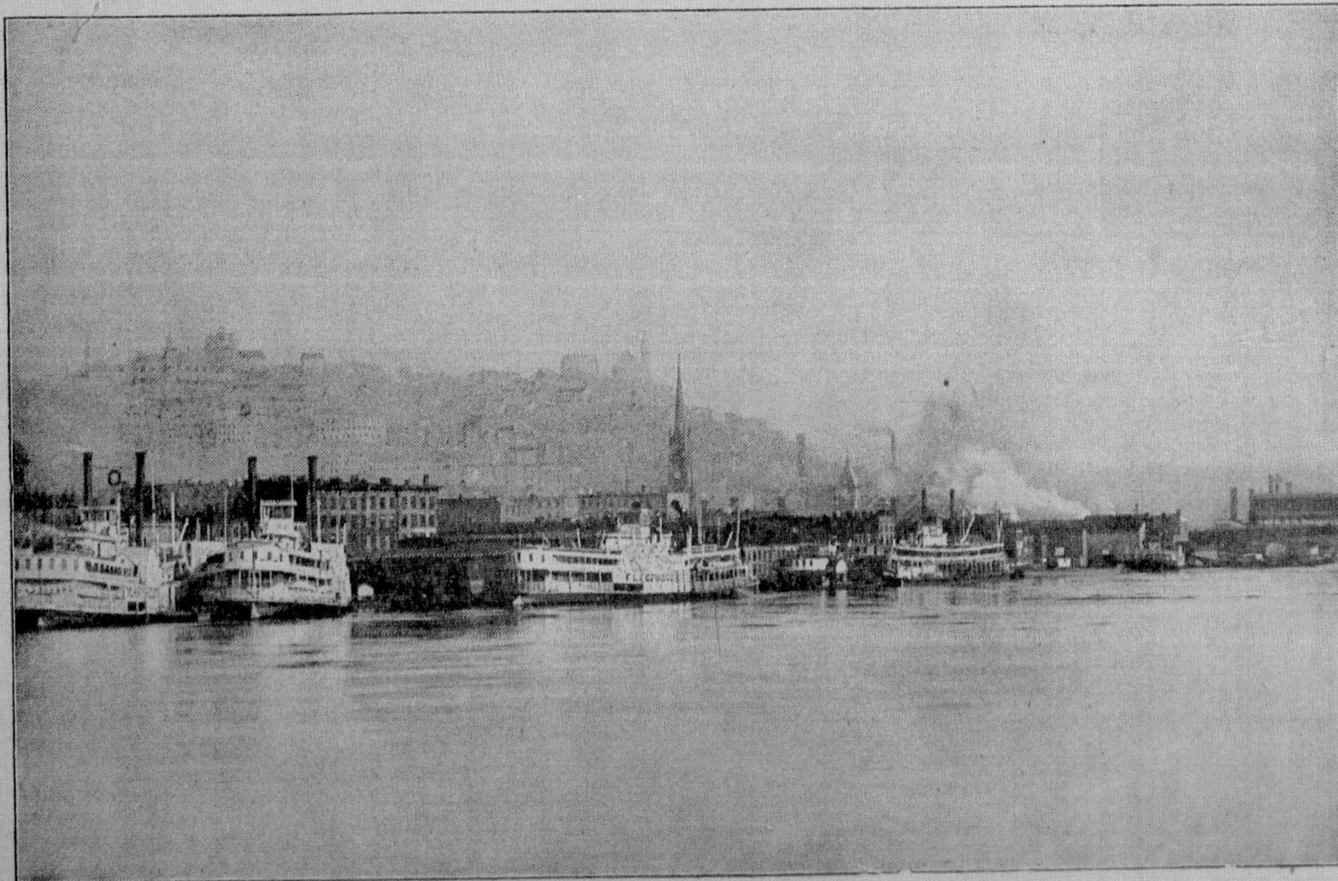

Ohio River, opposite Mount Adams.

demonstrator of anatomy, $5; graduation, $20. A spring session is also held, for which the fees are $30 additional. The branches taught are clinical dentistry, mechanical dentistry, anatomy, physiology, histology, pathology, therapeutics, chemistry, microscopy, operative dentistry, and hygiene. H. A. Smith is dean.

Ohio Mechanics' Institute. — On the south-west corner of Sixth and Vine Streets. The Institute was incorporated in 1829. From a small beginning, it encountered many drawbacks and difficulties from debt; but is now, and has been for years, on a solid foundation, owning the valuable building devoted to its uses. A large portion of the immense library it once possessed has been transferred to the Public Library. Five managers of the Industrial Exposition are chosen from the Ohio Mechanics' Institute. Besides the rooms devoted to the uses of the Institute in their large building, there is a public hall, known as Greenwood Hall, occupying the entire third story. The ground-floor is rented for business purposes. The structure is of Gothic architecture, ninety by seventy-five feet, and one hundred feet high. It is an ornament to the city.

Ohio Medical College Dispensary, one of the great charities of the city, is located in the building of the Medical College of Ohio. All sick persons who apply are supplied with medicines, and treated free of charge. An hour or more is devoted each day to this great humane work by the faculty of the college. From six thousand to eight thousand patients are treated annually. During the lecture-season students of the college are admitted to the clinic, but the dispensary is open every day during the year.

Ohio River, upon the banks of which Cincinnati is situated, is one of the most important rivers of the United States, and is formed by the confluence of the Alleghany and Monongahela Rivers at Pittsburg, Penn., whence it flows in a south-westerly direction, dividing Ohio, Indiana, and Illinois, on the right, from Virginia and Kentucky on the left. Its entire length is 950 miles, and it enters the Mississippi River 1,216 miles from the mouth of the latter river. Its most important tributaries are the Wabash, Cumberland, Muskingum, Kanawha, Kentucky, and Tennessee. Its medium breadth is 1,800 feet, and opposite Cincinnati its elevation above the level of the sea is 414 feet. The navigable waters of the Ohio and its tributaries are estimated at 5,000 miles; and the extent of area drained, at 200,000 square miles.

Old Men's Home.—A. M. Taylor of New Jersey left $10,000 for a home for aged and indigent men, provided $50,000 more should be raised for the same purpose. To secure this, an organization was effected, and a canvass for subscriptions begun and carried through successfully, the work being done almost wholly by Edward Sargent. In 1879 an arrangement was made with the trustees of the Widows' Home and Asylum for Aged and Indigent Women to erect a building supplying the needs of both institutions. (See Widows' and Old Men's Home.) The trustees are John Shillito, Anthony H. Hinkle, and Edward Sargent.

Old Streets, Boundaries, and Incidents.—In the winter of 1831–32 a flood submerged the whole lower level of the city. Water rose to the second stories of the highest houses on Front Street. Steamboats passed through Second (at that time Columbia) Street. A large number of the original citizens lived near the river; and it was not until the "miserable Yankees" came, and made a fuss about fever and ague, "and such aboriginal invigorators," that people who were "anybody" lived on the hill,—say Fourth Street. Front Street, from Walnut west to Elm, was lined by beautiful homes. The wharf was the meeting-place, especially Sunday morning. There the best townsmen exchanged the news; took a quiet "nip" at the "Orleans Coffee-house," situated just east of Main Street on the Public Wharf, and surrounded by a large open garden; and thence went to church. Joseph Darr, the proprietor of the coffee-house, just deceased, lived in and owned the large mansion south-east corner Seventh and Race. The chief business-streets were Main and Lower Market, now East Pearl. Pearl Street was opened in 1832; and at what is now its intersection with Main, stood a large tavern, with a large wagon-yard into which teamsters drove. This tavern was bought from Daniel Horne by merchants, who built a row of four-story brick stores, thought at the time to be the finest in America, some of which are still standing on the north side of the street. The projectors of this first great commercial enterprise were Goodman & Emerson, Carlisle & White, J. D. & C. Jones, C. & J. Bates, Foote & Bowler, Blachly & Simpson, Reeves & McLean, David Griffin, and John R. Coram. Pearl Street, west of Walnut, was opened in 1844. Fifth Street, except from Main to Vine, was occupied by cheap residences; and a wooden market-house filled the space now occupied by the Esplanade. About 1833

Broadway and East Fourth began to be pretentious as desirable residence streets. Prior to 1841 Fourth Street west of Walnut, as far as Plum, was a beautiful street. In 1841 improvements were made west of Plum, and gradually reached the "fence" which ended the street at what is now Wood Street. In 1832 Columbia (now Second) Street was merely a dirty creek, crossed by wooden bridges at all intersections west of Walnut. No business of importance was done west of Main. The wharfage was between Main and Broadway; and even as late as 1846 the wharf-space was a great mud-hole, sprinkled with coarse gravel. All transportation was done by river, by canal, or by country wagons. As late as 1842 the Little Miami Railroad opened the State of Ohio, and about 1848 the Madison and Indianapolis Railroad the State of Indiana. In 1840 streets beyond the canal were simply unmacadamized roadways. Central Avenue was then Western Row, which north of Court Street ran through pastures. Nearly every family kept a cow; and the cows were driven to the pastures in the morning, and were turned loose to wander home at night to be milked in the alleys and side-yards. The great characteristics of a city were not to be seen in Cincinnati until about 1848, when a "hog-law" drove those "first scavengers" from the streets. Ash-piles were condemned, and the city supplied with water and gas. Most of the houses were cheaply built, and but few men kept carriages. There were only a few schools worthy of note. The merchants often entertained customers at their homes, and the general habits of pioneer simplicity prevailed. Turnpikes from the city were built between 1834 and 1840, and many of the citizens of to-day remember the mud-roads to Walnut Hills. Prior to 1840, Clifton was unknown. Cumminsville, now the 25th ward, and Camp Washington, now the 24th ward, were all farms. The "sports" gathered at a mile race-track, south of the old Brighton House, where the John-street horse-car stables are. The principal drives were up the river-bank to "Corbin's," or down to old Joe Harrison's place. Only occasional pleasure-parties ascended the hills, and then chiefly towards Cleves. The "down-river" road found all the fast horses, and Joe Harrison gave them good cheer. A few elegant homes, some yet in good condition, lined the hill-side of the road which was approached by Front Street, and by a road, the Sixth Street of the present time. West of Western Row, Sixth Street was not improved much earlier than 1840. A great orchard stood on a high bank west of Park Street; milk-yards and brick-kilns generally occupied that locality. The pioneers of wealth in that street were Abraham M Taylor (who recently gave $10,000 towards the Old Men's Home), James Taylor, William Neff, J. P. Tweed, Ambrose Dudley, Pollock Wilson, H. W. Derby, and others. The great Barr Estate was north of Sixth Street, and was subdivided after 1843, and the Hunt or Pendleton Estate at the head of Broadway about 1846. In that neighborhood few houses were seen. The pork-houses were on Sycamore and Canal Streets; the wholesale dry-goods houses, on Pearl and Main Streets; and the large grocery-houses, on Main, Front, and Pearl Streets. Such is a faint outline of what the great city of Cincinnati was only forty years ago — *From Notes of George W. Jones.*

Opera-Houses. — See Amusements

Ophthalmic and Aural Institute, connected with the Pulte Medical College, is devoted to the homœopathic treatment of diseases of the eye and ear. The poor are treated free of charge.

Orangemen. — There are about eighty active Orangemen in the city. They constitute the True Blue Lodge, which meets semi-monthly at Odd-Fellows' Hall, north-east corner of Fourth and Home Streets.

Organ, the Great, in Music Hall, is one of the largest and finest in the world. It was built in Boston, but the artistic screen of wild cherry was designed and carved by residents of Cincinnati. It is 60 feet high, 50 feet front, 30 feet deep. It has 96 registers, 6,237 pipes, 32 bells, 14 pedal-movements, and 4 keyboards of 61 notes each. Its cash cost was $32,000. A description, with illustrations, in pamphlet form, edited by George Ward Nichols, is for sale by the superintendent of the hall, price ten cents. The organ can be visited week-days from four to 6 P.M. An organ concert, by George E. Whiting, takes place Wednesday and Saturday afternoons at half-past two o'clock; admission, 25 cents.

Orphan Asylum, the Cincinnati, the oldest charity of the kind in the West, was chartered in 1833. It is situated at Mount Auburn, and is conducted by ladies, but its finances are managed by gentlemen. The institution is Protestant, but not sectarian, and is supported by an endowment-fund, subscriptions, and contributions. The policy of the management differs somewhat from that of other orphan-asylums, in that it aims to secure greater chances of usefulness and respectability to the children, by keeping them in the institution longer than they are usually kept, and by giving them the benefits of a common-school education. A kindergarten, which had thirty children last year, is attached to the institution; and the older children attend regularly the public school on Mount Auburn, the average number of the latter being seventy. Between school-hours and during vacation, the children are trained in domestic work. About seventeen thousand children have been cared for by this institution since its organization. Mrs. A. D. Bullock is president, Mrs. George Fox recording secretary.

Orphan Asylums. — See Boys' Protectory, Children's Home, Cincinnati Orphan Asylum, Colored Orphan Asylum, German Protestant Orphan Asylum, Newsboys' Home, St. Aloysius' Orphan Asylum, St. Peter's and St. Joseph's Orphan Asylum, — all noticed in their alphabetical places.

Orpheus, the Cincinnati. — A musical association having about a hundred members of both sexes. Weekly practice-meetings are held in the hall of the German Mutual Insurance Company's building, at the south-west corner of Twelfth and Walnut Streets.

Out-door Poor. — So called because they cannot be admitted to the Infirmary. They are widows with families, and men out of work, whose families would suffer if not relieved by the city authorities. They are supplied with a limited amount of provisions and coal, on certificates issued by the sanitary police detailed for the purpose. The city is divided into twelve poor-districts. Provisions are issued from the Infirmary office, on Plum Street, between Seventh and Eighth Streets.

Overseers of the Poor. — Formerly the "out-door poor" had their wants attended to by a board of twenty-five overseers, one from each ward, at a salary of $600 each per annum. These overseers have been discontinued, and their duty devolved upon the sanitary police.

"Over-the-Rhine" is a name designating the district lying in the angle formed by the "elbow" of the canal, east of Plum Street, north of Canal or Eleventh Street, and south of the northern circle of hills. It contains part of the 9th, the 7th, 10th, 11th, and 13th wards. It is the most densely populated portion of the city, and is inhabited by about twenty-five thousand persons, almost exclusively Germans, and Americans of German descent. Music Hall is situated in this district. Innumerable variety-shows, beer-gardens, and other places of amusement and recreation, are in its precincts. It is a famous place of resort at all times, but especially on Sunday, for those who love excitement and beer. There is no sabbath "Over-the-Rhine." Nearly all the business-houses are kept open seven days in the week, and many saloons all night.

Painters. — A. W. Corwine, a miniature-painter, was, about 1820, the first artist of ability whose name occurs in the annals of Cincinnati; a few years afterward came Thomas Dawson; and about twenty years ago William Miller was a miniature-painter, well remembered by many of the present generation of Cincinnatians. A. Hervieu, who accompanied Fanny Wright on her second journey to this country, became a resident of the city, and was probably the first historical and landscape painter in the West. One of his large paintings was "The Landing of Lafayette in Cincinnati in 1825." All traces of this painting have been lost, but it is believed to have been taken to Europe. Hervieu was employed by Mrs. Frances Trollope; and only a few years ago his decorations could yet be seen on the panels of the doors of her country-house now standing on the south-west corner of McMicken Avenue and Dunlap Street. In the early part of the decade of 1830–40, James H. Beard began painting portraits, and tried various branches of art, until in 1846 he moved to New York; but since that time he has resided for short periods in this city, where Frank Beard, his son, did his first work. Miner K. Kellogg, and William H. Powell, the painter of "De Soto discovering the Mississippi River," were local contemporaries of Beard. E. Hall Martin, a native of this city, painted portraits and *genre* subjects. Thomas Buchanan Read, painter and poet, was one of the Cincinnati artists of forty years ago; his first attempts being in 1839, in sculpture. Somewhat later than Read, W. L. Sonntag, and W. W. Whittredge, known as Worthington Whittredge, made in Cincinnati their first efforts at landscape-painting, and were prominent among the local artists until the decade of 1850–60. Joseph O. Eaton about the same time was the painter of many excellent portraits and other works; but, after spending some years here, he moved to New York. John R. Johnson, born in Cincinnati, was also a contemporary, but remained to a later period until his removal to Baltimore. C. T. Webber, another of the same group, is still a resident of this city, where he has practised his profession for thirty years. His portrait of Gov. Charles Anderson is a noted specimen of great skill. Edwin C. Cridland, a pupil of Beard, began here about 1850. John R. Tait, a native of this city, has spent most of his time in Europe, and, after short periods of residence in Cincinnati, has become a resident of Baltimore. Mrs. Lily Martin Spencer was a well-known painter from 1850 to 1860. About the same period there were R. S. Duncanson, "a man of color as well as a colorist," who was a landscape-painter, having a high imaginative power; Charles R. Soulé, the portrait-painter; and A. H. Wyant, who began about 1858. J. E. F. Hillen, an unrivalled sketcher of trees and foliage, and Fabronius, an equal master of heads, have a place in the record of artists in this city about 1860; and G. Rossi, an Italian, was one of their contemporaries. Thomas C. Lindsay, a prolific landscape-artist, has pursued his industrious career in Cincinnati for at least twenty years. Henry W. Kemper, a landscape-painter, lately returned after an absence of fifteen years, was born here; and Dwight Benton, now a resident of Rome, dates his career as a landscape-artist from the time of his residence in this city, about 1865. George Sharples, artist and cotton-merchant, was devoted to landscape-painting for a few years in the present decade. John Aubrey has been engaged in painting portraits for the past twenty years. About 1860 Theo. Jones was a noted local caricaturist; and William P. Noble, born here, was devoted to the same work, as well as to painting in water-colors. William Winter, 1860–70, merits special mention for prominence in water-color portraits. E. D. Grafton, now so well known, has for many years been a painter in water-colors and an unrivalled arabesque artist. A majority of the later artists were educated at Munich. Franz Duveneck has acquired fame; and his works have been highly appreciated, especially in Boston. Henry Mosler has the honor of having some of his works admitted into the Paris Salon; and one of them was bought by the French Government for the Luxembourg Gallery. John Twachtmann has left here, and gone to New York, where he has met with much success. Henry F. Farny is a resident artist, of varied talent. J. H. Decamp is now a student at Munich; and Frank Strobridge, after a short life full of promise, died in 1879. Of the "Spanish-Roman Set," Alfred Brennan and Robert Blum are in New York; and Kenyon Cox is studying in Paris. Thomas S. Noble was a pupil of Couture, and is the painter of many works of merit. Among the many artists who have been here for brief periods were Eastman Johnson, F. C. Welch, William M. Chase, Victor Nehlig, John Mulvany, Ira C. Dennis, and E. F. Andrews.

Paris of America is a name really given to this city by "The Cincinnati Commercial." One Monday morning in the early part of 1878, in "The Commercial's" local columns, edited at that time by Edwin Henderson, appeared a long report of the varied and numerous amusements taking place on the Sunday preceding; and at the head of the report was the line "The Paris of America,"—a phrase eminently suggestive of Sunday revelry, and which at once became popular. Newspapers, railroads, shows, and advertisers have used it so much as an attractive catch-line, that it has become a generally recognized name for Cincinnati. The term has been occasionally applied to Cincinnati for more than ten years, and originated from an address by Judge George Hoadly, when he prophesied that Cincinnati would be "a city fair to the sight, with a healthy public spirit, and high intelligence, sound to the core; a city with pure water to drink, pure air to breathe, spacious public grounds, wide avenues; a city not merely of much traffic, but of delightful homes; a city of manufactures, wherein is made every product of art,—the needle-gun, the steam-engine, the man of learning, the woman of accomplishments; a city of resort for the money-profits of its dealings, and the mental and spiritual profit of its culture,—the Edinboro' of a new Scotland, the Boston of a new New England, the Paris of a new France." Shortly afterwards the phrase, "Paris of America," was applied to Cincinnati; and in "The Queen City," a history and guide of the city in 1869, George E. Stevens says, "It has been no idle fancy that has styled Cincinnati the 'Paris of America.'"

Parks.—There are nine public parks in the city limits: viz., Eden Park, Burnet-woods Park, Lincoln Park, Washington Park, Hopkins Park, Mount Lookout Park, Eighth-street Park, City Park, and Water-works Park; all of which are described in their alphabetical places.

Pendleton.—That portion of the city lying on the river-front, at the base of the hills, south-east of Walnut Hills, and east of Fulton, extending to Sportsman's Hall, three miles and a half from Fountain Square. It constitutes a portion of the 1st ward. At its eastern limit are the depots of the Columbia and Mount Lookout steam dummy railroad. The Elm-street line of horse-cars connect with the dummy. The Little Miami Railroad also has a station here.

Pharmaceutical Examining Board consists of three members, appointed by the Court of Common Pleas. They are chosen from ten pharmacists nominated by the Cincinnati College of Pharmacy. The province of the board is to examine applicants in chemistry, materia medica, and pharmacy, so as to determine their qualifications as retail druggists and dispensing pharmacists. The board grants two certificates, — a first-grade certificate authorizing the holder to register before this board and conduct a retail drug-business; and a second-grade certificate, making the holder a "qualified assistant pharmacist." Holders of first-grade certificates, and graduates of recognized colleges of pharmacy, are registered; and by a law enacted in 1873, and amended in 1875, all persons in the retail drug-business must be registered. The examining-board holds session bi-monthly, in February, April, June, August, October, and December.

Philosophical Society. — See Historical and Philosophical Society of Ohio.

Phœnix Club. — The largest and most fashionable of the Israelite clubs. It occupies a fine building on the north-east corner of Court Street and Central Avenue, to which the club removed when its former club-house on Walnut Street was torn down to make room for the new government buildings now being erected. The present building was remodelled in 1874, at a cost of $60,000. It contains, besides a large hall for balls and parties, 12 large social rooms, a restaurant, supper-room, billiard-rooms, library-room, and reading-room, the whole elegantly furnished. There are 240 members. Annual subscription, $60.

Physicians, Surgeons, and Dentists. — It often occurs that a stranger in a city has need of medical or surgical aid, and is timid about asking the advice of an acquaintance, or wants confidence in intrusting himself to practitioners unknown to him. For this reason the publishers have given below the names of some practitioners who rank unquestionably among the most highly esteemed, the most successful, and the most trustworthy persons of their profession; and the publishers wish to state very clearly that no personal or pecuniary considerations whatever, directly or indirectly, have influenced them in the selection of the names given. The men have already established their reputations by long residence and success, or by being intrusted with professorships at medical colleges and responsible appointments at hospitals. It is necessary to add that the list is only a small part of the large number of eminently respectable and able physicians, surgeons, and dentists, and that there are many practitioners in this city, whose names are not given for want of space, who, in the judgment of the ablest experts, rank equal in every particular to those whose names are found below. It is also necessary to warn a stranger, likely to be influenced by advertisements, to keep away from the doctors who advertise. For a person once getting into the hands of a quack — and quacks are numerous among the great advertisers in a profession — will very likely pay dearly for his experience. A person afflicted in any manner whatsoever can always safely intrust himself to the care of a regular practitioner in first-class standing; and to aid in finding such practitioners this list can be relied on.

General Surgeons. — W. W. Dawson, professor of surgery and dean at the Medical College of Ohio, and surgeon at the Good Samaritan Hospital; office, north-west corner Third and Broadway. P. S. Conner, professor of anatomy and surgery at the Medical College of Ohio, and surgeon at the Cincinnati Hospital; office, 159 West Ninth Street. C. S. Muscroft, sen., surgeon at the Cincinnati Hospital and the St. Mary's Hospital; office, 335 John. N. Pendleton Dandridge, pathologist at the Cincinnati Hospital; office, 57 East Fourth Street.

General Practitioners. — William Carson, physician at the Cincinnati Hospital; office, 53 East Fourth. C. G. Comegys, physician at the Cincinnati Hospital; office, 163 Elm. James T. Whittaker, professor of medicine at the Medical College of Ohio, and physician at the Good Samaritan Hospital; office, 100 West Eighth. Joshua W. Underhill, professor of Materia Medica and therapeutics at the Cincinnati College of Medicine and Surgery; office, 434 John Street. John A. Murphy, professor of medicine and dean of Miami Medical College, and physician at the Cincinnati Hospital; office, 163 West Seventh. Willian Clendenin, professor of anatomy at the Miami Medical College, and formerly the health-officer of Cincinnati; office, 136 West Seventh.

Gynæcologists and Obstetricians. — Thaddeus A. Reamy, professor of obstetrics and diseases of children at Medical College of Ohio, and gynæcologist at the Good Samaritan Hospital; office, 278 West Fourth Street. William H. Taylor, professor of obstetrics at the Miami Medical College, and obstetrician at the Cincinnati Hospital; office, 329 West Seventh Street. C. D. Palmer, professor of diseases of women and gynæcology at the Medical College of Ohio; office, south-east corner Baymiller and Findlay.

Aurists and Oculists.—Elkanah Williams, one of the most celebrated oculists in America, and professor of ophthalmology at the Miami Medical College; office, 64 West Seventh. W. W. Seely, professor of diseases of the eye and ear at the Medical College of Ohio, and ophthalmologist at the Good Samaritan Hospital; office, south-east corner of Fourth and Broadway. Joseph Aub, professor of diseases of the eye and ear at the Cincinnati College of Medicine and Surgery, and oculist at the Cincinnati Hospital; office, 84 West Seventh.

Homœopathists.—T. C. Bradford, who has practised homœopathy in this city for more than twenty years; office, 215 Race. J. D. Buck, professor of physiology and microscopy at the Pulte Medical College; office, 305 Race. S. R. Beckwith, a teacher of homœopathy for more consecutive years than any person in this country, and for several years professor of surgery at the Pulte Medical College, and Cleveland Homœopathic Hospital College; office, 161 West Seventh Street.

Eclectic Practitioner.—A. J. Howe, professor of surgery at the Eclectic Medical Institute; office, north-west corner Fourth and Main.

Dentists.—Jonathan Taft, author of several works on dentistry, and for many years dean of the Ohio College of Dental Surgery, and now professor of dentistry and dean of the dental college connected with the University of Michigan; office, 117 West Fourth Street. James Taylor, professor of dentistry at the Ohio College of Dental Surgery; office, 171 Elm Street. L. P. Meredith, a dentist of long experience and extensive practice, and author of several works on dentistry; office, 197 West Fourth Street. D. W. Clancey, clinical instructor at the Ohio College of Dental Surgery, north-east corner Seventh and John Streets.

Specialist in Diseases of the Throat.—Bernard Tauber, professor of acoustics and anatomy of the ear and larynx at the College of Music; office, 157 West Ninth Street.

Hosiery and Underwear Department.

THE STOCK IN THIS DEPARTMENT EMBRACES COMPLETE LINES OF

LADIES', MEN'S, AND CHILDREN'S

Cotton, Silk, Merino, and Wool Hose

IN ALL SIZES AND QUALITIES.

Underwear

OF ALL WEIGHTS AND QUALITIES.

Gloves.

Newest styles and colorings in Kid, Chamois, Dogskin, Pigskin, and Fur; also, Berlin, Cloth, Cashmere, and Silk Gloves

ALSO, IN THIS DEPARTMENT,

Men's Furnishing Goods

IN LARGE VARIETY.

Notion Department.

The great variety and range of goods classed under the head of Notions renders any thing like a complete list impossible.

Full assortments of staple notions constantly on hand, and all the novelties added as fast as they appear.

The John Shillito Company.

Physio-Medical Institute. — Located on the north-west corner of Seventh and Cutter Streets. The "doctrines of a vital force and the rejection of poisons are taught."

Pike's Opera-House, in the massive building belonging to the estate of the late Samuel N. Pike, on the south side of Fourth Street, between Walnut and Vine, was the most elegant hall in the city. It had a parquette, parquette-circle, dress-circle, gallery, and four proscenium-boxes. The dress-circle had eight box-stalls on either side, next the stage, each seating four persons. The whole seating capacity was two thousand. The hall is now used by the Cincinnati Chamber of Commerce. It is on the second floor, and is approached from Fourth Street by one wide and two narrow stairways. The building stands on the site of the old Pike's Opera-House, which was destroyed by fire in 1866. It is only one square south of Fountain Square, and is therefore easily accessible by all the street-railroad lines.

Pioneer Association, the Cincinnati, was organized in 1856, of ladies and gentlemen who had resided in Ohio prior to the 4th of July, 1812. Subseqently the limit for membership was changed to the year 1815. Quarterly business-meetings in March, June, September, and December, are held in the Council Chamber of the City Building. On the 4th of July, the birthday of American Independence; on the 7th of April, the anniversary of the settlement of Ohio; and on the 28th of December, the recognized date of the settlement of Cincinnati, — on all those days the formal and festive gatherings and excursions take place. Since the organization was formed, about four hundred members have died, and their funerals were attended by the surviving members. There are now about three hundred members; and the whole cost to each member for enrolment-fee and dues has been only $1. The president is John S. Perkins; and the secretary is John D. Caldwell, who, although not by birth entitled to membership, is, however, by adoption one of the most honored and active members, and has held his present position for almost a score of years.

Police. — The police-force of Cincinnati is controlled by the mayor. The executive officer is the superintendent, and next to him is the inspector. The patrolmen are directly controlled by 19 lieutenants and 13 sergeants, distributed among ten police-districts, each containing a station-house, to which a certain number of patrolmen report.

WOOLLEN DEPARTMENT.

In this department we offer full lines of the BEST KNOWN MAKES at very attractive prices.

FLANNELS.

WHITE, SCARLET, GRAY, AND BLUE, IN PLAIN AND TWILLS.
PLAID, STRIPED, PLAIN, AND PRINTED OPERAS, SHIRTING AND DRESS FLANNELS, ALL GRADES.

WOOLLENS.

CASSIMERES, REPELLENTS, LADIES' CLOTHS,
UNION AND ALL-WOOL BEAVERS,
FANCY CLOAKINGS, SUITINGS, BROADCLOTHS,
DOESKINS, ETC.

Of the best American and Foreign makes.

KENTUCKY JEANS, UNION AND ALL-WOOL FILLINGS.

Unequalled assortment.

BLANKETS.

WHITE BLANKETS,
From crib size to the largest made.

COLORED BLANKETS,
All shades and weights.

HORSE BLANKETS,
One and two strap, all grades.

THE JOHN SHILLITO COMPANY.

The rank and file of the force for the year 1882 numbered 283. Ten patrolmen are detailed as detectives, and do not wear uniforms while on duty. During the year 1882 the number of arrests made was 13,642. Of these, 9,427 were for crimes and misdemeanors, and 4,215 for safe-keeping; the latter being discharged without trial before the police-court. The salary of the superintendent is $2,500 per annum; inspector, $1,500; lieutenants, $900 each; and patrolmen, $800 each. The total cost of the department in 1882 was $271,310. It is probably the most efficient, and at the same time the least expensive, of the police-departments of this country. The cost to each resident is about $1, while in New York the cost is about $3.50.

Police-Stations. — The city is divided into ten police-districts, each having a station-house for the temporary confinement of arrested persons. At each station-house a certain number of policemen report, morning and evening, for roll-call. The station-houses are situated as follows: 1st district, Ninth Street, near Central Avenue; 2d, Hammond Street, between Third and Fourth; 3d, Bremen Street, between Fifteenth and Liberty; 4th, Third Street, west of Mill Street; 5th, corner Linn and Oliver Streets; 6th, Fulton; 7th, Walnut Hills; 8th, Corryville; 9th, Sedamsville; 10th, Cumminsville.

Population, according to United-States census, was in 1800, 750; 1810, 2,540; 1820, 9,602; 1830, 24,831; 1840, 46,338; 1850, 115,436; 1860, 161,044; 1870, 216,239. Of the population in 1870, there were 79,612 foreigners, including 49,448 born in Germany, 18,624 in Ireland, 3,526 in England, 2,093 in France. 210,335 were white, and 5,904 colored. In 1880 the population numbered 255,708.

Porkopolis is one of the names by which Cincinnati is known, and its origin is explained in the following manner: About 1825 George W. Jones, president of the United-States branch-bank, and known as "Bank Jones," was very enthusiastic about the fact that 25,000 to 30,000 hogs were being killed in this city every year; and in his letters to the bank's Liverpool correspondent he never failed to mention the fact, and express his hope of Cincinnati's future greatness as a provision-market. The correspondent, after receiving a number of these letters, had a unique pair of model hogs made of papier-maché, and sent them to "George W. Jones as the worthy representative of Porkopolis." The hogs were kept in the bank until it closed, and were then taken care of by Mr. Jones, who a few years before his death handed them over to John W. Coleman, one of the largest slaughterers at the time; and he in turn passed them over to H. A. Bowman, superintendent of the Miami stock-yards, who leaves them at the office of Samuel Davis, jun., & Co.

Pork-Packers' Association of Cincinnati dates its organization Oct. 30, 1872, and has for its object the promotion of the interests of the provision-trade by securing concert of action and a free interchange of opinion, and by submitting recommendations as to rules for the government of the provision-trade of this city to the Chamber of Commerce for consideration. Its members comprise the leading pork-packers of Cincinnati, and to its deliberation the present code of laws for the government of the local provision-trade is largely traceable. It was the first to take the lead in granting reciprocal judicial privileges to the members of other commercial organizations, adopting a like rule throughout the country. It has made exhibitions at Vienna and at the Cincinnati Industrial Exposition, and has always been influential in the council of the National Pork-Packers' Association. The room used is set apart for the association by the Chamber of Commerce, to which it is a recognized adjunct; all members of the Association being members of the Chamber, and all members of the Chamber having free access to all privileges of the Association-rooms.

Portsmouth, Big Sandy, and Pomeroy Packet Company, the Cincinnati, owns eight boats. Of these "The Ohio, No. 4," "The Telegraph," and "The Potomac" make daily trips to Pomeroy, O.; "The Bostona" and "The Fleetwood," daily trips to Huntington, W. Va., where they connect with the Chesapeake and Ohio Railroad; "The Bonanza," tri-weekly trips to Portsmouth, O.; "The Wildwood," tri-weekly trips to Maysville, Ky.; and "The City of Portsmouth," daily trips (except Sundays) to Chilo, O. The company also does a general towing-business, and for this purpose owns three boats, "The T. W. Means," "The Etna," and "The Cobb Cecil," and about twenty barges. "The A. L. Norton," also owned by this company, is used for transient passenger business. The president is John Kyle, the secretary T. M. Holloway, and the superintendent Louis Glenn.

Post-Office Statistics. — The total receipts of the Cincinnati post-office for the year 1882 were $623,062.48, and the total expenses only $191,742.34. There were 36,931 money-orders issued, from which

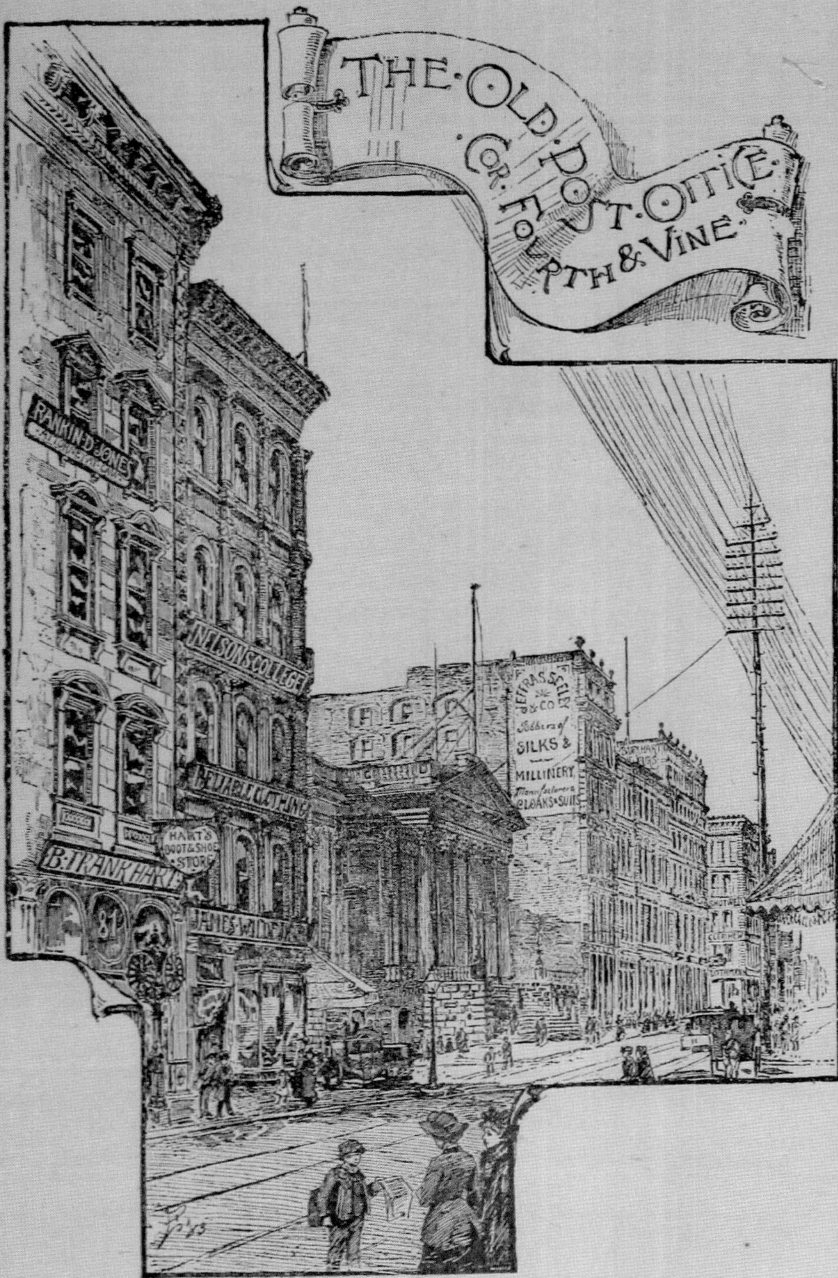
THE·OLD·POST·OFFICE·
COR. FOURTH & VINE.
RANKIN D. JONES
NELSON'S COLLEGE
RELIABLE CLOTHING
HART'S BOOT & SHOE STORE
B. FRANK HART
81
JAMES WALDE
SILKS &
MILLINERY
CLOAKS & SUITS

the total receipts, with the fees therefor, were $531,629.62; number of money-orders paid were 195,564; amount paid out on orders, $2,521,809.70; number of letter-carriers employed, 100; total number of pieces mail-matter handled, 28,701,952; number of letters advertised, 24,727; sent to Dead-Letter Office, 263,015; total number of pieces mail-matter distributed, 50,369,450; second-class matter mailed by publishers, 2,785,315 pounds; postage on second-class matter, $57,056.00; number of letters registered, 38,932; number of registered letters received for delivery, 152,316; number of registered packages handled in transit, 328,206.

Post-office, the, is in the building on the south-west corner of Fourth and Vine Streets, and occupies the basement and the west half of the first floor; in which latter are the registry and money-order departments and the offices of the postmaster and his secretary. The present quarters are much too small; and the post-office, with all its various departments, will be moved into the building now being erected by the United-States Government, as soon as it is completed. Col. S. A. Whitfield is postmaster. (See Custom-House, and see Government Building.)

Pottery, Artistic. — Manufacturing in Cincinnati has become a recognized and important industry. At the Industrial Exposition held in this city in 1882, the most exquisite and tasteful designs and rare specimens were exhibited, and attracted marked attention from lovers of the beautiful in art. Numerous and large orders were given from all parts of the United States for the productions of our potteries, most prominent among which is the "Rookwood Pottery," situated at 207 Eastern Avenue; Maria Longworth Nichols, proprietor.

Pottery Decoration has gained for the city a name contributing somewhat to its reputation in art-matters. The work has been accomplished by amateurs, almost exclusively by ladies. The owners of the potteries have assisted their efforts; but as yet the potters have failed to take the lead in the matter, and have confined themselves to the production of undecorated wares. The variety and superior qualities of the clays of Ohio and the neighboring States make possible the building-up of a great industry at a place where unrivalled facilities are afforded for the creation of artistic products from materials as well suited for the purposes as any in the world. Robert Clarke & Co. have just published the eighth edition of "China

Painting," a valuable manual for amateurs, by Miss M. Louise McLaughlin of this city.

Pottery Club. — An organization of ladies, amateurs in art-work, formed April, 1879, for the decoration in under-glaze painting of pottery made from the clays of the Ohio Valley. Miss M. Louise

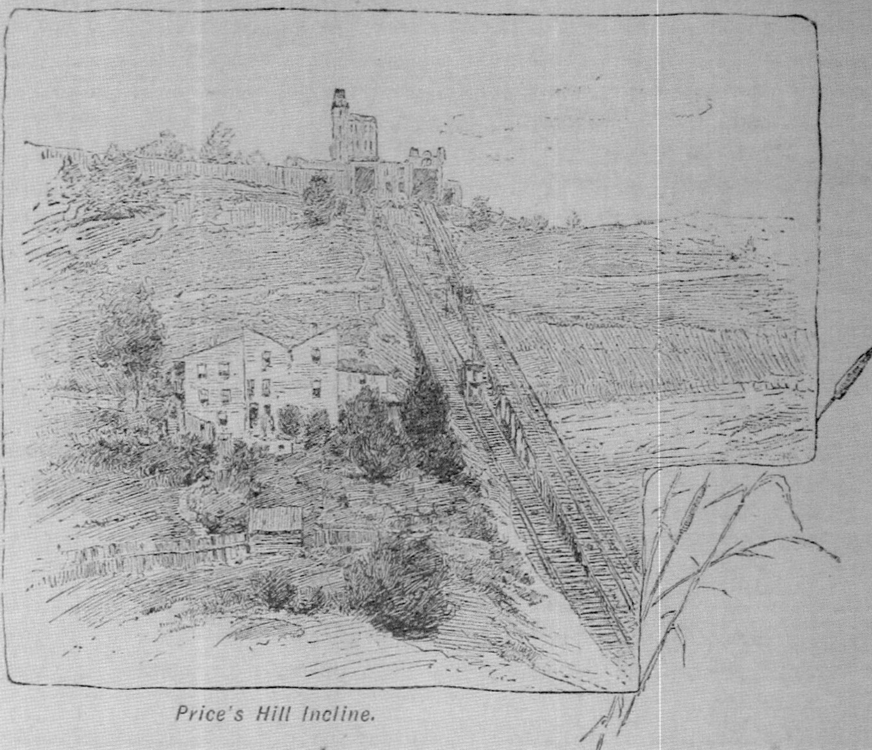

Price's Hill Incline.

McLaughlin is president, Miss Clara Newton secretary. The club meets Tuesdays and Thursdays at the Women's Art Museum Association Rooms.

Prevention of Cruelty to Children and Animals, the Ohio State Society for, was organized in May, 1873. Its principal office is in Cincinnati, at No. 55 West Fourth Street. Arrangements are now being perfected to establish branch-offices throughout the State of Ohio. During the ten years since its organization, it has done a noble work in decreasing the number of cases of brutality to animate beings. The society is supported largely by subscriptions. Life-

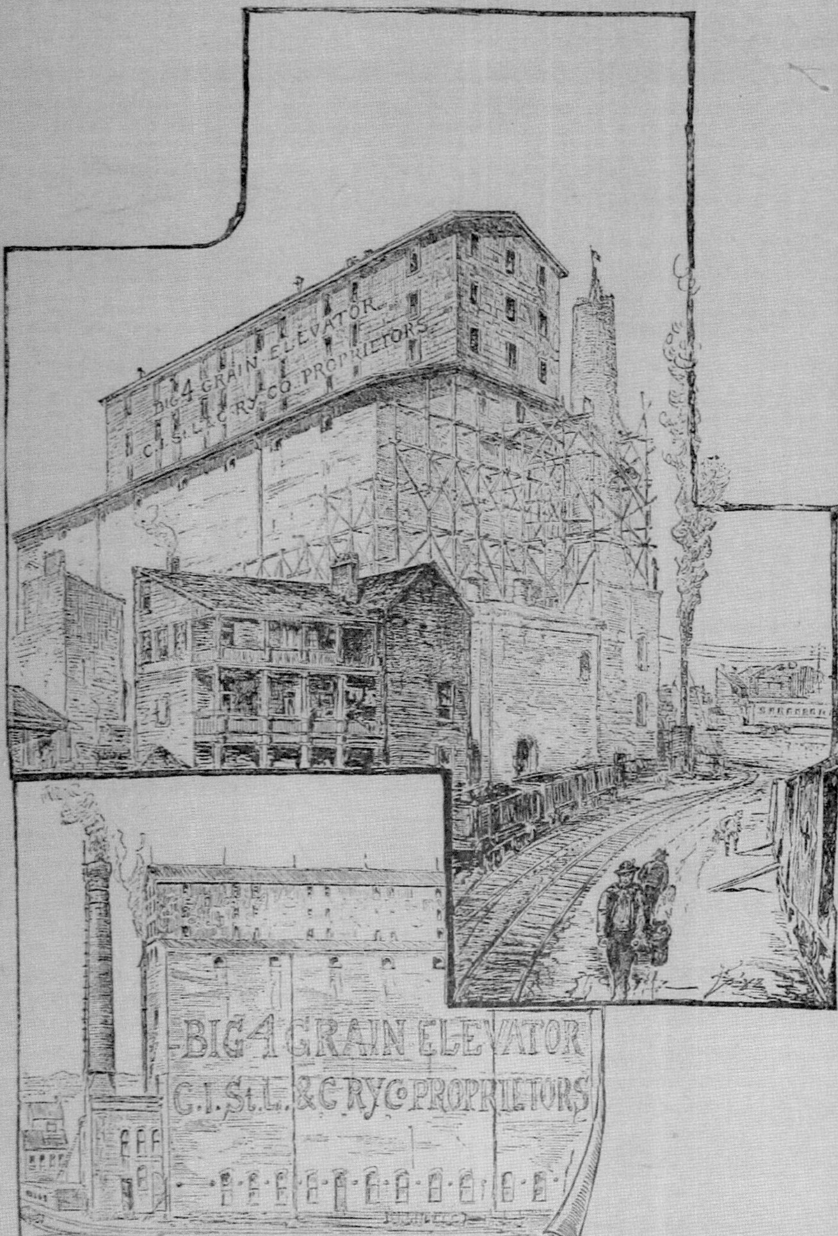
BIG 4 GRAIN ELEVATOR
C.I.St.L.C.RY.CO. PROPRIETORS
BIG 4 GRAIN ELEVATOR
C.I.St.L.&C.RyCo PROPRIETORS

members pay $100; active members $5 a year, and children $1 a year. It also has recently begun publishing "The Humane Appeal."

Price's Hill is on the west bank of Mill Creek, overlooking the Ohio River. Its height above the river is about four hundred feet. The high ground continues westward beyond Warsaw, a distance of four miles. It is covered with elegant private residences, convents, schools, and colleges. Its summit is reached by Price's-hill Inclined-plane Railway, the foot of which is at the junction of Eighth Street and State Avenue. The Warsaw Pike, winding around the hill by easy grades, is also a means of reaching the top. There are grounds, pavilion, and terrace connected with the Price's-hill House at the summit, and music is often furnished there. Picnics and pleasure-parties also make use of the grounds. The views of the river and surrounding country are not surpassed by any in this city. The Eighth-street line of horse-cars stop at the foot of the inclined plane.

Protestant Churches. — The Protestant churches are less encumbered with debts than those of any other large city. Seventeen of the twenty-three Protestant denominations are wholly out of debt for their churches, while the debt of all the Protestant churches amounts to less than $115,000. The Protestant churches have a total membership of about 21,000, a Sunday-school attendance of about 25,000, and property valued at nearly $3,500,000.

Provisions. — As a great provision-market, Cincinnati ranks second to but one city in the world; and as a market for the best quality of meats, bringing the largest prices, the city ranks first. In the winter season of 1880–81 there were 522,425 hogs packed here; the cost of which was $6,446,228. There were 26,596 barrels of hog-meat, and 65,627 packages of lard produced. During the year ending Aug. 31, 1881, the imports and exports were as follows: —

	Imports.	Exports.
Hogs, number of	1,053,216	304,170
Pork, barrels of	3,599	37,300
Lard, pounds of	13,003,365	37,702,839
Meats, pounds of	50,489,141	110,643,940

During the summer season, about 150,000 hogs are packed. For the year ending Aug. 31, 1881, the live-stock statistics are as follows: —

	Receipts.	Shipments.
Cattle	186,632	73,556
Sheep	324,727	238,167
Horses and mules	24,429	20,398

In the provision trade, — that is, slaughterers, packers, and curers of meats, — there are 173 firms, with an invested cash capital of $4,230,000. They occupy real estate valued at $3,837,244; employ 1,950 persons; and the value of their product for 1881, including lard, was $14,242,739. Among the most prominent firms in this trade are Samuel Davis, jun., & Co., office and packing-house corner Court Street and Broadway; Evans & Kinney, office room B, Pike's Opera-House, and packing-house adjoining the United-Railroads Stock-Yards; Evans, Lippincott, and Cunningham, office and packing-house corner Bank and Patterson Streets; James Morrison & Co., office and packing-house corner of Bank and Riddle Streets; Joseph Rawson & Son, packing-house on Spring-grove Avenue, near the United Railroads Stock-yards, office and warehouses 300 & 310 Sycamore Street. There are also a number of firms who do a commission business in provisions; and prominent among these is the firm of William H. Davis & Co., 271 and 273 Sycamore Street, who are also curers of hams and salt meats on commission account. F. A. Laidley & Co. are not only extensive pork-packers, but are also large jobbers in all kinds of provisions. The packing-house is on the Colerain Pike, and office No. 85 West Second Street. (See Stock-Yards.)

Public Library and Reading-room. — Vine, between Sixth and Seventh Streets. It is under the control of the chairman of the Board of Public Education, and six persons appointed by that board. It contains 108,000 volumes and 12,000 pamphlets, and is free in every particular. About $60,000 dollars a year is spent for its support ($18,000, derived chiefly from a tax of one-tenth of a mill, is spent yearly for books). Books, pamphlets, manuscripts, etc., are constantly donated to it. It is open every day, from eight A.M. to ten P.M. The library is one of the best-arranged and most flourishing, and the reading-room one of the most complete and comfortable, in this country. The building is fire-proof, and is one of the largest

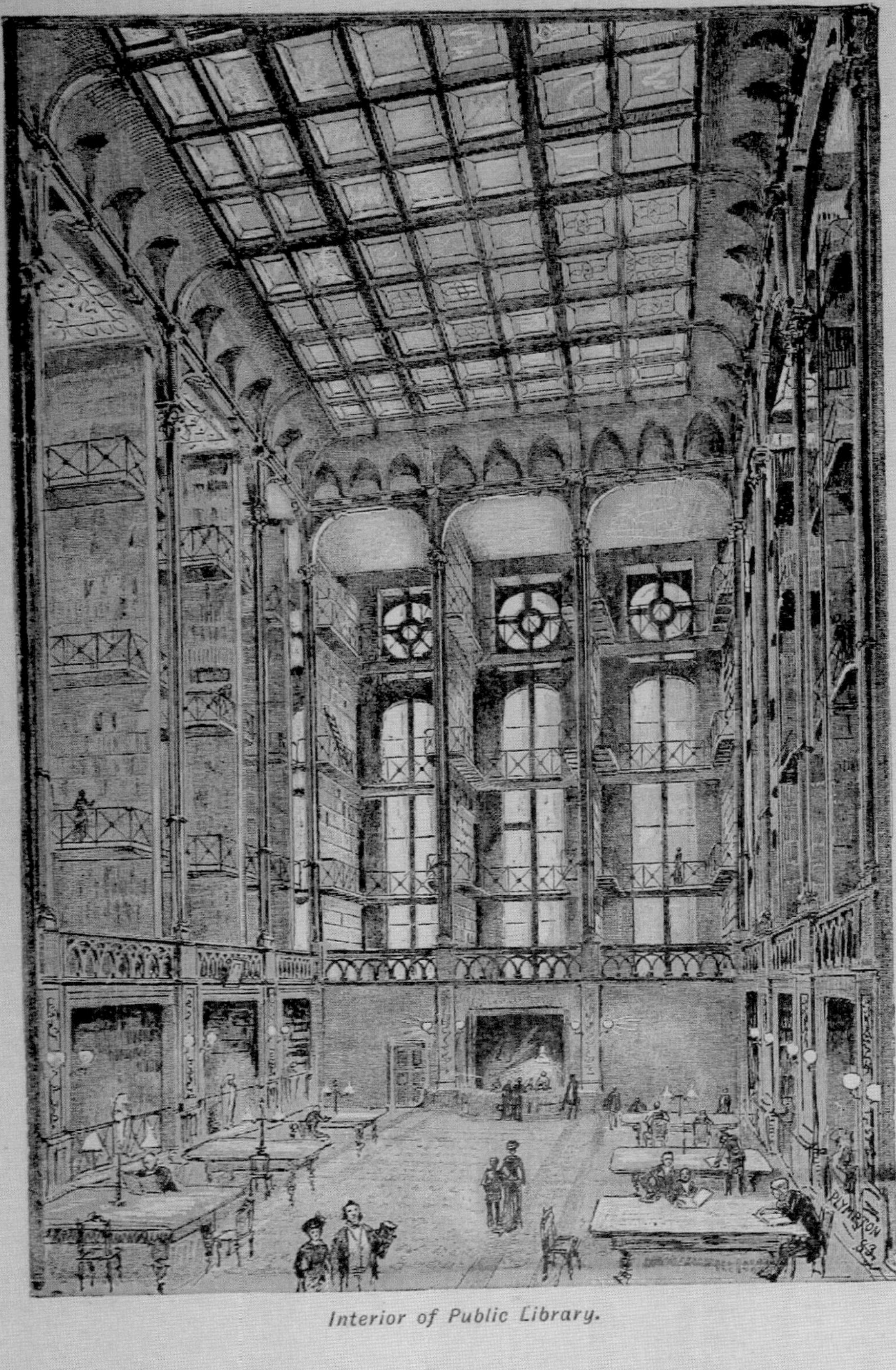

Interior of Public Library.

and finest in this city. It has cost, with the ground, $400,000. One branch of the library has been opened at Cumminsville, and another will probably be opened within a year at Columbia. To the librarian, C. W. Merrill, is due much of the success of the library, as well as many of the improvements.

Publishers. — There are four large publishing-houses in this city, besides several firms publishing subscription-books, and a number of booksellers, and newspaper and printing offices publishing books and pamphlets of various kinds. The four great establishments are those of Robert Clarke & Co., Van Antwerp, Bragg, & Co., Western Methodist Book Concern, and Wilstach, Baldwin, & Co. The three last named are referred to in their alphabetical places in this book. Robert Clarke & Co.'s is the leading bookselling and general book publishing house in the South-west. Their establishment occupies the large five-story stone-front building, No. 65 West Fourth Street. This firm is known throughout the United States as one of the most trustworthy and most successful houses in the book-trade. Mr. Clarke has been connected with the house since 1855, when he bought Tobias Lyon's interest in the firm of Lyon & Patterson; the style of firm changing to Patterson & Clarke. In 1857 Mr. Clarke bought Mr. Patterson's interest, and carried on the business in his own name. At that time the store was in Bacon's Building, corner of Sixth and Walnut Streets, and the business was chiefly in second-hand and foreign books; this being the first house in Cincinnati to import books direct from London and Paris. In 1858 R. D. Barney and J. W. Dale united with Mr. Clarke; and the new firm, under the style of Robert Clarke & Co., bought the business of Henry W. Derby & Co., law-book publishers, and dealers in the miscellaneous books published by Harper & Brothers, and Derby & Jackson. They then moved into the store occupied by Derby & Co., 55 West Fourth Street, and began business as publishers of law-books, and wholesale and retail booksellers. In 1867 the business was removed to its present quarters. In 1872 Howard Barney and Alexander Hill were admitted to the partnership. This house has published over 150 volumes of law-books, one of which was the celebrated Fisher's Patent Cases, the highest-priced law-books ever published in this country, — 6 volumes, at $25 a volume; and also about a hundred volumes of miscellaneous books, including the invaluable Ohio Valley Historical Series, edited by Mr. Clarke, and issued in eight handsome volumes. Many publications of this firm rank equal in style and value to any published in the United States. The third floor of the establishment is devoted exclusively to works known as Americana, of which a fine catalogue has been issued. Besides their publishing and bookselling departments, Messrs. Clarke & Co. have an extensive book-bindery, book and job printing-office, and stationery department.

Pulte Medical College. — Corner Seventh and Mound. Organized in 1872. Homœopathic instruction in all branches of medical science. The building is said to be one of the largest and best-appointed for its purposes in this country. There are twenty-five rooms for college purposes, including halls, lecture-rooms, museum, etc. Main amphitheatre seats two hundred. The Homœopathic Free Dispensary and Cincinnati Hospital are at the service of students. Sessions from October to March. Fees vary.

Queen City is known, the world over, as one of the accepted and appropriate names of Cincinnati. This name was given in recognition of the fine situation, the lovely surroundings, the excellent climate, the fertile soil of the neighborhood, and the bright prospects for the future greatness of the city, and also in appreciation of the early development of enterprise, culture, refinement, and prosperity among the citizens. The name has been generally used with reference to this city for fully fifty years; but just when and by whom it was originated, the publishers are unable to learn. In 1838 a book entitled "Tales from the Queen City" was published in Cincinnati. Longfellow paraphrases the words in his poem on "Catawba Wine," in the verse reading as follows —

"And this Song of the Vine,
This greeting of mine,
The winds and the birds shall deliver
To the Queen of the West,
In her garlands dressed,
On the banks of the Beautiful River."

Queen City Club is composed of about three hundred leading professional and business men. Its club-house, corner Seventh and Elm, is one of the most elegant and commodious in the country. It cost, with real estate and furnishing, about $170,000. It contains rooms for conversation, billiards, cards, chess, and other games, besides reading and dining rooms. Its restaurant is conducted *à la carte.* A reception and dining room is reserved for the wives and families of the members. Each member holds at least one share of stock of the value of $250, and pays annual dues of $75, with a credit of $15 as interest on his stock. Five members are elected yearly to serve for three years as a board of management, and this board alone has the right of accepting or rejecting applications for membership. Visitors must be introduced by members.

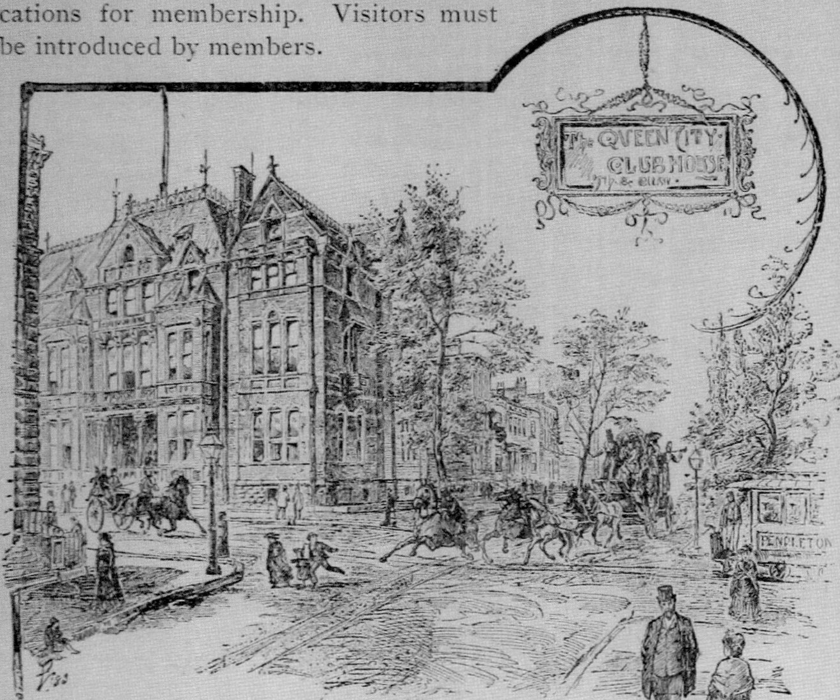

Reading-rooms. — The largest and most comfortable public reading-rooms are those of the Public Library and of the Young Men's Mercantile Library Association. There are also good reading-rooms at the Cincinnati Gymnasium, the Chamber of Commerce, and the Young Men's Christian Association.

Red Men, the United and Improved Order of, is a benevolent organization, dispensing its benefits after the manner of the Odd Fellows and other similar bodies. What it has to do with the aborigines, is known only to the members. There are eight tribes

CLOAK AND SHAWL DEPARTMENTS.

All the latest Paris styles in Cloaks and Costumes are received as soon as introduced, and our assortment is always the largest in the market.

We are extensive manufacturers of Cloaks, our workrooms being on a large scale. Shapes and styles receive our closest attention.

Our facilities are such that we can produce at lower cost than most manufacturers, an advantage of which we always give our customers the benefit.

DOLMANS, CARRIAGE WRAPS,
SEAL-SKIN SACQUES,
CIRCULARS. JACKETS,
RAGLANS,
FUR-LINED CIRCULARS, ETC.

Endless variety and unrivalled low prices.

THE JOHN SHILLITO COMPANY.

and one encampment of the United Order, and four tribes of the Improved Order, in Cincinnati. Nearly all the tribes have a separate place of meeting.

Reformed Presbyterians. — Although there are two churches styled as above, and both designating themselves the First Church, they differ somewhat from each other. Both of them fifty years ago formed one church; but in 1833 a division took place, and since that time there have been two distinct churches. Much of that time the "Plum-street congregation" has been without ministers, and consequently the growth has been small. In 1854 Robert Patterson was installed pastor, and after he served two years a vacancy of twelve years followed. In 1868 James Y. Boice was installed pastor. Up to this time the church-building was on George Street; but Mr. Boice began in the basement of a new building, a beautiful little stone church, situated on Plum Street, between Eighth and Ninth Streets, and now occupied by the congregation over which A. G. Wylie, D.D., is pastor. The "John-street congregation" comprises a small society worshipping on Clinton, east of John Street. Their doctrine is that the United States is not a Christian government, and therefore they cannot consistently vote at any election. They hope to have the Lord Jesus Christ recognized in the Constitution. J. M. Foster is pastor.

Relief Union, the Cincinnati. — This great charity was founded in 1850, and has been in continual and successful operation ever since. It is supported by voluntary contributions, the greater portion coming from life-members, a number of whom pay amounts ranging from $100 to $1,000 annually. As much as $40,000 has been collected and disbursed in a single year. Since 1873, however, the receipts have not been so large, by reason of the panic in that year, and the death of several of the former large contributing members. The society operates through a local visiting committee of two in each ward, who visit each applicant, and satisfy themselves as to their needs. The necessaries of life are supplied to the extent the fund will allow, without regard to color, sex, nativity, or religion. The Union has an office in the City Buildings, whence supplies are issued.

Reservoirs. — There are five reservoirs connected with the waterworks system. The two largest of these are in Eden Park, both capable of holding 100,000,000 gallons of water. They are constructed in one of the natural ravines, across the mouth of which an immense wall of solid masonry has been thrown. Their construction cost the city nearly $4,500,000. They supply that portion of the city north of Third Street to the hills. The old reservoir, on Third Street at the foot of Mount Adams, is a superstructure of solid limestone masonry. It is located in Water-works Park. Its capacity is but a tithe of that of the great reservoirs, and it is kept full by constant pumping. It supplies the district south of Third Street, and a portion of the West End. The other two reservoirs are immense boiler-iron tanks, located in the angle formed by the junction of Vine Street and Auburn Avenue, Mount Auburn; that being the highest point of ground in the vicinity, and about 467 feet above low-water mark. Water is lifted to these reservoirs by a pumping-engine located at the junction of Hunt and Effluent-pipe Streets, which draws its supply from the great reservoirs in Eden Park. These reservoirs supply the districts of Mount Auburn, Corryville, and Walnut Hills. A line of ten-inch pipe is also laid from these reservoirs down Vine Street to Fourth, at which point the pressure is 200 pounds to the square inch. The fire-plugs along this line are connected with it, and can throw water farther than a steam-engine can. The Tyler-Davidson Fountain is supplied from this source. A sixth reservoir, on Price's Hill, in the western part of the city, will soon be completed.

Revision, the Board of, meets the first Monday of each month. Its province is to take under consideration any vital interest of the city, scrutinize the official conduct of city officers, and report its action to council. It is composed of four members: viz., Thomas J. Stephens, mayor and *ex officio* president; Michael Ryan, president board of aldermen; L. L. Sadler, president board of councilmen; James M. Dawson, city solicitor.

Riverside. — A suburb adjoining the western corporation line, fronting on the Ohio River, six miles from Fountain Square. It contains many elegant country residences. It forms a separate election precinct in the county. Riverside can be reached by the Ohio and Mississippi, the Cincinnati, Indianapolis, Chicago, and St. Louis railroads, the Storrs and Sedamsville horse-cars, and the Lower River-Road, an excellent macadamized turnpike. The drive is a beautiful one; giving a charming landscape of river, and hillsides dotted with lovely suburban houses, vineyards, and private parks.

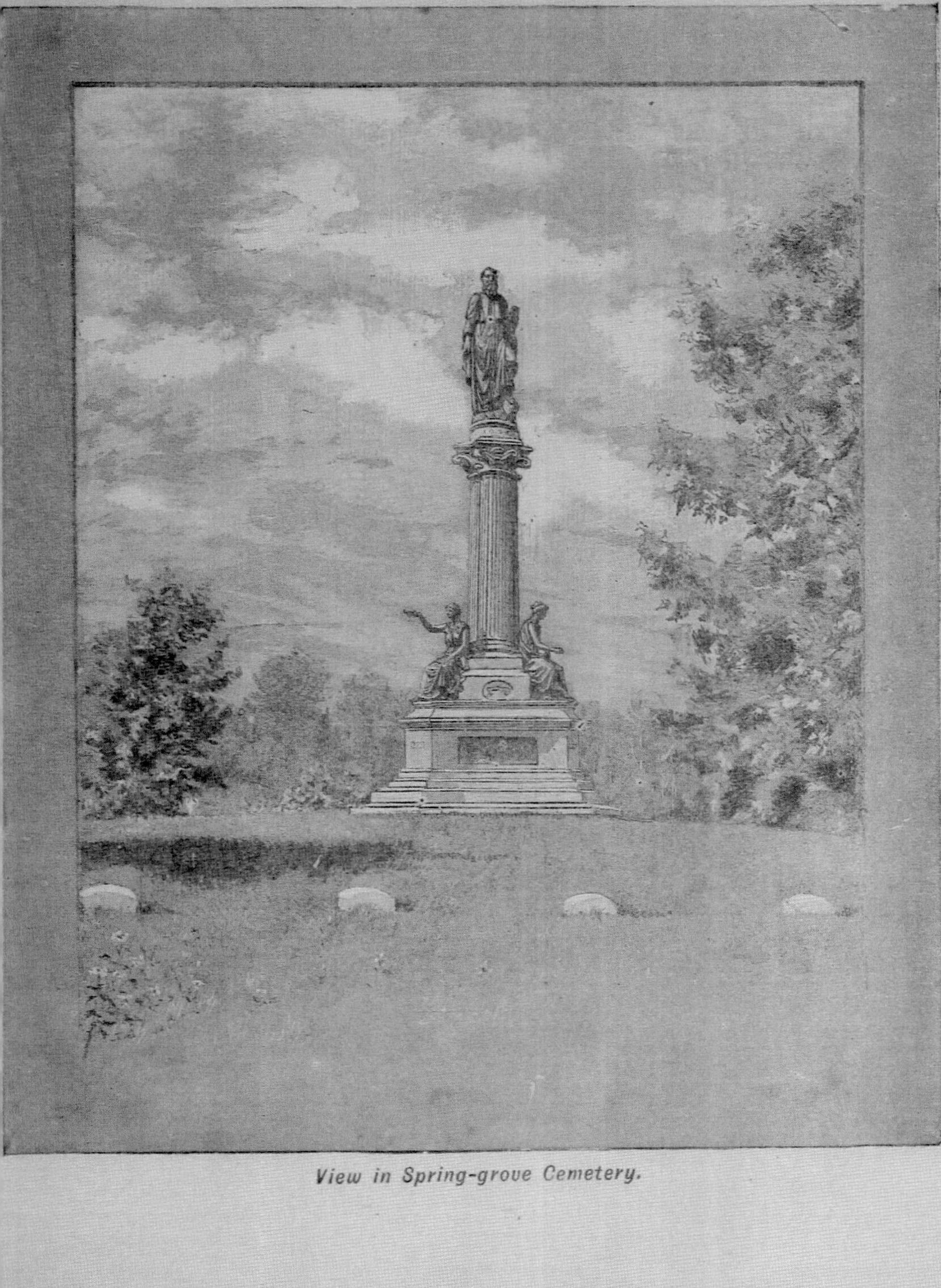

View in Spring-grove Cemetery.

Robinson's Opera-House, on the north-east corner of Ninth and Plum Street, is a very handsome building devoted to music and the drama in the city. Its seating capacity is 2,300. The auditorium contains a parquette, parquette-circle, balcony, and gallery, besides four large private boxes. The theatre was built in 1872 by John Robinson, circus-manager. The cellar was built expressly to provide winter-quarters for animals used in the circus. The main entrances are on Ninth Street. The Seventh-street or blue line of horse-cars pass the building going east; the Elm-street and the Eighth-street lines pass within one square. The Opera-House overlooks the City Park, and is in the midst of what is known as the "church region."

Royal Insurance Company of Liverpool, Eng., although a foreign company, has not only a national reputation, but also a local history. In 1852 an agency of the company was given to the late Dr. John S. Law, who continued the business in his own name until 1871; when, upon the formation of a partnership with his son John H. Law, who had been at work in the office since the agency was established, the style of the firm was changed to John S. Law & Son. In 1877, at the death of the senior member, the business passed into the hands of John H. Law. For the entire period of twenty-seven years, the Royal has had a most enviable record in this city; and its standing to-day is equal to that of any insurance company in the world. All losses in this neighborhood are paid without reference to the home office; and the best indemnity possible is offered by this company, with assets amounting to almost $33,000,000, — of which nearly $3,000,000 are kept in the United States. Moreover, the stockholders are individually liable to the full extent of their private fortunes. The losses paid by the Royal already exceed the enormous sum of $35,000,000.

Safe-Deposit Company of Cincinnati occupies one-half of the National Lafayette and Bank of Commerce building at 20 West Third Street. The safes are thoroughly fire and burglar proof. They are thirty-five feet long, twelve feet and a half wide, and seven feet high, and are composed of five alternate layers of steel and iron, and so put together that no screw or nut penetrates more than three layers. Constant work for eighteen months was required to construct these immense safes. They have four combination-locks of different makes. Every safeguard is adopted; and the place is watched day and night on both the inside and outside. The renters of boxes and depositors of securities have every convenience for handling their property quietly and unobserved. The Safe-Deposit Company was organized in 1866, and was one of the first corporations in the United States to provide for rich and poor people the means of absolute security against fire and burglary at a moderate cost. Its capital stock is $100,000. The president is Henry Peachey, and secretary Samuel P. Bishop.

Sanitarium, the Cincinnati. — A private hospital for the treatment of mental and nervous diseases, at College Hill, O. It was opened in 1873, and since that time has established its character as a permanent institution, having appointments unsurpassed by those of any similar institution in the country. Four hundred persons have already been patients at the sanitarium. The building, erected originally for the Ohio Female College, is an elegant and attractive structure of brick with stone facings, three stories in height above the basement. Close by the main building are five two-story cottages. All the apartments in the main building and in the cottages are well furnished and comfortable. It is the only strictly private insane-asylum in the West, and is in charge of Dr. W. S. Chipley, who has had thirty-four years' experience in the treatment of the insane. The charges vary with the accommodations furnished. The Sanitarium can be reached by a drive over Spring-grove Avenue, or by the Cincinnati, Hamilton, and Dayton Railroad and College-hill Narrow-gauge Railroad (fare forty cents round trip). John L. Whetstone president, Val. P. Collins secretary, and John F. Elliott treasurer.

School-books. — See Van Antwerp, Bragg, & Co.

School of Design of the University of Cincinnati was founded by Charles McMicken. In 1853 an association known as the Ladies' Academy of Fine Arts received from Mr. McMicken $1,000 to be spent for casts, which were to be given to a school of design whenever one should be founded in this city. Some years later the casts, as well as pictures owned by the academy, were handed over to the School of Design which had just been founded. The school prospered as much as its limited means allowed. Later, Joseph Longworth endowed the school with $100,000; i.e., the Old Observatory property perpetually leased to the Passionist Fathers, and yielding seven per cent on $50,000, and the other $50,000 being given in United-States bonds. Then the facilities and number of teachers were increased. In 1871 the school was placed under control of the University of Cincinnati, and since that time it has been remarkably successful. In 1882 there were nine instructors and nearly four hundred pupils. To this school is due much of the credit for the elaborate designs and carving on the organ in Music Hall. Instruction is free to residents. Non-residents are charged $30 a year for attendance on the day-classes, and $15 for attendance on the night-classes. The hours are every week-day, from nine A.M. to one P.M., and from seven to nine P.M.; and the sessions are the same as those of the University of Cincinnati. The rooms are in College Building, and can be visited by permission of the principal, Thomas S. Noble.

Schools, Public. — The total number of children enrolled for attendance at the public schools in 1882 was 37,996. The average daily attendance of the number enrolled was 78 per cent. To accommodate this vast number of pupils, the city provides 37 district or primary, 4 intermediate, and 2 high-school buildings, besides 5 buildings for colored schools, and the University of Cincinnati. The city is divided into 27 districts for white, and 5 districts for colored pupils; the 7th, 8th, 15th, 16th, 17th, 24th, 25th, and 26th districts having two buildings each, the 21st district four, and the remaining districts one each. The buildings are nearly all elegant, new, and commodious, one of them alone costing $85,000. The average cost of each of the buildings may be placed at $40,000. To impart instruction to the youth of the city, 633 teachers are required, whose salaries range from $400 to $2,600 per annum. Pupils passing through the public schools must attend six years in the district, three in the intermediate, and four in the high schools; when, on graduating from the high school, they can enter the university. Examinations are required in passing from one year's grade to another, from the district to the intermediate, and from the latter to the high schools. In addition to the ordinary English branches, German, music, and drawing are taught in the district and intermediate, and French, Latin, and Greek in the high schools. The schools are governed by the Board of Education. This board also controls the public library, the normal school, and the school for deaf-mutes; the latter being one of the only two schools of the kind in the country supported chiefly by a municipal corporation as part of its school-system. Night-schools are held in fifteen of the districts, three being for colored pupils. The total expense of the schools for the year 1882 was $784,405.98

The superintendent is John B. Peaslee. (See University of Cincinnati, Hughes High School, and Woodward High School.)

Schools, other than Public. — There are within the city limits four business colleges, one dental college, one law-school, seven medical and surgical colleges, one college of pharmacy, one college and four conservatories of music. There is also the St. Joseph College, St. Xavier College, Mount St. Mary's Seminary, Young Ladies' Academy of St. Vincent de Paul, — all Roman-Catholic institutions; Lane Theological Seminary, of the Presbyterian denomination; Cincinnati Wesleyan College, — a Methodist-Episcopal young ladies' institute; and Hebrew Union College. Besides the above, there are numerous private schools in and around the city, and several colleges and seminaries distant only a few miles from the city Among the most prominent private schools in the city are the Chickering Institute for boys; the Collegiate School for boys, under direction of Babin & Rix; Miss C. E. Nourse's family and day school for girls; Bartholomew English and Classical School for girls; Miss S. J. Armstrong's Mount-Auburn School for girls; and Mount Auburn Young Ladies' Institute, under direction of H. Thane Miller.

Sculptors. — The earliest in this city was Frederick Eckstein, a Prussian by birth, and a resident in this city fifty years ago. He was a man of great eccentricities, among which was one of valuing his works at a precise sum of odd dollars and cents, with amusing exactness. From him Hiram Powers acquired the first rudiments of the art. Powers began between 1830 and 1840 the work which afterwards gave him such world-wide fame; and to Nicholas Longworth he was indebted, not only for patronage, but also for aid to go to Italy to pursue his profession. S. Clevenger, about 1840, made many excellent portrait-busts, notably that of President Harrison, now in the Young Men's Mercantile Library Rooms. Thomas D. Jones resided here for many years; and his busts of Thomas Ewing, Judge McLean, Thomas Corwin, and many others, attest his skill. Ed Brackett was well known as a sculptor in Cincinnati in the early part of the decade 1840–50. N. F. Baker, a Cincinnatian by birth, studied in Italy; and his statue of "Cincinnatus," on the front of the building occupied by Chatfield & Woods, on Fourth Street, and that of "Egeria" in the lake at Spring-grove Cemetery, are carefully executed works of art. Louis T. Rebisso, of the School of Design,

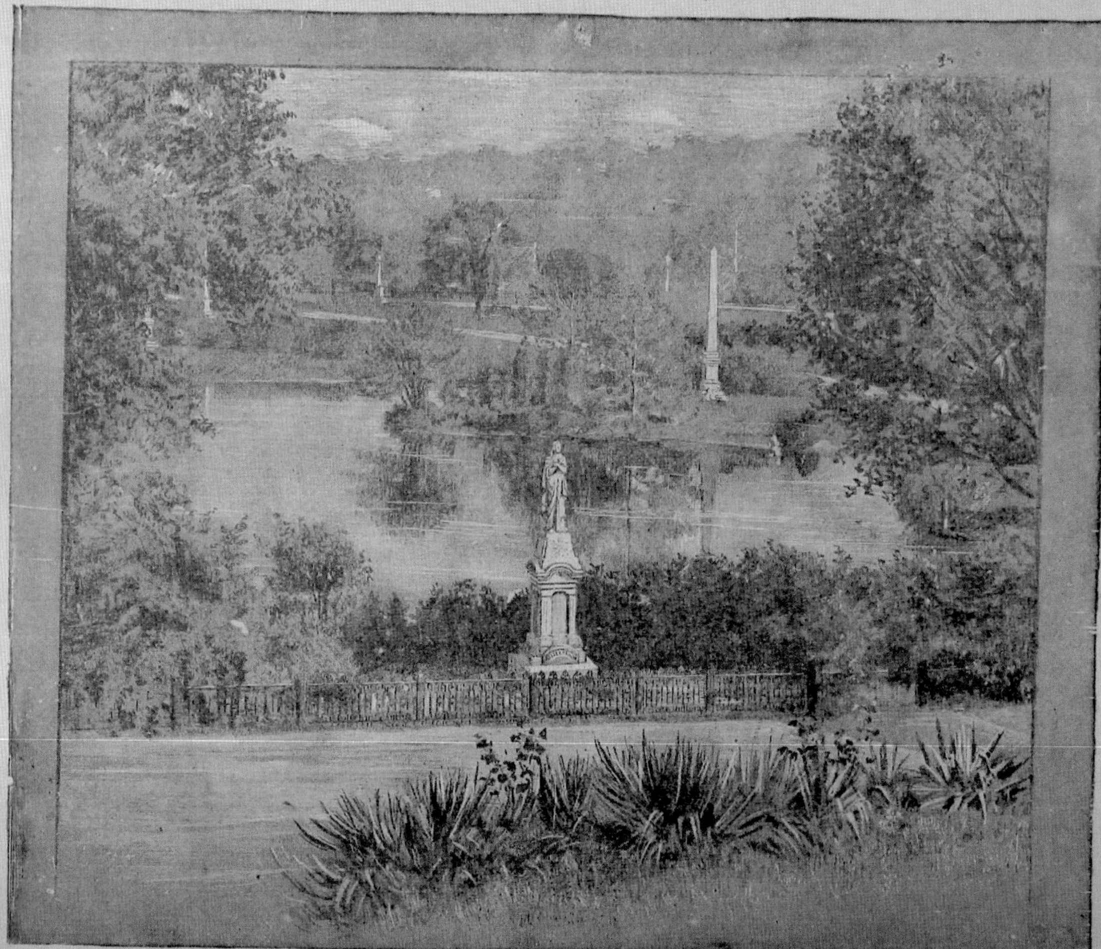

View in Spring-grove Cemetery.

is a sculptor of considerable ability. His most celebrated work is the colossal equestrian bronze statue of Gen. McPherson, lately erected in Washington, D.C. Moses J. Ezekiel is the well-known sculptor of the colossal marble statue of "Religious Liberty," temporarily placed in Fairmount Park. L. Fettweis is a resident sculptor, born in Cincinnati, and trained in the German art-schools. Frank Dengler, one of the greatest of young American sculptors, recently died after a short career, during which his great talents were appreciated even in art-loving Boston. August Mundhenk, recently returned from Europe, is a sculptor, who has established a foundery for casting bronze-work. H. K. Brown was for a short period a resident here, and Preston Powers now has a temporary studio in this city.

Second Presbyterian Church, on the south-west corner of Eighth and Plum Streets, is one of the finest of the church edifices of Cincinnati. The corner-stone was laid in 1873; and the church was first occupied Jan. 3, 1875, and dedicated April 11, 1875. The buildings is of Blue-hill limestone, in the Gothic style of architecture; its spire is 205 feet high; and its seats are arranged in amphitheatre form, for the accommodation of 1,100. The organ is a very fine instrument, and cost, without the case, $10,000. The total cost of the church and its furniture was about $275,000, and the society is wholly out of debt. The society was organized in 1816; and its preliminary meetings were held at the residence of Judge Jacob Burnet, on the site of the present Burnet House; and for the first two years its services were held anywhere that accommodations could be found. In 1818 a little frame building was erected on Walnut Street, above Fifth Street, where services were held until 1830; when a second building, a neat brick edifice, having a steeple with a clock paid for by the city council, was erected on Fourth Street, between Vine and Race Streets. The building cost $28,000, and the land $5,000; but the land was sold in 1871 for $160,000, and the society built the beautiful edifice already described. The following is a list of the regular pastors: David Root, 1820–32; Lyman Beecher, 1832–43; John P. Cleveland, 1843–45; Samuel W. Fisher, 1846–58; M. L. P. Thompson, 1859–65; James L. Robertson, 1867–70; Thomas H. Skinner, 1871; James Eells, 1883.

Sedamsville. — A portion of the 21st ward, west of Mill Creek, fronting on the Ohio River, and south of the western range of hills, three miles and a half distant from Fountain Square. It is a manufacturing district, containing several large distilleries and saw-mills. It was formerly a part of Storrs Township. The Third-street line of horse-cars and the Eighth-street line make connection with the Storrs and Sedamsville line, the former at the bridge over Mill Creek, on Sixth Street, and the latter at the junction of Eighth Street and State Avenue.

Sewerage. — The natural advantages of Cincinnati for surface drainage are admirable, the rolling character of the site favoring it. But sewers were found necessary on the slopes from the central plateau, and all the principal streets running down to the Ohio have sewers from Seventh Street to the river. Part of the district north of Seventh and east of Plum has surface drainage into the Miami Canal, which empties into Eggleston-avenue Sewer; and part is drained by the Sycamore-street Sewer and its branches. North of Liberty Street the drainage is into the mammoth Liberty-street Sewer, which empties into the McLean-avenue Sewer. West of Central Avenue, north of Seventh, and south of Liberty, lateral sewers are laid, which lead to the immense McLean-avenue Sewer, now being constructed to the river. The sewerage system is almost perfect. Sewers range in size from 1 foot to 12 by 14 feet. The total number of lineal feet of sewer laid under the present system by the city, excluding that laid by private citizens, of which there is a large amount, is 204,161, — nearly 39 miles.

Shakspeare Club, organized in 1851, is the oldest organization in the city for the purpose of giving weekly readings from Shakspeare and other dramatic poets, and is also a leading amateur theatrical club; its entertainments always having been noted for care taken in their preparation, and skill in their presentation. It will probably hereafter use the hall of the Allemania Club; for the season of 1878–79 the Melodeon Hall having been used. There are about twenty active members, who take part in the entertainments, and bear the deficit for the expenses proportionally. Associate members pay $10 a year for the privileges of the club. George W. Pohlman is secretary. Strangers can be invited by members.

Shelter House. — See Casino.

Shillito's Mammoth Dry-goods House is one of the interesting sights in Cincinnati. There are only a few business buildings in the United States as magnificent as this structure, which was opened

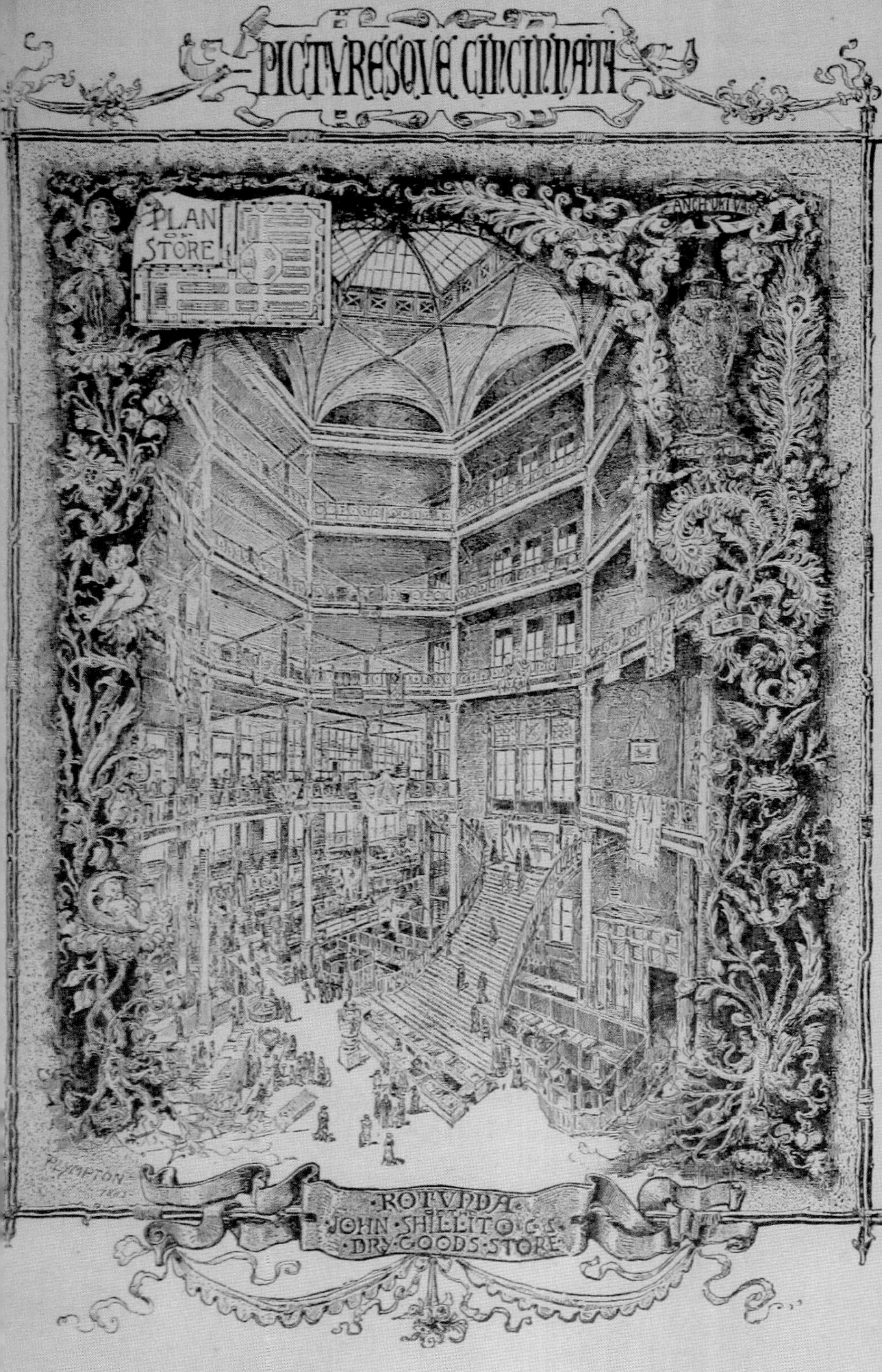
PICTURESQUE CINCINNATI
PLAN OF STORE
PLYMPTON
·ROTUNDA·
JOHN·SHILLITO·CO'S·
·DRY·GOODS·STORE·

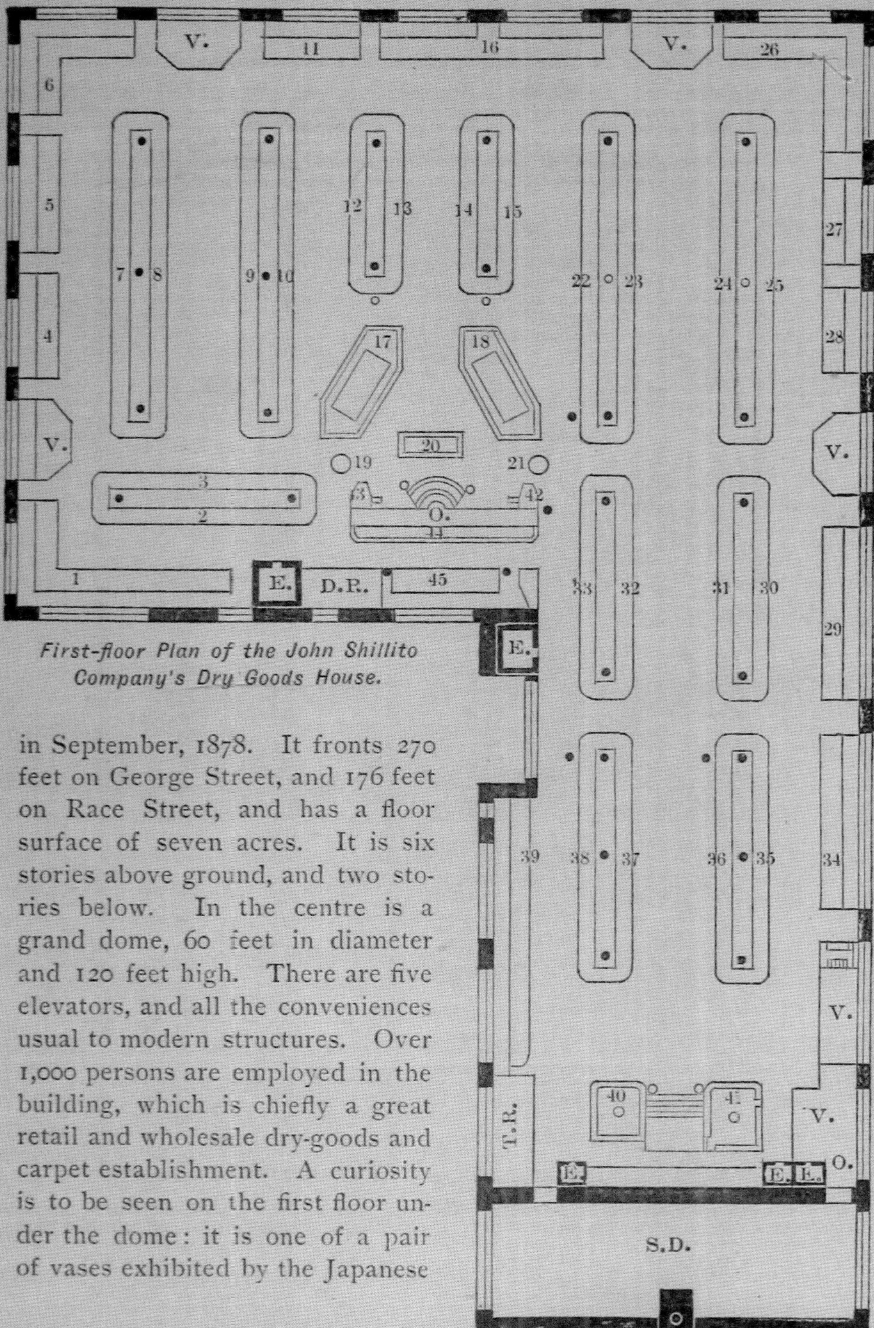

First-floor Plan of the John Shillito Company's Dry Goods House.

in September, 1878. It fronts 270 feet on George Street, and 176 feet on Race Street, and has a floor surface of seven acres. It is six stories above ground, and two stories below. In the centre is a grand dome, 60 feet in diameter and 120 feet high. There are five elevators, and all the conveniences usual to modern structures. Over 1,000 persons are employed in the building, which is chiefly a great retail and wholesale dry-goods and carpet establishment. A curiosity is to be seen on the first floor under the dome: it is one of a pair of vases exhibited by the Japanese government at the Centennial Exposition in 1876, and is one of the largest pieces of lacquered porcelain ever made in Japan.

Sinking-Fund Trustees, the Board of, comprises five of the

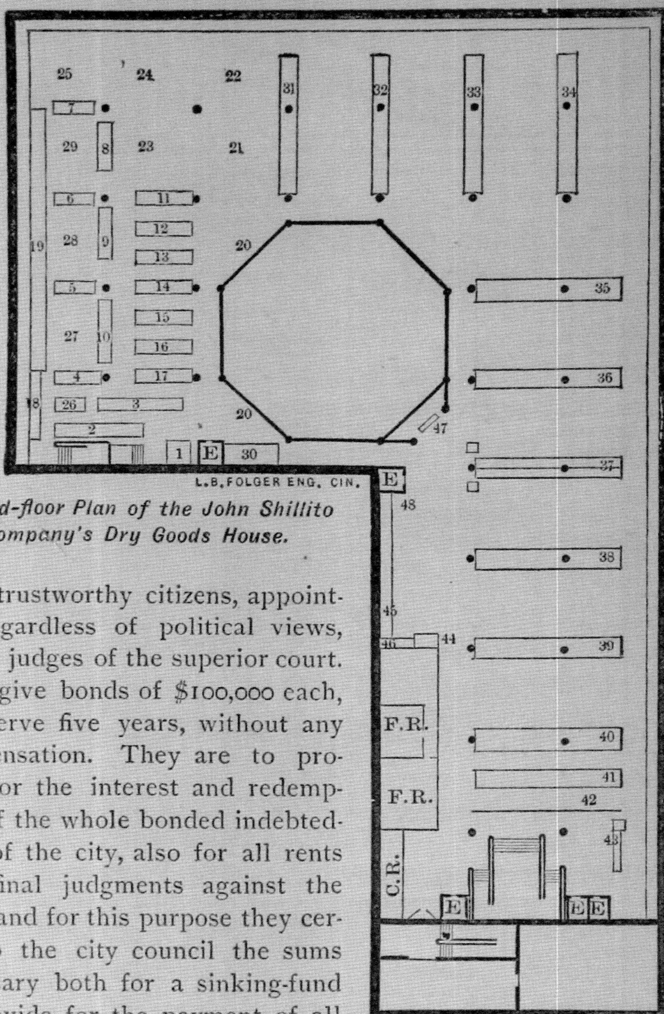

Second-floor Plan of the John Shillito Company's Dry Goods House.

most trustworthy citizens, appointed, regardless of political views, by the judges of the superior court. They give bonds of $100,000 each, and serve five years, without any compensation. They are to provide for the interest and redemption of the whole bonded indebtedness of the city, also for all rents and final judgments against the city; and for this purpose they certify to the city council the sums necessary both for a sinking-fund to provide for the payment of all the city's bonds, and for the payment of the interest on all the bonded indebtedness. Then the city council is required by law *to* place in the tax ordinance the several sums so certified in preference to any other items. They are to receive the net earnings of the Southern Railroad, and also to take charge of rents due the city. The total receipts of sinking-fund appli-

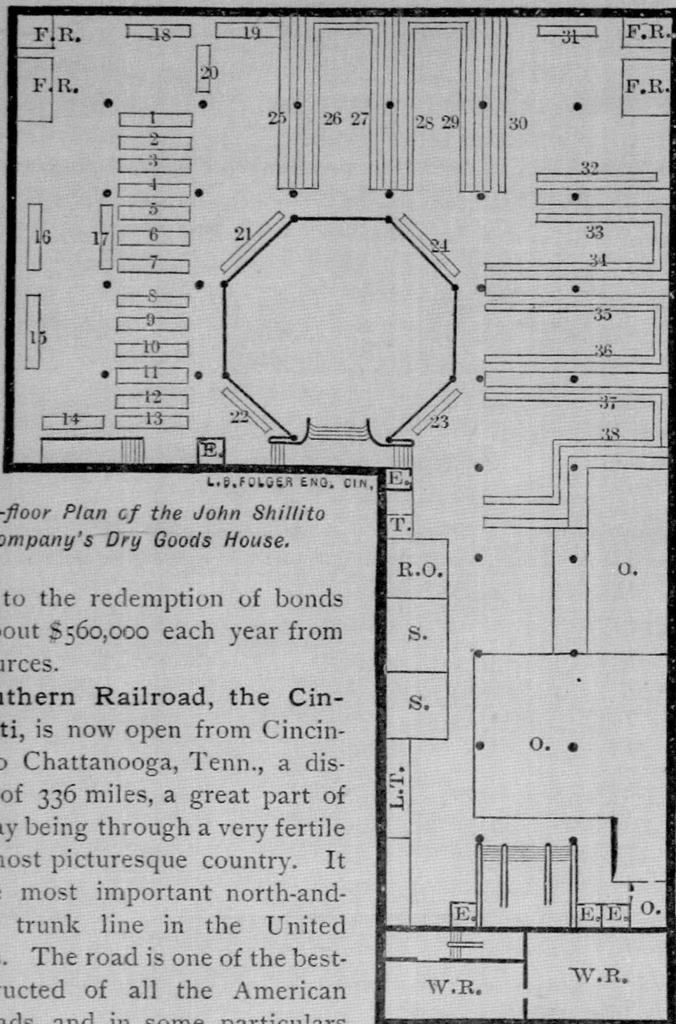

Third-floor Plan of the John Shillito Company's Dry Goods House.

cable to the redemption of bonds are about $560,000 each year from all sources.

Southern Railroad, the Cincinnati, is now open from Cincinnati to Chattanooga, Tenn., a distance of 336 miles, a great part of the way being through a very fertile and most picturesque country. It is the most important north-and-south trunk line in the United States. The road is one of the best-constructed of all the American railroads, and in some particulars shows a remarkable piece of engineering. It crosses the Ohio River over the Southern Railroad Bridge; and between the terminal points it crosses 47 wrought-iron bridges and viaducts, 13 wooden bridges, and passes through 27 tunnels, one of which is 4,700 feet long, and through deep cuts in rock, and over ground filled up in many places. It is thought to be one of the best pieces of railroad engineering and construction in this country. The principal contractors were R. G. Huston & Co. The Southern Railroad makes connections with all roads centring at Cincinnati and at or near Chattanooga, as well as several important connections between those cities. The uniform charge for local passenger travel is three cents a mile. This whole railroad passing through three States, and built at a cash cost of $18,000,000, is owned in fee simple by Cincinnati, — the only city in the world that has built a railroad of this magnitude. It is managed for the city by a board of five trustees, consisting of Miles Greenwood, president, R. M. Bishop, E. A. Ferguson, Henry Mack, and A. H. Bugher. The trustees are appointed by the superior court of this State. They give bonds of $100,000 each, and the whole pay for the board amounts to $5,000 a year. The road has been leased for a term of years to a corporation known as the Cincinnati, New Orleans, and Texas Pacific Railway Company: the officers being John Scott, president and general manager; Harry Peters, secretary and treasurer. The offices are in the Albany Building, No. 130 Vine Street. The depot is situated at the corner of McLean Avenue and Gest Street, and is reached by the Eighth-street line of horse-cars.

Spencer Township is situated east and north-east of Columbia, and east of Cincinnati Township, and is bounded on the south by the Ohio River, and on the east by the Little Miami. In this township are Pendleton, Columbia, East Linwood, Russells, and Red Bank.

Sportsman's Hall. — See East-End Garden.

Spring-grove Cemetery, situated near Cumminsville, was consecrated in 1845. Its area was 166 acres of undulating surface and sandy soil, and cost $16,000; but it has since been increased to 600 acres, and is now the largest cemetery in the United States, and has over 33,000 interments. It is probably the most picturesque large cemetery in the world. The numerous springs and groves suggested the name "Spring Grove." A handsome entrance-gate leads from the broad Spring-grove Avenue into the grounds. The "park plan" suggested by A. Strauch, the deceased superintendent, was a plan to relieve the ground of the heavy encumbered air of a churchyard, and

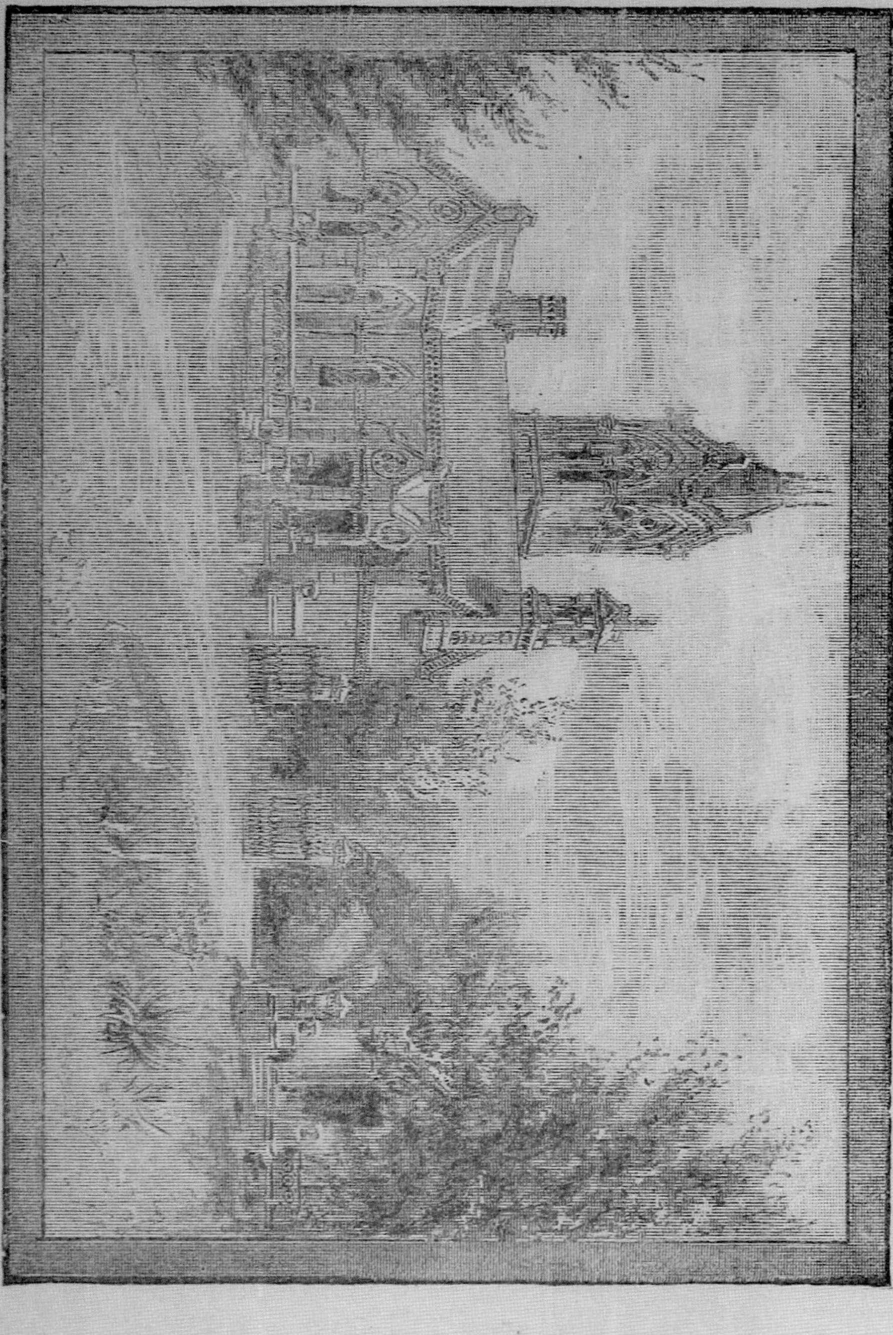

to present the appearance of a natural park. The plan was successful; and Spring Grove is now beautifully laid out, with far-stretching lawns, trees, miniature lakes, and shrubbery, and ornamented with stately monuments, chapels, vaults, and statues. The Dexter Mausoleum is an elaborate Gothic chapel of gray sandstone. From a balustrade surrounding the chapel, a charming view is obtained of the ornamental waters and surrounding landscapes. The Soldiers' Monument, erected in 1864, is a bronze statue on a granite pedestal, and represents a soldier standing on guard. A beautiful mortuary chapel in cruciform shape, 108 feet long and transepts 66 feet long, with walls of blue limestone and trimmings of sandstone, was contracted for in July, 1879, at a cost of $40,000. The graves are generally arranged in circles, and are numbered and recorded. There are about 7,000 lot-holders. The office for permits to visit the cemetery, and to buy lots, is No. 2 Pike's Opera-House. Horse-cars to cemetery, Baymiller-street, John-street, and Freeman-street lines; fare, 10 cents. Steam-railroads, Cincinnati, Hamilton, and Dayton, and the Baltimore and Ohio Railroads; fare, 20 cents. The president of the association is Henry Probasco, the treasurer John Shillito, and the secretary S. B. Spear. Superintendent, William Falway.

Springer Music Hall. — See Music-hall and Exposition Building.

Springer Statue. — See Statues.

Spring Lake. — A suburban resort on the Avenue, between Spring-grove Cemetery and Chester Driving-park, adjoining both. The grounds are large and elegant, divided into lawns, groves, and flower-gardens. The lake is supplied from natural springs, and furnishes the water-supply for the beautiful lakes in Spring-grove Cemetery. Spring Lake was formeriy the residence of the late Platt Evans. It can be reached by the Spring-grove Avenue horse-cars. Accommodation-trains on the Cincinnati, Hamilton, and Dayton, Dayton Short-line, and Cincinnati, Washington, and Baltimore Railroads, stop near the main gate.

St. Aloysius' Orphan Asylum (German, Roman Catholic). — Situated on the Reading Road in Avondale, about four miles and a half from Fountain Square. It is a large three-story brick building, with accommodations for 300 orphans. Inside the building is a chapel, where the children attend daily services. Father Hyronimus, assisted by the Sisters of Notre Dame, conducts the asylum; but the finances are managed by a board of trustees, of which Dr. B. Mosenmeier is president, A. H. Haarmeyer treasurer, and W. J. Overbeck secretary. Any member's child when an orphan is taken care of until of age; i.e., a boy until 21 years, and a girl until 18 years of age. At a proper time employment is found for the orphans, and they are watched over by committees appointed for that purpose. There are now 260 boys and girls at the asylum. The support of the institution comes from 2,200 active members, paying $3.25 a year; "a Washington-birthday celebration," a "Fourth-of-July picnic," and an "anniversary." At the three entertainments, about $7,000 are raised. The asylum is about two squares from the depot of the Cincinnati, Washington, and Baltimore Railroad (fare, 25 cents).

Springer Statue. — Upon the west side of the vestibule of Music Hall, midway between the south and central entrances to the main hall, stands the Springer Statue erected to commemorate the munificence of Mr. Reuben R. Springer. The statue, which is six feet three inches in height, represents Mr. Springer standing in a graceful and easy position, with his right hand resting on a stand upon which are carved emblems of Music, Art, and Industry. The left hand holds a scroll, on the inner page of which can be discerned a section of Music Hall set in bas-relief in gilt. The immediate base, four inches in thickness, with the statue itself, is of one piece of pure white Carrara marble. The pedestal, a dark red marble traversed with streaks of light green and white, affords a strong contrast to the pure white of the statue resting upon it, though mined only a short distance from each other. The size of the pedestal is three feet nine inches high, three feet wide, and two feet three inches long. On the four sides appear in bas-relief in delicate gilt letters the word "Springer" at the front, "Music" at the right, "Industry" at the back, and "Art" at the left. The base upon which the entire work rests is a fine Maryland gray granite, octagonal in shape, and sloping from the pedestal. The size of the base is four feet by five, and one foot three inches high. The entire height of the work as it stands in place is eleven feet and seven inches. The wall decorations in the rear, in striking contrast to the surroundings, with a neat railing enclosing the statue, add very much to the effect. The statue is the work of Preston Powers of Florence, Italy, where it was executed, and is recognized as the best effort of this eminent artist. It was unveiled and presented to the trustees of Music Hall, Monday, May 15, 1882.

St. Francis de Sales Church and School. — Corner of Woodburn Avenue and Madisonville Pike. The corner-stone was laid June 30, 1878, by Archbishop Purcell, in the presence of nearly 10,000 persons. The exterior of the church is now finished, with the exception of the

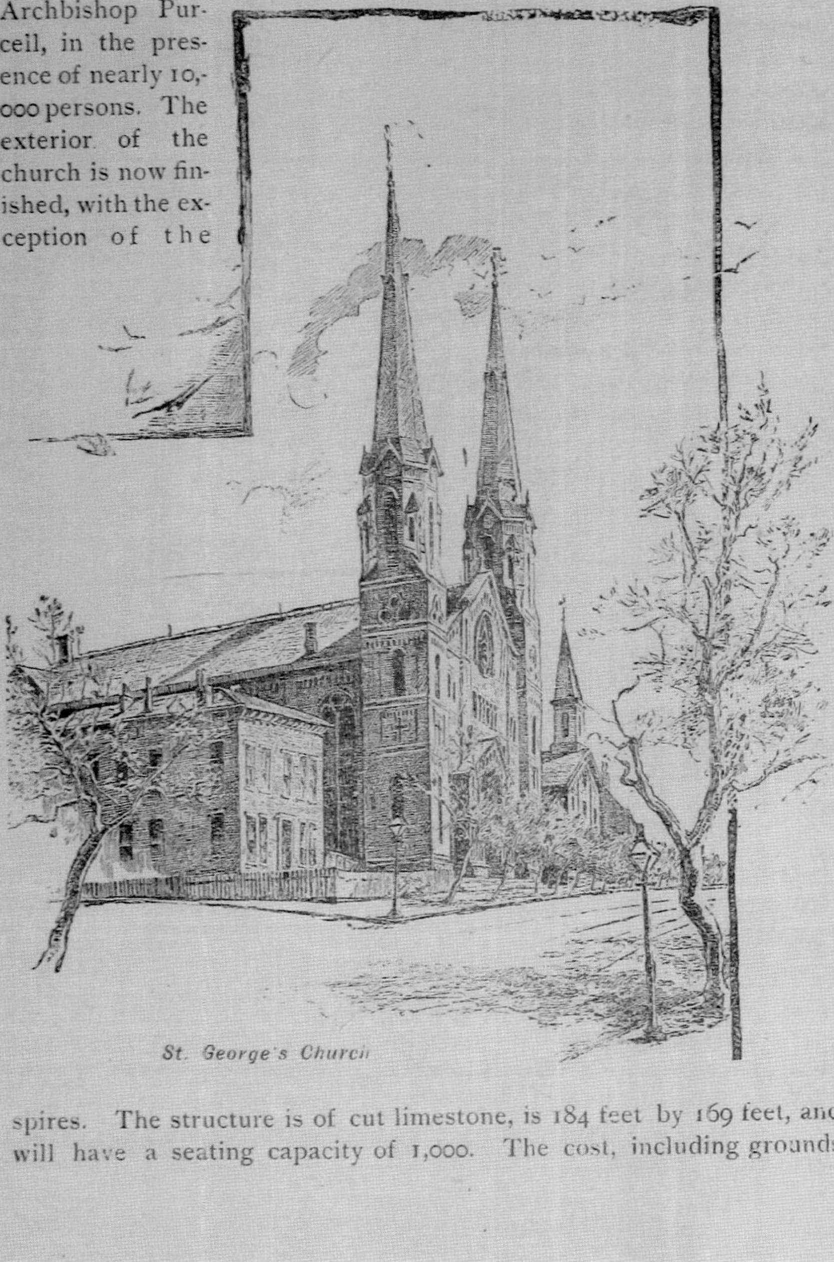

St. George's Church

spires. The structure is of cut limestone, is 184 feet by 169 feet, and will have a seating capacity of 1,000. The cost, including grounds and schoolhouse, will be $118,000; and it is claimed that it will be the handsomest church-edifice in Hamilton County. The parochial school adjoining has been occupied since Jan. 1, 1878, and is under the charge of the Sisters of Charity.

St. Mary's Hospital is under control of the Sisters of the Poor of St. Francis. It is situated on the north-west corner of Baymiller and Betts Streets. It was established in 1869, though not completed until 1873. There is room for 500 beds, besides a number of rooms for private pay-patients. The medical staff consists of five physicians and surgeons. The attendance is furnished by the Sisters.

St. Nicholas, the, of which E. N. Roth is proprietor, is the *bon-ton* restaurant and *café*, and one of the most comfortable hotels in the city. The restaurant, although not as grand as the *Café Anglais* in Paris, the *Café Royal* in London, or Delmonico's in New York, holds the same position in Cincinnati that the restaurants named hold in their respective cities. The *café* on the lower floor, with entrance on Race Street, is a popular resort for gentlemen desiring a first-class meal in little time and at prices somewhat lower than those charged in the restaurant. The hotel is conducted on the European plan, the charges for rooms ranging from $1 to $2.50 per day. The building was in former times two old-fashioned residences built with full thought about comfort; and the rooms and halls, besides being elegantly furnished, are spacious, airy, and luxurious. The location, on the south-east corner of Fourth and Race Streets, is very convenient. In the gentlemen's sitting-room is an elaborate painting, seven by twelve feet. Besides being a specimen of fine art, it is a queer subject, and is said to have an interesting history. The inscription reads "Pauline Bonaparte, by Devouge, 1811." It represents Madame Bonaparte, life-size, almost nude, and seated upon a sofa. The painting is said to have belonged to Joseph Bonaparte, and was sold, upon his return to France, to Nicholas Longworth, by whom it was sold at auction, and finally bought by Mr. Roth of the St. Nicholas.

St. Paul's Church (Methodist-Episcopal) is part of the old Western charge, established in 1835. The congregation at that time met in a brick chapel on the north-west corner of Fourth and Plum Streets, and enrolled about seven hundred members. Here so faithfully were the threatenings of the law, as well as the promises of the gospel, preached, that the place became known as the "Brimstone

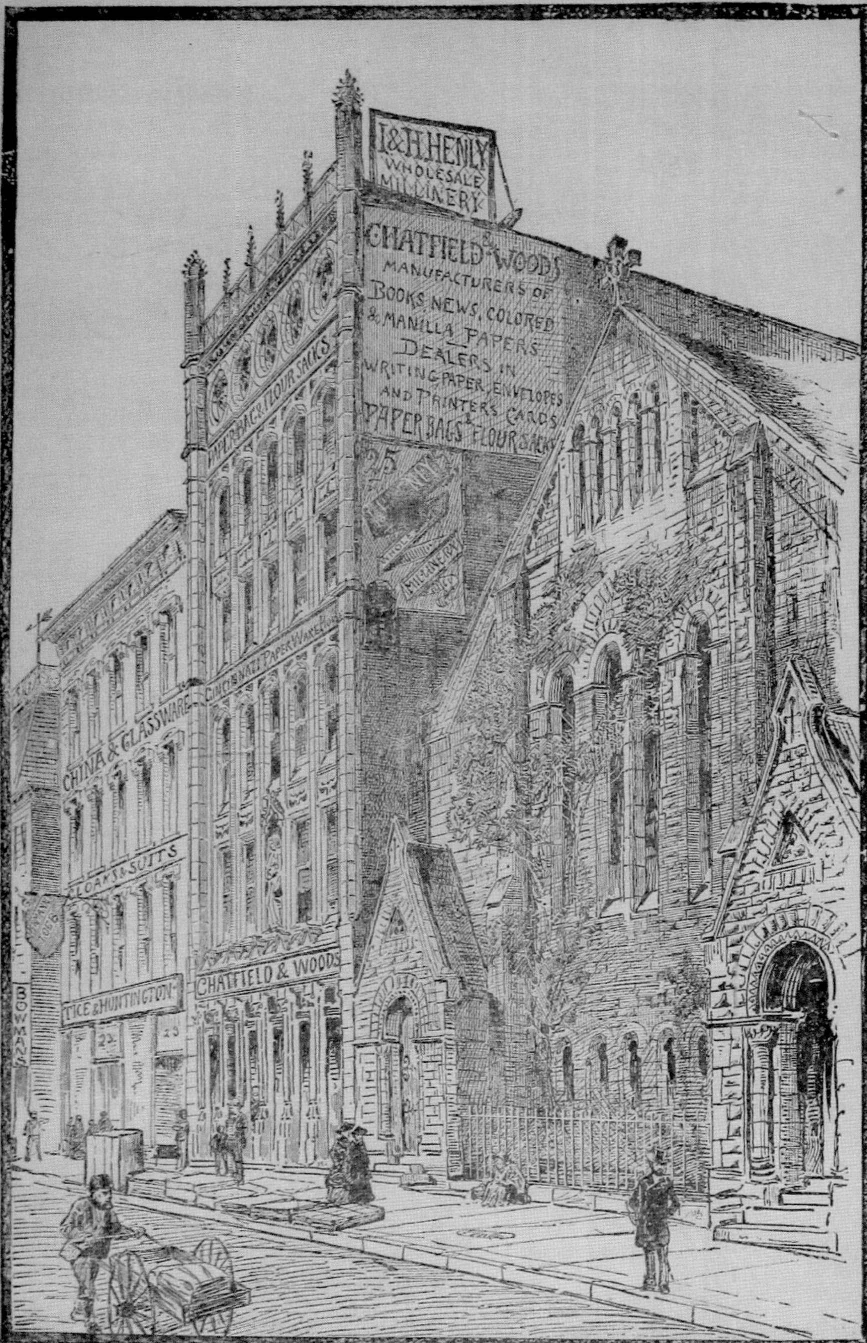

St. Paul's Church. (Torn down 1883.)

Corner." When a new church building became necessary, ground was purchased on Central Avenue; and here, in 1844, was erected Morris Chapel. Outgrowing this, the trustees obtained a lot on the corner of Seventh and Smith Streets, and in 1868 began the erection of St. Paul's Church and parsonage. The building is of blue limestone, and is one of the handsomest in the city. The membership numbers nearly six hundred persons.

St. Paul's Protestant-Episcopal Church.—Organized Aug. 1, 1828, under the Rev. Samuel Johnston, the first Episcopal minister settled in the city, and the first rector of Christ Church, which he left with a number of his parishioners to form this church. It was incorporated in 1831. The building, situated on the south-east corner of Seventh and Plum Streets, is of stone and brick in the Romanesque style, and has two unfinished towers or spires, giving it an odd appearance, at the same time an agreeable one. There are about three hundred communicants. Salmon P. Chase was for many years secretary of the society, and teacher and superintendent of the Sunday school. The rector is Samuel Benedict, D.D.

St. Peter's and St. Joseph's Orphan Asylum.—In the northern part of Cumminsville, about three squares from the Cincinnati, Hamilton, and Dayton Railroad depot. The building is a large four-story brick structure, surrounded by nearly twenty acres of the society's property. The average number of children in the asylum is 350; and the annual expenses are between $16,000 and $18,000. Children, one or both of whose parents are dead, are admitted, usually without charge; but when the surviving parent or friends are willing to pay, a moderate charge is made. The institution is conducted by the Sisters of Charity, and is supported by public charity. A bazaar and a picnic, held once a year, are the chief sources of income; but the St. Peter's, St. Joseph's, and the St. Xavier's orphan societies, as well as many individuals, make liberal contributions yearly. The asylum is also known as the Cumminsville orphan asylum, or as the Catholic orphan asylum. It can be reached by the Cincinnati, Hamilton, and Dayton Railroad (fare 15 cents), and by the Cumminsville and Spring-grove line of horse-cars (fare 5 cents).

St. Peter's Cathedral, situated on the corner of Plum and Eighth Streets, in point of beauty and architectural correctness is thought the finest church structure in the city. It is 200 feet in length by 91 in width. The roof is supported by 18 freestone pillars,

3½ feet in diameter and 33 in height. The main walls are built of Dayton marble, while the basement is of blue sandstone. The steeple is 221 feet high, and in the gracefulness of its proportions is unsurpassed by any spire in this country. An altar of Carrara marble, with two angels on each side,—the work of Hiram Powers,

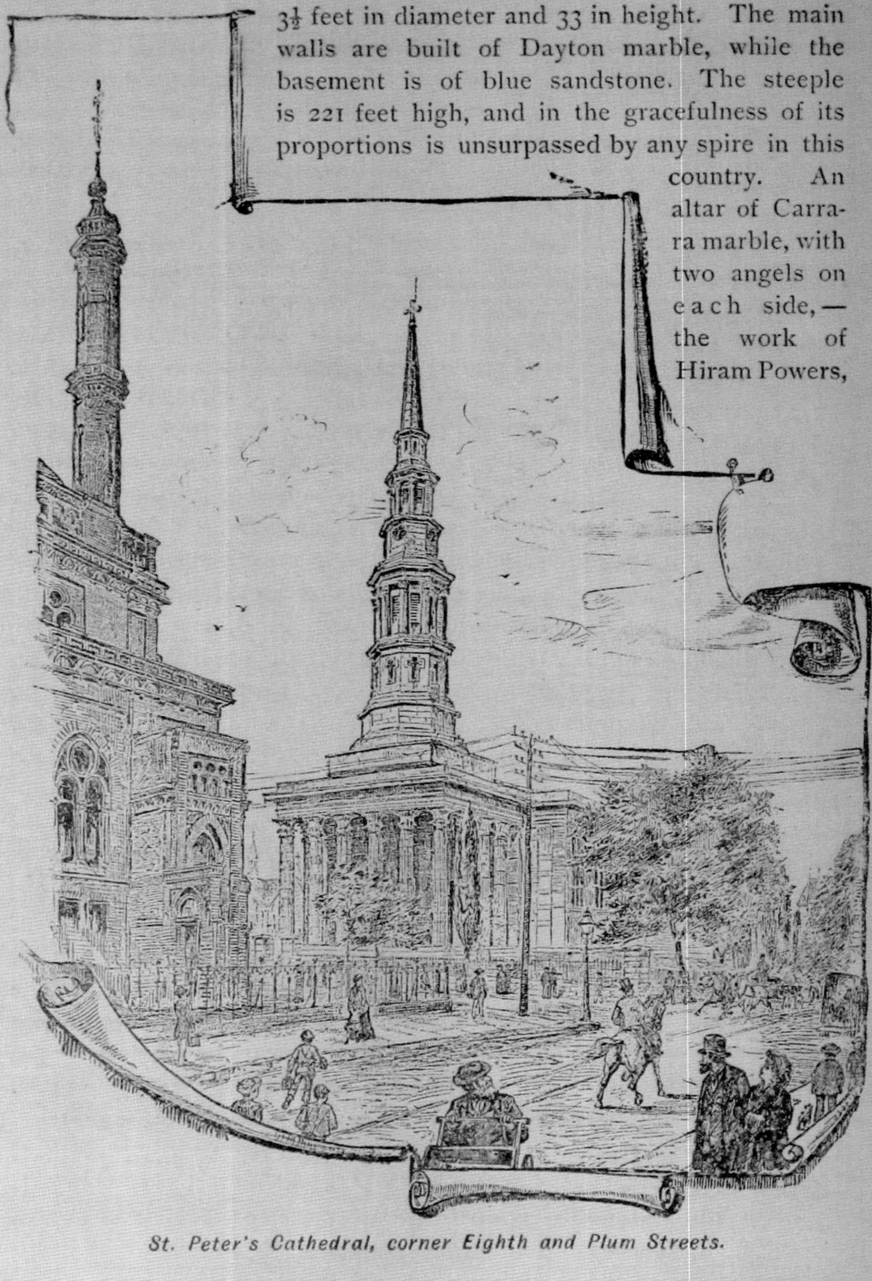

St. Peter's Cathedral, corner Eighth and Plum Streets.

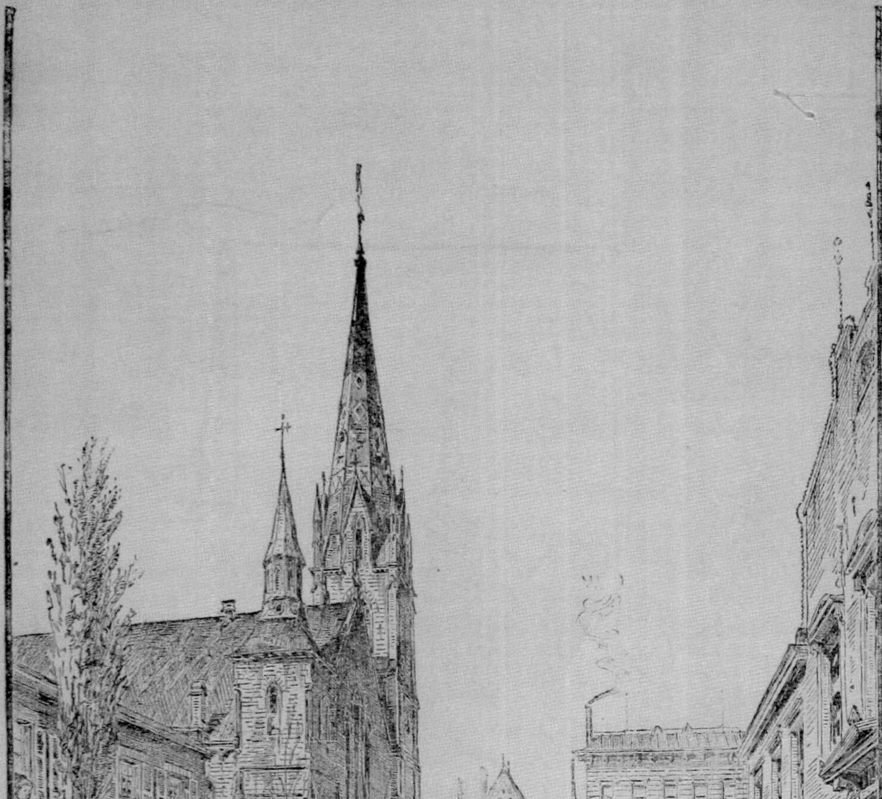

St. Paul's Methodist-Episcopal Church.

— occupies the west end of the cathedral. Opposite is an organ having 44 stops and 2,700 pipes. Some fine paintings, interesting alike for their historic and artistic merits, may be seen in the cathedral. "St. Peter liberated by an angel," by Murillo, was taken during the Peninsular War from the Spaniards, and presented by Cardinal Fesch, uncle of Napoleon I., to Bishop Fenwick. The cathedral was begun in 1839, consecrated in 1844. It has a seating capacity of 1,600, and, including the grounds, cost $244,000. (See Chimes.)

St. Xavier College was established in 1831, under the name of the Athenæum, by the Right Rev. E. D. Fenwick, D.D., the first bishop of Cincinnati. In 1840 Archbishop Purcell placed it in charge of the Fathers of the Society of Jesus, who have managed it ever since. There are two distinct courses of instruction, — the classical and the commercial. The former is designed especially to qualify young men for professions, and aims at imparting a thorough knowledge of the classics; and the latter is designed to qualify young men for a business career. In all departments for the year 1882–83 there were about 240 students, all of whom were day-scholars. Although under Roman-Catholic management, the college is open to young men of all denominations, and only the Catholic students are required to attend mass. The building, owned and occupied by the college, is a large brick structure on Sycamore Street, at the corner of Seventh. In it is a fine library of more than 14,000 valuable volumes.

Stadt Theatre. — See Turner Hall.

State Banks. — See Banks.

Steam Dummy Railroads. — The Columbia and Mount Lookout steam dummy railways start from the East-end Garden, in Pendleton, at the end of the Elm-street line of horse-cars. The Columbia line pursues its course east to Columbia. The Mount Lookout line branches off at Delta Station, one mile from Pendleton, and runs north to Mount Lookout and East Walnut Hills.

Steamboats and Packets. — The steamboat business of the Queen City of the West is one of large dimensions, embracing all the river trade from Pittsburg to the Gulf. The lines are as follows: The New-Orleans line of eleven boats, departing Tuesday, Thursday, and Saturday; the Memphis line of six boats, departing on Monday, Wednesday, and Friday; the United-States mail line of four boats, two boats making daily departures for Louisville, and one each day for Madison. Three boats ply regularly between Cincinnati and Pomeroy, making daily departures except on Sunday. From Cincinnati to Huntington the line consists of two boats making one departure daily. One boat makes tri-weekly trips Monday, Wednesday, and Friday, for Vanceburg. One boat leaves once each week for the Kanawha Valley, and three boats for the Tennessee River. A peculiar and attractive feature of the passenger business is the large excursion traffic in the winter season to New Orleans and all points South, forming a pleasant, healthful, and instructive relaxation from the cares of business and household duties. The total number of steamboats (including tow-boats) plying on the river for the year 1881 was 206, with a tonnage of 58,153. The tonnage of steamboats and barges manufactured in Cincinnati during the year 1880–81 was 11,236, as against 5,970 for 1879–80; a most gratifying increase, and giving promise of a brilliant future.

Storrs Township, so called, but now a portion of the city, the 21st ward, extends from the west bank of Mill Creek along the river front west to Riverside. Its western border-line is also the corporation line of Cincinnati. Sedamsville, Fairmount, Lick Run, and Warsaw were in this township.

Street-Railroads. — See Horse-Cars, Inclined Planes, Narrow-gauge Railroads, Steam Dummy Railroads.

Streets, Avenues, and Alleys. — The length of the streets, avenues, and alleys of the city, improved and unimproved, will be a matter of surprise even to most of the inhabitants. By an improved street is meant one paved with bowlders, limestone blocks, wooden blocks, macadamized, or gravelled. By unimproved is meant that the street is graded, but not yet finished with a hard surface. Jan. 1, 1881, the city civil engineer reports that there were, within a small fraction, $101\frac{2}{5}$ miles of streets and alleys paved with bowlder stone, $83\frac{1}{4}$ miles of macadamized (broken limestone) avenues, streets, and alleys; $6\frac{3}{4}$ miles of limestone-block-paved avenues, streets, and alleys; 7 miles of wooden-block streets; $12\frac{2}{5}$ miles of macadamized turnpikes: total miles improved avenues, streets, and alleys, $210\frac{3}{4}$; miles of unimproved avenues, streets, and alleys, $199\frac{3}{4}$: total miles improved and unimproved streets, avenues, and alleys, $410\frac{1}{2}$. (See Old Streets, etc.; and see Landmarks, etc.)

Sunday is a characteristic day in Cincinnati. No city in this country is more alive on Sunday than is Cincinnati. From this fact the name "Paris of America" has been firmly attached to it. It is true that the wholesale and the better class of retail business-men shut their business-places; but in many parts of the city there are retail shops open during a part or the whole of Sunday; while "Over-the-Rhine" there is no cessation from business on any day of the week. Throughout the city, the hotels, eating-places, barber-shops, cigar-shops, fruit-stands, and bar-rooms are open the forenoon or all of the day. Amusements at any time of the year are never wanting. In summer, crowds go to the hill-top resorts, to the Zoölogical Gardens, to the concert and beer gardens, to base-ball games and other athletic sports, and on railroad and steamboat excursions. In the winter, crowds go to the hill-top resorts, which then provide shelter, warmth, and music; to beer-saloons, where some sort of music is generally furnished; to club and private parties; and they also go skating, sleigh-riding, etc. During the greater part of the year, the cheap places of amusement, styled by themselves "opera-houses" and "theatres," are open Sunday afternoons and evenings; and during the winter, occasional attractions are offered at the better class of theatres by way of concerts, lectures, and theatrical performances. The demoralizing "free shows," consisting of a low variety entertainment, the expenses of which are paid out of the profits on sales of liquor and tobacco, are open the year round. The public libraries and reading-rooms do good work by attracting many persons to read books and papers. The Young Men's Christian Association, the Women's Christian Temperance Union, and the Young Men's Hebrew Association, keep open their places; and the two first named hold services at various hours. The social club-houses are open on Sunday; and members, with friends from outside the city, resort to them. While knowing that there are such varied and so many amusements, it must not be forgotten that a large part of the community are constant and devout church-going people. There are over a hundred and fifty congregations holding regular service, one, two, or three times a day,—except during the hot season. Then there are many Sunday schools, and some Jewish people known as Reformed Israelites, holding their services on Sunday. In the afternoon and evening a large part of the people, even the better class, will drive out on the road, or visit the public parks; and the railroad and steamboat lines make Sunday their special day on which to bring in excursions from neighboring places. And so it is that the Sunday life in this city very clearly shows the metropolitan character of Cincinnati.

Surgeons. — See Physicians.

Suspension Bridge. — See Bridges.

Sycamore Hill. — That part of the city lying on Sycamore Street in its ascent to Mount Auburn. The ascent begins near Liberty Street, and the summit is reached at Saunders Street, half a mile distant. Sycamore Hill is very steep in some places. In early days it was the entrance to the city by way of the Lebanon Pike.

Taxes. — For the year 1882, the real and personal property on the grand duplicate for taxation in Cincinnati amounted to $166,986,-105; in Hamilton County, outside the city, it amounted to $38,480,-771; total, $205,466,876. The total levy by the city, for all purposes, on the property within its limits, is 18.96 mills on the dollar. To this must be added the state levy, 2.90 mills, and the county levy, 1.96 mills; making a total of 23.82 mills, or $2.38.2 on each hundred dollars. The rates of taxation in the townships outside the city vary from 7½ to 20 mills, or from 75 cents to $2 on each hundred. The city-tax levy for 1882 was divided as follows: —

	MILLS.
General fund	1.13
Police	1 60
Superior court	.06
Fire-department	1.39
Light	1.38
Workhouse	.20
Sanitary purposes	.25
Parks	.07
Sewerage	.10
Street-cleaning	.50
Redemption of city debt	.50
Hospital	.48
Infirmary	.40
House of Refuge	.22
Street-repairs	1.10
Redemption Southern Railroad bonds	1.16
Interest on city debt	4.46
School, Library, and University	3.96
	18.96
Add state levy	2 90
Add county levy	1 96
Total	23.82

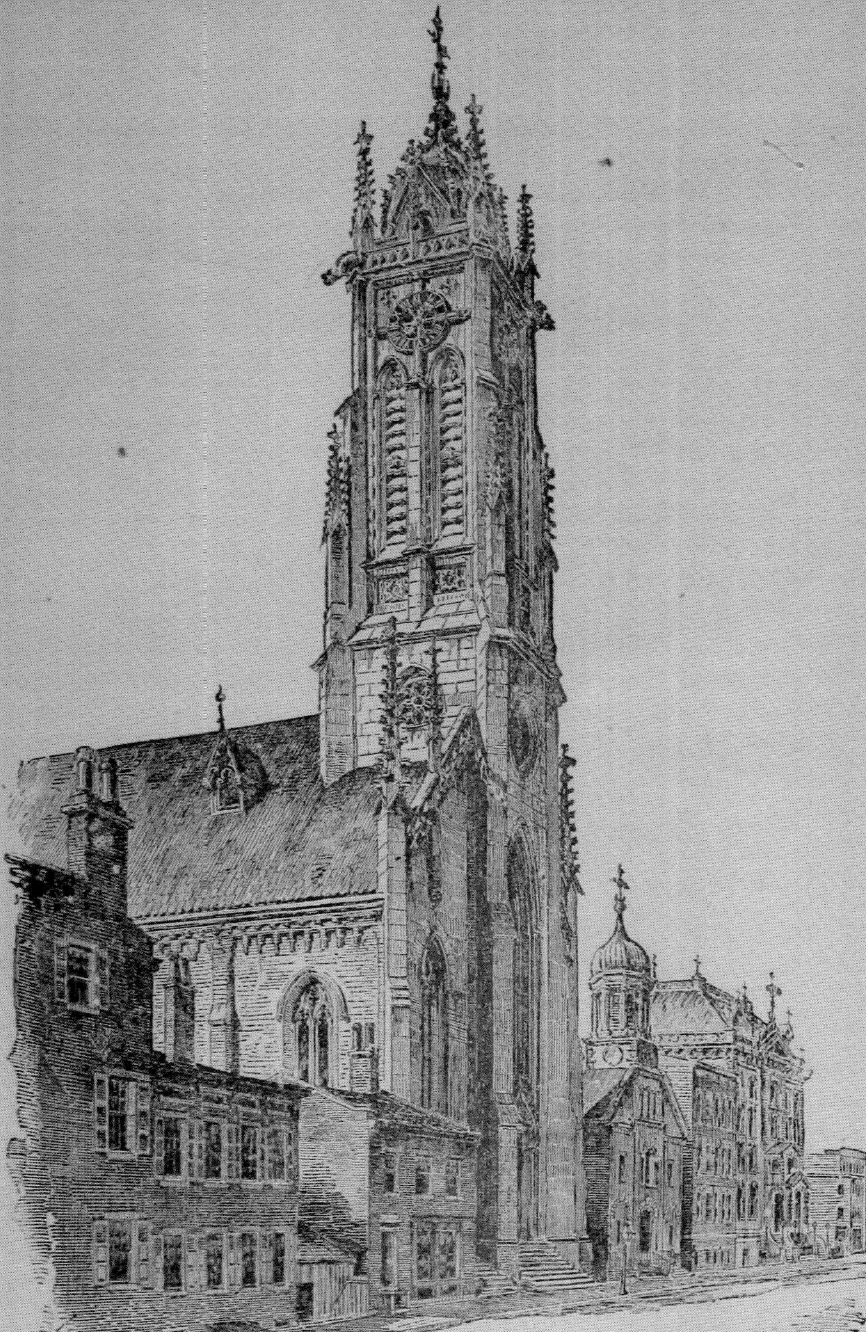

St. Xavier College.

Telegraph and Telephone Offices. — American District Telegraph Company, 165 Vine Street; Baltimore and Ohio Telegraph Company, 57 West Fourth Street; Bell Telephonic Exchange, 43 West Fourth Street; Board of Trade Telegraph, 22 West Fourth Street; City and Suburban Telegraph Association, 43 West Fourth Street; Western Union Telegraph Company, north-west corner Fourth and Vine Streets.

Temperance Organizations. — There are six lodges of Good Templars, and five divisions of Sons of Temperance, in Cincinnati. They hold weekly meetings in their separate halls, which are scattered in every portion of the city, from Columbia to Cumminsville. The Women's Christian Temperance Union, the Cincinnati Temperance Reform Club, the Women's Temperance Union of Walnut Hills, and the Templars of Honor, also hold weekly meetings. The central meeting-place is the hall of the Women's Christian Temperance Union, No. 115 West Sixth Street. Meetings are held here every Sunday afternoon.

Theological and Religious Library Association was organized in 1863. Its extensive and valuable collection of books and pamphlets is in alcoves specially assigned to them in the Public Library. The president is George F. Davis, and the secretary is John D. Caldwell.

Third National Bank of Cincinnati is number twenty of the national-bank system. It began in July, 1863, with a cash capital of $300,000, which was increased in 1864 to $500,000. In May, 1871, it purchased the building and business of the Bank of the Ohio Valley, which was organized in 1858, immediately after the failure of the Ohio Life and Trust Company. In 1871 the capital was increased to $800,000, at which amount it stands to-day. The surplus is about $320,000, and the deposits about $3,500,000. The dividends have averaged twelve per cent a year, and the stock is very largely held by those directly connected with the management of the bank. The Third National does a legitimate banking business, and deals in foreign and domestic exchange, European letters of credit, gold and currency drafts on California, and United-States and Cincinnati bonds. It is also the United-States and City of Cincinnati depository. The office is 65 West Third Street.

Thoms' Hall. — A public hall on the west side of Central Avenue, between Fourth and Fifth Streets, in the second story. The build-

CARPET DEPARTMENT.

The assortments include all the newest designs in floor-coverings of all grades, embracing the popular styles in

PERSIAN, INDIAN, AND GERMAN PIECE CARPETS,

AXMINSTERS, WILTONS,

BODY AND TAPESTRY BRUSSELS,

WITH

WOOL CARPETINGS IN THREE-PLY,

EXTRA SUPER, AND SUPER,

COTTON AND WOOL INGRAINS,

HEMP AND DUTCH CARPETINGS,

MATTINGS, RUGS, AND MATS,

OIL CLOTHS, LINOLEUMS, ETC.

Buyers will always find, in this department, complete and attractive assortments at the

LOWEST PRICES.

THE JOHN SHILLITO COMPANY.

ing was once owned by Morris Chapel, Methodist-Episcopal Church congregation; but the society, becoming too large to be accommodated in the hall, sold the building to J. C. Thoms, who converted it into a convenient hall for small entertainments.

Tobacco. — As a tobacco-market Cincinnati ranks among the first, while as a centre of trade in white tobacco she is the largest market in the world. Manufacturers from the sea-board and Western cities draw heavily on this city for their supplies of this particular class of tobacco. It is doubtful if any other commodity is now so peculiarly connected with the prosperity of the city as this. All the lines of transportation, warehouse-men, insurance companies, banks, manufacturers, merchants, and shop-keepers in general find in it important contributions to their business. The tobacco business of Cincinnati, in all its branches of chewing and smoking goods, shows a considerable increase over the year 1881, both in production and taxes paid. The production in Cincinnati, Covington, and Newport was as follows: Fine cut and plug, 4,702,159 pounds; smoking-tobacco, 2,064,150 pounds; number of cigars and cigarettes, 127,253,970. Taxes paid were as follows: Fine cut and plug, $712,370.44; smoking-tobacco, $330,437.17; cigars and cigarettes, $754,596.61. These figures show an increase over 1881 in the aggregate taxes paid on all three commodities of $20,366.84.

Trades' Assembly. — A central organization, composed of three delegates from each of fourteen trade-unions which have asked for membership. The assembly holds semi-monthly meetings at Bricklayers' Hall, corner of Central Avenue and Court Street. Only a small proportion of the various trade-unions of the city belong to the assembly. It is devoted to the interests of workingmen, and takes an active part in political affairs.

Trinity Church, on Ninth Street, between Race and Elm, was, like St. Paul's, a part of the Western Charge. A church for this portion of the work was built in 1837, on the site of the present building. The lot was purchased of Luther Rose, and up to 1841 the Western Charge remained undivided. After that year separate pastors were appointed for the two churches. Trinity Church, so named, was erected in 1859–60, and was the first regularly constituted Methodist congregation which introduced the system of family or promiscuous sittings. Up to that time the men and women were in all cases required to sit apart in public worship. Trinity also introduced the first church-organ into Cincinnati Methodism.

Turner Hall, owned and occupied by the Turnverein, is a large building, Nos. 513 to 519 Walnut Street. It was finished in 1859, at a cost of $35,000. The hall proper, which is in the third story, is fitted for, and is used as, a German theatre, known as the Stadt Theatre, and is in great demand for political conventions, balls, etc. The building contains also, on the rear of the ground-floor, a gymnasium fitted with all the appliances for athletic exercises usually found in gymnasiums. In the second story rear is a large hall, in which the meetings of the Turnverein and of numerous other societies, singing-clubs, and building associations, are held. There are also several large committee, cloak, and other rooms on the second floor. On the ground-floor front are a large saloon and reading-rooms. In the rear of the building is a large garden, with pavilion for music, and tables for refreshments, to which there is an entrance from Allison Street. The building is maintained by rents received for its various halls, and the proceeds of the saloon.

Turnverein, the Cincinnati. — A German society for the promotion of athletic exercises. It was organized in 1848, and now numbers about five hundred members, many of whom are honorary and contributing. The active members are divided into classes: one consisting of all above the age of eighteen years; another, of youths between the ages of fourteen and eighteen; and the third, of children under fourteen years. Each class has its time for practice in the gymnasium, where competent teachers are employed every night. The association has its own band, selected from the members who are musicians, and a cadet-corps of youth between fourteen and eighteen years of age. These latter are drilled in the manual of arms and military movements. The uniform of the cadets is a dark-gray coat, pants, and cap; and that of the adult Turners is simply an unbleached linen short sack-coat, worn with any other colored garments. The Turnverein owns the Turner Hall.

Tyler-Davidson Fountain, the, is one of the objects in Cincinnati in which the citizens take the utmost pride. It is the grandest fountain in the United States, and by far the noblest work of art in the city. It was unveiled in 1871, and was donated to the city by Henry Probasco, as a memorial of his brother-in-law, Tyler Davidson, who for many years had the project under consideration. It stands in the centre of the esplanade, on Fountain Square. The massive base and the circular basin are made of porphyry, quarried and polished in Europe. The fountain itself is cast in bronze, of condemned cannon procured from the Danish government. The castings weigh twenty-four tons. The diameter of the basin is forty-three feet, and the weight of porphyry eighty-five tons. The height of the fountain above the esplanade is thirty-eight feet. The bronze pedestal on the base of porphyry is square; the four sides bearing representations in relief of the four principal uses of water, — water-power, navigation, the fisheries, and steam. The pedestal is surmounted by four semi-circular bronze basins, each pierced in the centre by a single jet an inch in diameter. From the centre of the four semi-circular basins rises a second bronze pedestal, surmounted by a square column, on which stands the Genius of Water, a draped female figure, with outstretched arms, from the palms and fingers of whose hands the water falls in spray into the four semi-circular basins. On either side of the square column is a group of figures of heroic size. The eastern group represents a mother leading a nude child to the bath; the western group, a daughter giving her aged father a draught of water; the northern group, a man standing on the burning roof of his homestead, with uplifted hand, and praying for rain; the southern group, a husbandman with an idle plough, and at his side a dog panting from heat, supplicates Heaven for rain. There are life-size figures in niches at each corner of the bronze pedestal beneath the semi-circular basins. One represents a nude boy with a lobster, which he has just taken from a net, and is holding aloft in triumph with one hand; another, a laughing girl, playing with a necklace of pearls; the third, a semi-nude girl, listening to the sound of the waves in a sea-shell which she holds to her ear; the fourth, a boy well muffled, strapping on his skates. There are four drinking-fountains, equi-distant on the rim of the porphyry basin. Each is a bronze pedestal, surmounted by a life-size bronze figure. One represents a youth astride a dolphin; the second, a youth kneeling, holding one duck under his left arm, and grasping by the neck another; the third is that of a youth, around whose right leg a snake has coiled, which the youth has grasped with his left hand, and is about to strike with a stone that he holds in his right. The fourth figure is that of a youth kneeling on the back of a huge turtle, and grasping it by the neck. Water issues from the mouths of the dolphin, duck, snake, and turtle. The fountain was designed by August von Kreling of Nuremberg, and cast by Ferdinand von Müller, director of the Royal

Bronze Foundery of Bavaria. The cost of the fountain itself was $105,000 in gold. Together with the esplanade, the total cost was over $200,000. All horse-cars pass by or quite close to the fountain.

Union Bethel, the Cincinnati. — Nos. 30 to 36 Public Landing, east of Sycamore Street. The Bethel owns the Bethel Church building, which was erected in 1869, at a cost of $35,000. In front stands the main building, erected in 1872, at a cost of $45,000. The whole property cost $134,000. The Bethel is supported by subscriptions and contributions. David Sinton gave it $113,000, and two fairs netted $72,000. Membership, $10 a year, $50 for life Only members vote for directors. The Bethel comprises a church, undenominational, services Sundays, 11 A.M., 7.30 P.M., and Thursday evenings 7.30; a sabbath school, probably the largest in the world, for its average attendance is over 2,200, meets Sunday afternoons, 2.30; the "Young Men's Home," open every day from 6 A.M. to 12 P.M.; "Newsboys' Home," and the Merchants' Dining-Rooms furnish meals and lodging at the lowest possible prices; and the profits, if any, go to the relief-department, which provides meals and beds to the worthy needy poor. Thomas Lee has been identified with the institution for fourteen years, and has been its superintendent and pastor for the past eleven years.

Union Central Life-insurance Company of Cincinnati. — The only local life-insurance company. It was incorporated in 1867, with a capital stock of $100,000; and Jan. 1, 1883, the gross assets were $1,837,090.96; and according to the New-York standard, its surplus was $270,614.68, and its amount of assets to each $100 of liabilities was $117,27. Its income for 1883 was $495,158.02. The laws of Ohio restrict its investments to mortgages upon unencumbered real estate, worth, exclusive of buildings, double the amount loaned thereon, Government bonds, and loans upon its own policies. Its stockholders are liable for double the amount of their stock. Its policies, after three annual payments, are also by law made incontestable, except as to age or fraud. The superintendent of insurance is required to examine the company annually. The company owns the office-building on the south-east corner of Fourth Street and Central Avenue. The president is John Davis, and the secretary E. P. Marshall, succeeding John Cochnower and N. W. Harris, who held the same offices from the time the Union Central began business.

Union Insurance Company of Cincinnati was organized in

1855 in Kentucky, as the Mercantile Insurance Company of Covington; but in 1859 it re-organized in Ohio under the present name. The company's capital was $100,000, with twenty per cent paid in. Since 1859 the remaining eighty per cent has been earned, and cash dividends averaging seven and a half per cent a year have been paid, besides $20,000 surplus accumulated. Nearly $1,000,000 have been its receipts for premiums, and nearly $600,000 its payments for losses. The first secretary of the company, A. C. Edwards, served until 1873, when he was elected vice-president. In 1875 he was elected president, which office he now holds. Mr. Edwards's successor as secretary is Joseph T. Blair, who has held the position since 1873. The company does only a fire business, having discontinued its marine business. Office, 66 West Third Street.

United Brethren Churches. — First German, Clinton and Baymiller, Jacob Ernst, pastor; Second German, 729 Eastern Avenue, Gottlieb Fritz, pastor.

United Railroads Stock-yard Company was incorporated in 1871, with a capital of $500,000. Fifty acres of land were bought on the west side of Spring-grove Avenue in the 24th ward. About two-thirds of the property lies between the avenue and Mill Creek, and one-third on the west side of Mill Creek, the whole being connected by the company's own bridge. These yards are surpassed in size, arrangement, and management, by but few stock-yards in the world. They have cost about $750,000, and have accommodations for 5,000 cattle, 10,000 sheep, and 25,000 hogs. The receipts each year amount to nearly 1,000,000 hogs, 300,000 sheep, 160,000 cattle, and 10,000 calves. Almost all railroads make connections with these yards. A brick building contains the stock-yards' office, the Avenue Hotel, and offices rented to live-stock dealers. The officers of the company are J. L. Keck president, and John H. Porter secretary and treasurer. The Cumminsville and Spring-grove horse-cars pass the yards.

United-States Internal Revenue Collector's Office occupies Rooms 6, 7, 8, and 9, on the second floor of the Johnston Building, south-west corner of Fifth and Walnut Streets. The first district of Ohio comprises Hamilton County; and in this district, April 30, 1878, there were 3,248 persons who held licenses as retail liquor-dealers, and 4,214 as retail tobacco-dealers. Out of the whole number, more than one-half were Germans. The following are the statistics for this district for the year ending July 1, 1882: —

SOURCES.	REVENUE.
10 distilleries	$9,008,267
359 tobacco, cigar, and snuff factories	1,034,025
21 breweries	707,190
Licenses	138,379
From liquors and tobacco	$10,887,861
From all other sources	39,281
Revenue of this district	$10,927,142

Moreover, the revenue of this county alone from liquors and tobacco is fully one-thirteenth of the entire revenue of the United States. The cost of collecting the revenue here is one and one-seventh per cent. The United-States collector is C. B. Montgomery, who has about ninety deputies and other employés under him.

United-States Mail-Line Company, the, established upwards of fifty years, runs a line of steamboats between Cincinnati and Louisville, and carries the mail between those cities and to intermediate points on and in the vicinity of the Ohio River. It owns five boats, — three first-class side-wheel steamers, the "United States," "Gen. Lytle," and "Ben Franklin;" and two stern-wheelers, the "Louis A. Shirley" and "Gen. Pike." Four boats are in service all the time, daily trips being made to Louisville and to Madison, Ind. One first-class boat is held in reserve. Fare to Louisville, $3.50; round trip, $6. The freight carried is at all-rail rates, the company carrying the insurance. Connections are made with all railroads in both cities, and coupon-tickets sold on the steamers. During the fifty years the company has been in active business, but three accidents accompanied by loss of life have occurred on its steamers. It is the oldest navigation company on the Western waters. Wharf-boat at foot of Vine Street. Thomas Sherlock president.

United-States Marine Hospital Service, established by Act of Congress July 16, 1798, and re-organized by Acts approved June 29, 1870, and March 3, 1875, is the medical department of the mercantile marine; and is charged, under the direction of the secretary of the treasury, with the duty of looking after the health-interests of the officers and seamen employed on all American vessels engaged in the foreign, coastwise, and inland trade. The object of the establishment of this service was to encourage fit persons to become seamen by affording care and treatment to such as may while following their vocation become sick or disabled. The present surgeon-general of the marine-hospital service is Dr. John B. Hamilton. In addition to the care of the sick and disabled of the mercantile marine, the medical officers of the marine-hospital service are, under the laws of the United States, further charged with the medical care of seamen of the revenue-cutter service, and with the physical examination of officers of the revenue-cutters of the United States, and of the keepers and crews of life-saving stations; and finally they are required to aid in the enforcement of quarantine, under the direction of the secretary of the treasury. Original appointments into the medical corps are made to the grade of assistant surgeon only, and after thorough examination into professional qualifications by an examining board of surgeons of the service; and the medical officers are assigned to duty wherever their services may be required from time to time. The relief-stations of the service are nearly 100, and the number of seamen cared for are from 15,000 to 18,000 each year. During the year 1882, the patients of the service numbered nearly 20,000. Medical officer in charge of the service at the port of Cincinnati, Surgeon Walter Wyman.

United-States Custom-House and Post-Office. — See Custom-House, and see Post-office.

United-States Signal-Service was organized by Act of Congress approved Feb. 9, 1870, directing the secretary of war to provide for taking meteorological observations at military stations in the interior, and at other points in the States and Territories, and for giving notice on the northern lakes and on the seacoast, by telegraph, of the approach and force of storms. Gen. Albert J. Myers, chief signal-officer of the United-States Army, was directed to carry into effect the duties above mentioned that had been imposed upon the secretary of war. The Cincinnati office is in Rooms N and 63, Pike's Opera-house building.

University of Cincinnati, the, is organized under the act passed by the General Assembly of Ohio, April 16, 1870, "to enable cities of the first class to aid and promote education;" and which authorizes any person or body corporate, holding any estate or funds in trust for the promotion of education or any of the arts and sciences, to transfer the same to the city as a trustee for such purpose; thus affording a means of consolidating various existing funds, which separately are of little or no avail for their intended purposes. In accordance with this act, a university board was appointed January, 1871. This board immediately received an estate which had been left in trust for the city by Charles McMicken in 1858. Since then the endowment of the university has been increased by important donations from the Cincinnati Astronomical Society, Joseph Longworth, John Kilgour, and Julius Dexter, and by a bequest from the Rev. Samuel J. Browne. With these funds and others, with the assistance of the city, the university accumulated nearly $1,000,000 worth of property. It consists of three departments: the academic, or department of literature and science; the school of design, or art department; and the observatory, or astronomical department. There were in the academic department, during the year 1882–83, five post-graduate students, fifty students in undergraduate courses, and thirty-nine students in special courses. The university is free to residents of both sexes, and a moderate charge is made to non-residents. Samuel F. Hunt is chairman of the board of directors, and Thomas Vickers is rector of the university. (See Observatory, and see School of Design.)

Van Antwerp, Bragg, & Co. conduct the largest publishing-house in the world devoted exclusively to school-books. Their establishment, fronting at 137 Walnut Street, includes four large buildings of seven floors each. In these is done every part of the work of editing, making, and publishing school-books, which have received the highest awards at the world's fairs held at Vienna, Philadelphia, and Paris. About four million books are made each year, and are sold in every State and Territory in the Union. They are more extensively used than any other school-books published. Some of the principal text-books of this house are McGuffey's and Harvey's Readers and Spellers, Ray's and White's Mathematical Series, Eclectic Geographies, and Copy-books, Venable's and Thalheimer's Histories, — forming a part of the well-known Eclectic Educational Series. The new edition of McGuffey's readers, just prepared for the press at a cost of $30,000, is probably the best series of readers in every particular that has ever been published. The firm dates its foundation from 1830, and is now composed of Lewis Van Antwerp, C. S. Bragg, H. H. Vail, Robert F. Leaman, A. Howard Hinkle, and Harry T. Ambrose.

Vine-street Hill. — A name given to that portion of the city lying on Vine Street in its ascent to the summit of the northern hill.

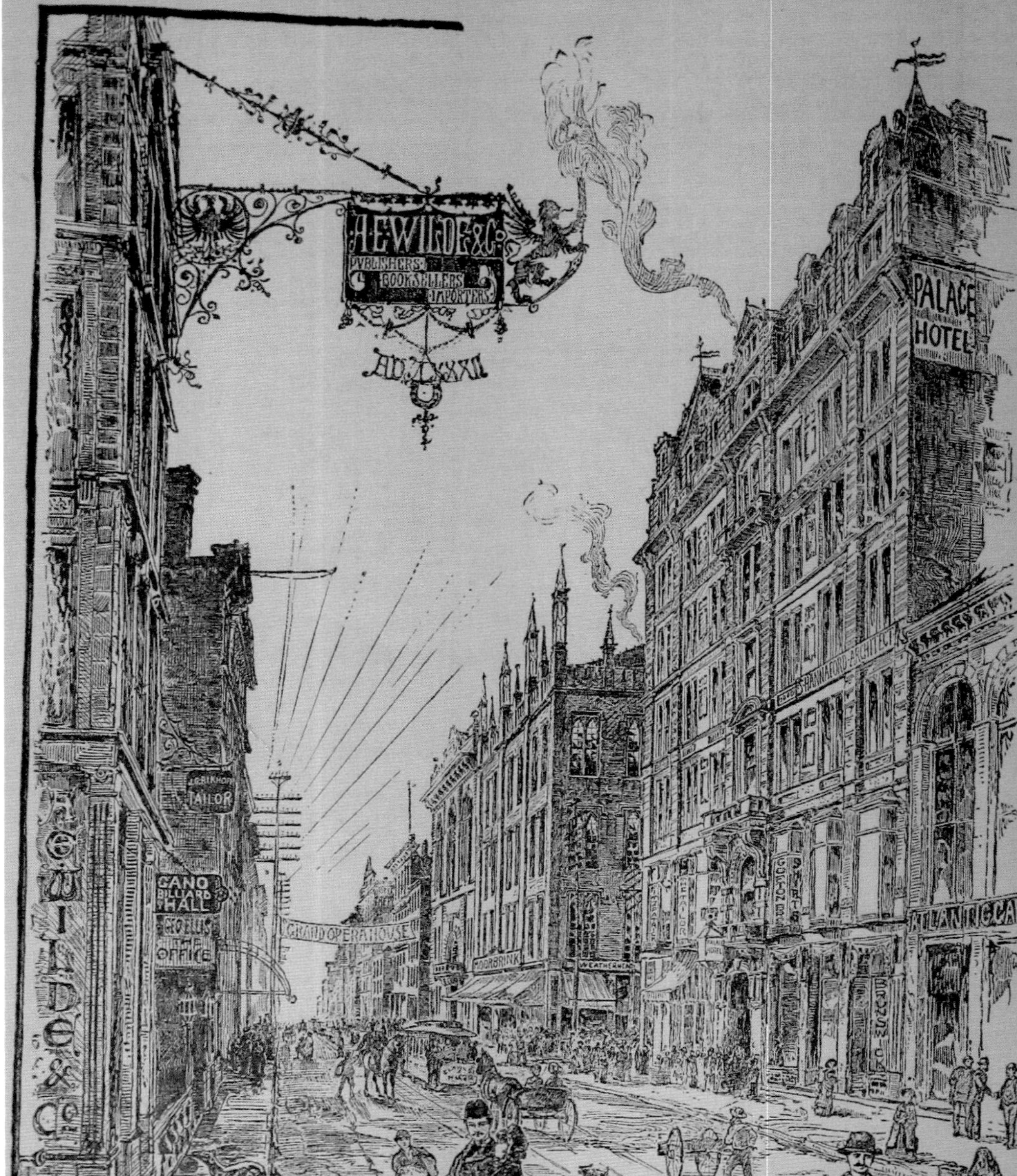

Vine Street, looking South.

It extends from the junction of Vine Street and Hamilton Road to McMillan Street, Corryville, a distance of three-quarters of a mile. Vine Street ascends the hill at a grade of four hundred feet to the mile, and was cut through at a great expense. This portion of Vine Street in early days was known as the Carthage Pike.

Washington Park. — The square between Race and Elm Streets, extending from Twelfth northwardly nearly to Fourteenth Street. It is opposite the Music-hall building. The four and a third acres occupied by the park, as well as that on which Music Hall stands, was formerly a cemetery, but its use as such was discontinued about the year 1840. For twenty years it was neglected, and overgrown with briers and weeds. In 1861 the bodies of the dead were removed, and the work of turning it into a park begun. It was graded down, sodded, and a substantial iron fence eight feet in height built around it. Later a spray fountain was built in its centre, and a drinking-fountain consisting of a huge bowlder perforated for water-pipes placed near by. Serpentine walks of screened gravel were made, and the park thrown open to the public. It is filled with noble elms and sycamores of a century's growth or more, being the natural forest-trees. It has ornamental iron gates on the four sides. The monument to Col. Robert L. McCook stands on the western edge of the lake containing the fountain. The park is the favorite of German children, being in the midst of the German district; and thousands daily seek its generous shade during sultry weather. It is well supplied with rustic benches and other seats. *Horse-cars,* — Elm-street and Vine and Twelfth Street lines. (See Monuments.)

Water-Works. — Cincinnati has reason to be proud of her water-works. The pumping-house is located on the river-bank, on East Front Street, immediately east of the Little Miami Railroad Depot. It contains seven large pumping-engines, the largest being known as the "Shields" engine, which has a cylinder eight feet in diameter and twelve feet stroke, with a pumping capacity of 20,000,000 gallons per day, each revolution lifting into the reservoirs 1,880 gallons. This is said to be the largest steam-engine in the world. The other six engines have each about half the capacity of the Shields. Water is lifted from the Front-street pumping-house into the old reservoir at the foot of Mount Adams and the two mammoth reservoirs in Eden Park. This pumping-house is a curiosity well worth being seen. A second pumping-house, located at the intersection of Hunt and Effluent-pipe Streets, receives a supply of water from the Eden-park reservoirs, and lifts it to the immense boiler-iron reservoirs on Mount Auburn, from which the portion of the city on the northern hills is supplied (see Reservoirs). The consumption of water during the year 1882, for all purposes, in the city, was 7,126,569,266 gallons. Of the vast amount, revenue was received for only about one-half. The public institutions, fountains, fire-department, and leakage consumed the other half. The water-works are owned and operated by the city, through the board of city commissioners. The length of street-mains already laid, ranging in diameter from three inches to forty inches, is 180 miles. The average price of water to consumers is twelve cents per 1,000 gallons.

Water-works Park. — For many years this was the only park in the city. It lies on the southern slope of Mount Adams, facing the Ohio River, between which and the park is the Front-street pumping-house. The old reservoir, a structure of solid masonry, occupies the most elevated portion. The grounds contain about three acres, and are tastefully ornamented with flowers, trees, and shrubbery. It is now but little used, greater attractions being found in Eden Park, close at hand.

Weather House. — See Casino.

Wesleyan College, the Cincinnati, a college for young women, and controlled by the Methodist-Episcopal Church, was founded in 1842, and until 1865 occupied the building on Vine Street, between Sixth and Seventh, now known as Aug's Club-House. That property is owned by "The Cincinnati Enquirer," and the former chief recitation-room of the college used as "The Enquirer's" mechanical department. On the abandonment and subdivision of the old Catherine-street burying-ground, the college association erected an elegant college building, which was completed in 1868, on a portion of the abandoned ground, on the west side of what is now known as Wesley Avenue, in the rear of Christie Chapel Methodist-Episcopal Church. The building is of Gothic architecture, four stories high besides the mansard roof, 90 feet wide, and 180 feet front on Wesley Avenue. The building and site are valued at $225,000, the building alone having cost $135,000. The courses of study comprise the primary, academic, and collegiate, music, drawing, and painting. Boarding-pupils are accommodated in the college building. The average daily attendance during the year is about 225. Many Cin-

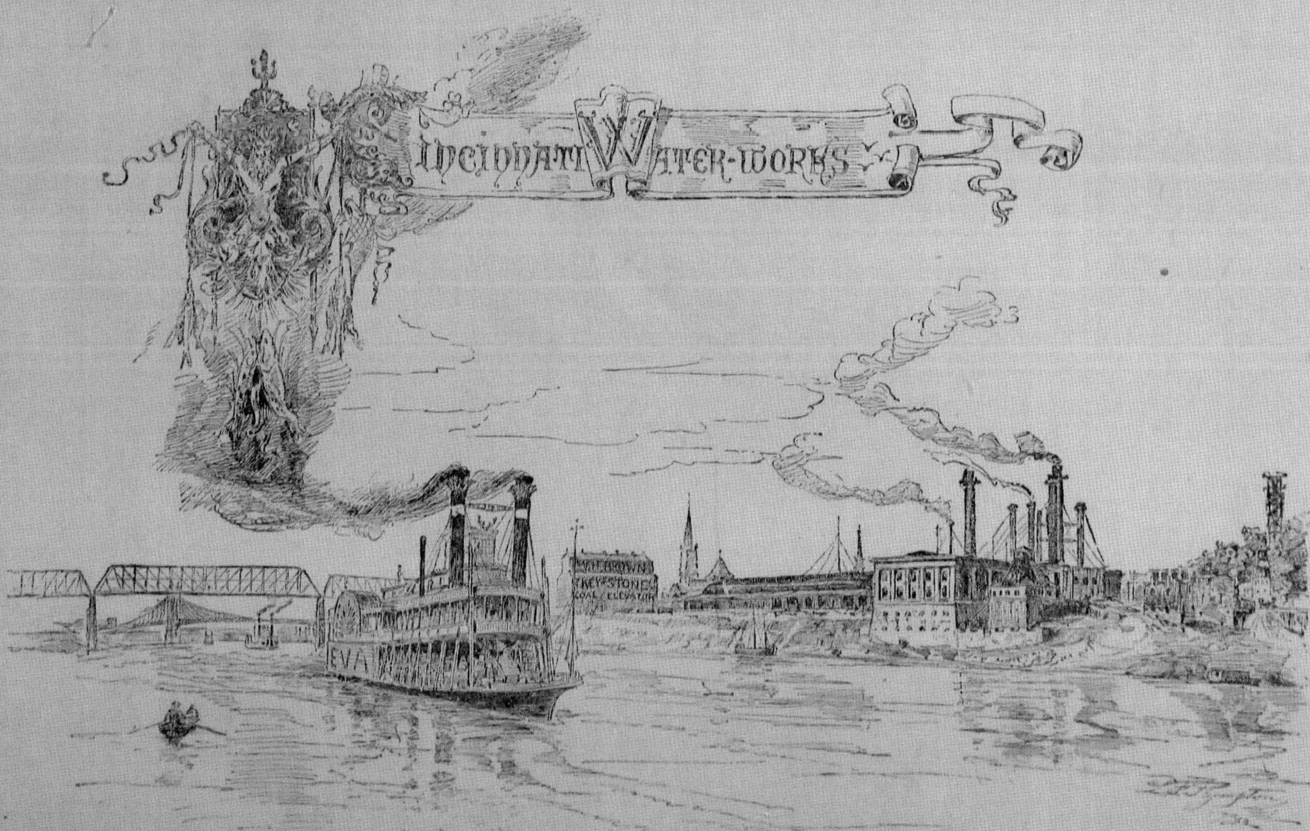
Cincinnati Water-Works
EVA
KEYSTONE
COAL ELEVATOR

cinnati ladies prominent in charitable and educational works are alumnæ of this college: among them may be mentioned the wife of President Hayes.

Wesley Chapel is the mother-church of Methodism in Cincinnati. The first class was organized in 1804, and consisted of only eight persons; but so rapid was the growth of the church, that in less than two years the leaders of the society determined to secure a lot, and erect upon it a house of worship. They accordingly purchased from James Kirby, lots eighteen and nineteen on the north-west corner of Fifth Street and Broadway, at that time in the midst of open fields. Kirby's deed was dated Sept. 25, 1805; and the grant was made by himself and wife to William Lynes, Robert Richardson, Christopher Smith, James Gibson, and James Kirby, as trustees. A small stone house was put up; and, when this became too small, a brick addition was built in the rear. In process of time, even this was outgrown; and in 1829 the present building was erected. The membership of the church was then 1,250. The little class of 1804 has now grown into 20 churches, with over 5,000 members.

West End, the. — This term was originally applied to that portion of the city west of Central Avenue and north of Sixth Street to Court; the partially settled territory north of the latter street being known as Texas, in which stood the Bull's-Head Tavern, now at the corner of John and Findlay Streets. The march of improvement and population drove out most of the Texas slaughter-houses, soap-factories, and tanneries; and the entire district has been rebuilt with substantial and many elegant private residences, churches, and other public buildings. The term "West End" is now applied to all that portion of the city north of Fourth Street, and west of John to the Mill-creek bottoms. It contains about one-half the population of Cincinnati.

Western Insurance Company of Cincinnati holds a perpetual charter granted in 1836; but did not begin business until 1854, when twenty per cent on the capital of $100,000 was paid in. In four years the company's earnings made the capital full paid, and since 1858 semi-annual dividends have always been paid. The total dividends amount to over $310,000, and the average is twelve and a half per cent a year. Fifteen consecutive semi-annual dividends were ten per cent each, and eleven consecutive semi-annual dividends were eight per cent each. The net assets of the Western are $183,547.

The first president of the company was T. F. Eckert, who held the position for twenty-four consecutive years until his death in 1878. His successor is F. X. Reno, who previously had been the secretary. Charles F. Runck is secretary. Office, 82 West Third Street.

Western Methodist Book Concern was established in Cincinnati in 1824, to publish and circulate religious books and periodicals, chiefly in support of the Methodist-Episcopal Church, to whom the property belongs, and by whose General Conference the agents and editors are elected. The buildings include a beautiful four-story freestone building fronting at 190 West Fourth Street, in which on the first floor is the magnificent Methodist Bookstore, and on the uppers are the editors' and agents' rooms; and also a back-building, five stories high, containing one of the largest and most complete book and job printing and binding establishments in the West. The agents are Walden & Stowe.

Western Society for the Suppression of Vice has for its object the enforcement of all laws for the suppression of the trade in and circulation of obscene printed matter and pictures and articles of indecent and immoral use.

Western Tract Society aims "to supply an evangelical literature, and to apply it for the reformation and salvation of men." It was commenced in 1852, and publishes tracts and papers for the sabbath-school and for the family. It is undenominational. The principal paper is "The Christian Press." Place of business, 176 Elm Street.

Wharves. — Along the eleven miles of river-front, there are many wharves, popularly called landings. Most of these, in number and extent of lineal feet, are private property, and are used for log-rafts, coal-boats and barges, and lumber. The extensive coal-dealers, who have elevators, generally own their landings. So also with the Marine Railway and Dry-dock Company, and the large saw-mill owners of Pendleton, Fulton, Columbia, and Sedamsville. The Public Landing — that owned by the city — extends from a point a short distance east of the water-works, west to Mill Creek. The greater portion of this is leased to private parties, ferries, steamboat-lines, and others. The Public Landing proper extends from Broadway to Race Street, and within this limit all general steamboat traffic is confined. The city maintains a wharf-master and wharf-register to collect wharfage-fees and to look after its wharf-interests in general.

Widows' and Old Men's Home is situated in Walnut Hills, and is one of the largest and finest structures of its kind in this country. It consists of two wings, one of which is occupied by the Widows' Home and Asylum for Aged and Indigent Women, and the other by the Old Men's Home. The building is of brick, 237 feet by 181 feet, three stories, and cost $80,000. This home is the result of the amalgamation of these two associations. The former was organized in 1848, incorporated in 1851, and, until 1879, owned and occupied a building on Highland Avenue, Mount Auburn. The building became too small to accommodate all applicants; and in 1879 the management of the Old Men's Home proposed the creation of a common fund, with which to erect a commodious building in Walnut Hills, which should be sufficiently large to accommodate both institutions. This was done, and resulted in the building above described. The corner-stone was laid July 2, 1879, and the structure was completed September, 1880. The conditions of admission to the Widows' Home are the possession of a good character, and payment of $100 by the applicant, who must not be under 60 years of age. To the Old Men's Home the same conditions apply, as to age and respectability, with this addition: charges of admission are, from 60 to 65 years of age, $300; from 65 to 70, $250; over 70, $150. The inmate also transfers to the home all personal or real property he may be possessed of, save such as is necessary for his personal expenses. There are at present 9 inmates in the Old Men's Home, and 60 in the Widows' Home. The home is under the supervision of a board of lady managers, with gentleman trustees, and is supported by endowment-funds and donations, the latter being swelled by the private fortunes of some of the inmates. Mrs. P. Mallon is president, and Mrs. N. A. Jeffras secretary. The home can be reached by the Walnut-hills and Mount-Adams inclined-plane horse-cars.

Widows' Home, the Bodmann German. — Located on Highland Avenue, Mount Auburn; and named after Mr. Ferdinand Bodmann, one of Cincinnati's prominent German merchants. The buildings were formerly used as an American Widows' Home, and the problem of its successful management was a matter much thought of and frequently discussed by Mr. Bodmann. His daughter, Mrs. J. B. Gibson, in the spirit of her father, actuated by a desire to ameliorate the lonely condition of worthy German widows, took a positive step towards bringing to a practical issue the thoughts of many years, and in 1881 purchased the buildings, remodelled them, and presented them to a representative assemblage of German ladies of Cincinnati to be used as a Widows' Home. Steps were immediately taken to incorporate the Home, which was accomplished July 8, 1881, with Louis Ballauf, Charles Jacob, jun., And. Erkenbrecher, Ferdinand Vogeler, and John B. Gibson as incorporators. The object of the incorporation is to provide a home for aged and helpless German Protestant widows who are alone in the world. The conditions of admission are the payment of $100, and the possession of a good character by the applicant. The buildings are of brick, four stories in height, and contain fifty-four rooms and accommodations for about a hundred inmates. They are surrounded by about two acres of ground beautifully laid out and ornamented. There are at present sixteen inmates. The Home is under the supervision of three trustees and twenty-eight lady managers. It has an endowment fund of between $15,000 and $20,000. Reached by Main-street horse-cars and Mount-Auburn Inclined-plane, also by Elm-street and Walnut-hills horse-cars. Visitors admitted.

Wilstach, Baldwin, & Co. are publishers of law, medical, scientific, and miscellaneous books, as well as manufacturing stationers. The business was established in 1842, and the firm name changed to its present style in 1870. The firm is composed of Charles F. Wilstach and F. H. Baldwin. In manufacturing blank-books and office-supplies for railroads, banks, and other corporations, mercantile houses, and municipalities, this is the leading house in the South-west. The manufacturing department occupies two large buildings, — one 25 by 80 feet, four stories high; and the other 30 by 80 feet, five stories high. The sales and ware rooms occupy two large floors, each 42 by 120 feet. The establishment gives employment to about 100 hands. The bindery is one of the largest and best in the city, and is in charge of Mr. Wilstach, who for eighteen years was president of the Ohio Mechanics' Institute, for nearly four years mayor of Cincinnati, and was the president of the first of the present series of the Cincinnati Industrial Expositions.

Women's Art-Museum Association. — See Art.

Women's Christian Association is an institution not only worthy of all the support it receives, but also entitled to the most liberal encouragement that the people can afford. Its object is the temporal, moral, and religious welfare of women dependent on their own exertions for a livelihood. To further this object, three departments have been established, — a business-women's boarding-house, a committee on employment, and a committee on city-missionary work. The boarding-house is not a charity-home; but it is a comfortable home for women desirous of paying their way, and at the same time of living in a very respectable yet economical manner. $3.50 a week is the maximum price, except for single rooms, when the prices vary from $4 to $5. The house, at 100 Broadway, with accommodations for forty ladies, is owned by the association. A number of young ladies attending the College of Music and the schools are among the boarders. The employment-bureau is at 267 West Fourth Street, and is open from nine A.M. to four P.M. During the year 1882, there were 1,662 applications for situations filed, and 726 situations found. The mission committee have organized three "mothers' meetings," the work of a Bible-reader, who is really a city missionary, and visiting committees. A mothers' meeting is a place where the poor women of a neighborhood are gathered together, to learn to sew, while conversation about general and religious matters is carried on.

Woman's Christian Temperance Union is a re-organization of the "Women Crusaders." It was organized in 1875, to promote temperance sentiment by preaching the gospel to those addicted to drinking, and to those engaged in the liquor-traffic. It holds regular meetings at its hall, 115 West Sixth Street, on Sunday, Tuesday, and Thursday afternoons, at four o'clock. The Reform Club, an outgrowth and auxiliary of the Union, meets in the same hall Saturday evenings at eight o'clock. Any person can attend the meetings. Since 1875 about 5,700 persons have signed the temperance pledge of the Union and of the Reform Club. The dues of the Union are sixty cents a year; but the main support comes from collections, donations, and from sustaining members.

Women's Dispensary Association. — A free dispensary for the treatment of diseases peculiar to females, in charge of lady physicians of the homœopathic school, and open daily at 306 Linn Street.

Woodburn, a beautiful village on the hills in the eastern part of the city, is three miles distant from the Post-Office, and may be reached either by the Walnut-hills or by the Eden-park street-cars. It is the residence of some of the wealthiest Cincinnatians, whose handsome houses and well-kept grounds make this one of the most beautiful of the suburbs. At the corner of Woodburn Avenue and

Madisonville Pike is the handsome Catholic Church of St. Francis de Sales.

Woodland Garden. — See East-end Garden.

Woodward College. — The predecessor of Woodward High-School, under the presidency of William Woodward, its founder. In 1853 the old college building was torn down, to make room for the elegant high-school building which now occupies the site. The alumni of the college, of whom many are living in the city, designate themselves "Old Woodward Boys."

Woodward High-School, founded by William Woodward, is located on Franklin Street, between Broadway and Sycamore. Promotions to enter the school are made from pupils who pass a satisfactory examination in the intermediate schools. Pupils to be eligible for attendance must reside in the district lying north of Clark Street, and east of Central Avenue from Clark Street to the Ohio River. On the other side of this line, high-school pupils must attend the Hughes High-School. The high-schools are managed by the union board of high-schools, composed of six delegates from the board of education, five delegates from the board of trustees of the Woodward Fund, and two delegates from the trustees of the Hughes Fund. The average number of pupils in attendance at Woodward is about four hundred and twenty-five. French, German, Latin, and Greek are taught, and all the elements of a first-class common-school education. Graduates are admitted to the University of Cincinnati without examination.

Woodward Monument. — See Monuments.

Workhouse, the Cincinnati, is an immense building situated on the Colerain Pike, in Camp Washington, adjoining the House of Refuge. It consists of a central structure five stories high, with wings, the height of three stories, in which are the cell-rooms, each wing ending in a building of four stories. The frontage of the whole edifice is 510 feet. The south wing contains the cells for male prisoners, ranged in a single block of six tiers, reached by iron stairways. This block contains 360 cells. The north wing, similarly arranged, contains 240 cells for female prisoners. The main building contains the office, the family-rooms of the resident superintendent and secretary, and the prisoners' kitchen. A chapel stands immediately in the rear of the central structure, into which a Catholic altar can be wheeled when occasion requires. Services are held every Sunday

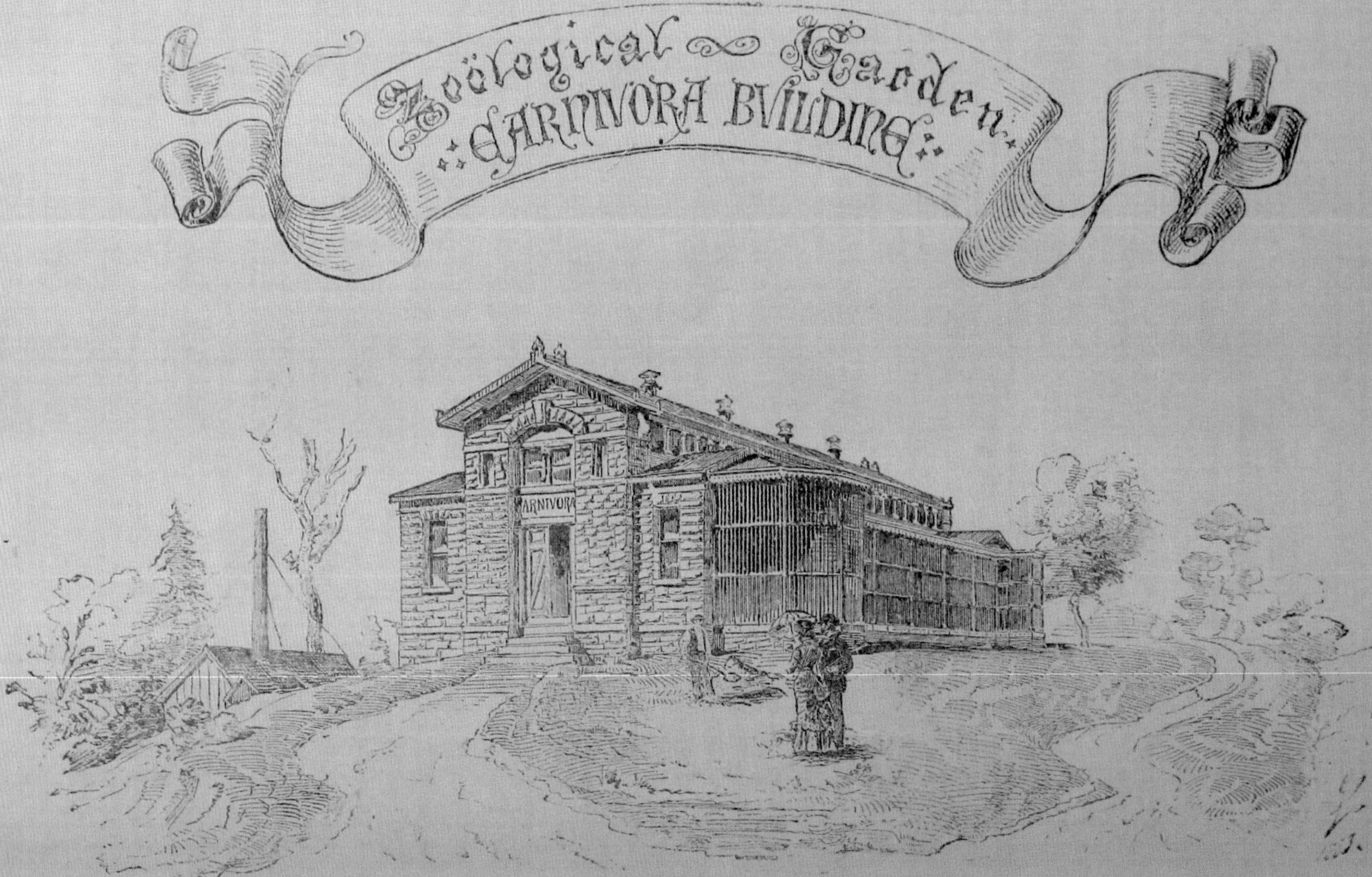
Zoölogical Garden
CARNIVORA BUILDING
CARNIVORA

morning at ten o'clock; and, although none are required to be present, there is scarcely any one absent. The grounds back of the prison are surrounded by a wall of masonry fifteen feet high. Within this enclosure are the workshops, founderies, blacksmith's-shop, tool-houses, guard and other houses of sufficient size to give employment to all prisoners the workhouse will accommodate. Commitments are made by the police-court and court of common pleas for all crimes and misdemeanors the punishment for which is of a less grade than imprisonment in the penitentiary. The grounds contain 26 acres. The daily average number of prisoners is about 460. The Workhouse is managed by a board of five directors, appointed by the mayor, and confirmed by the council. *Horse-cars*, — the Avenue line; fare, 5 cents from the city.

Workmen, Ancient Order of United. — A mutual benefit and insurance association, in which the members receive weekly sick-benefits, and at death the widow or other heirs receive the sum of $2,000. The qualifications for membership are a good moral character and sound health, the latter determined by an examining surgeon. The order is very strong in Cincinnati, there being 22 lodges. In the State there is an aggregate membership of about 2,700, and in the entire order about 66,000. Annual dues, from $4 to $6; assessment for each death, $1.10.

Yale Club, founded in 1863, is said to be the oldest regularly organized alumni association in this country. Its object is to bring together the graduates of Yale College, at least once a year, so as to keep alive the memories of Alma Mater. The annual dinner takes place during the Christmas vacation, in order that instructors, graduates, and undergraduates, who are in the city for the holidays, may be present. The young members have formed a Junior Yale Club, as a branch of the older club; and in the spring an informal supper is held at Boman's, at which about twenty members are present. At the regular dinner as many as seventy-five persons have been present.

Young Men's Bible Society of Cincinnati, one of the oldest local institutions of the kind, was founded in 1834, as an auxiliary to the American Bible Society, when Salmon P. Chase was elected its president, which position he held for ten years. The object of the society is to circulate the Holy Scriptures, without note or comment. During the year 1881–82 there were distributed 3,035 Bibles and 6,388 Testaments; 552 Bibles and 1,170 Testaments were donated.

The membership-list embraces the names of prominent clergymen and laymen of every denomination, as the society is non-sectarian in its character. The rooms are at 176 Elm Street.

Women's Exchange, an enterprise started Feb. 1, 1883, and patterned after similar organizations in the East, has for its object the establishment of a headquarters where women desirous of contributing towards their own support may deposit for sale articles of their own home-production, such as embroideries, paintings, potteries, canned fruits, specimens of culinary art, etc. It is managed by a board of thirty directors, and is located at 247 Race.

Young Men's Christian Association was established Oct. 4, 1848, and is the oldest association of this kind on the American continent. It has occupied the present premises, a large five-story, stone-front building, situated on the south-east corner of Sixth and Elm Streets, since 1874. The association hall has a seating capacity of 300, and has two reading-rooms, with a library of 1,500 volumes; besides which there are social parlors, with chess and parlor-croquet rooms, baths, etc. Prayer-meetings are held week-days at twelve o'clock, and Saturday, Sunday, and Monday evenings at eight o'clock. Bible-classes are taught on Sundays at four P.M., and Thursdays at eight P.M. Free lectures and concerts and other entertainments once a week. Services are held by the committees at the hospitals, jail, and workhouse. Cottage meetings and open-air services are also held. The city missionaries and Bible-readers hold services the first Monday evening in each month. Gospel temperance-meetings are held on the last Monday evening of the month. Sunday-school teachers' class meets for study every Saturday at twelve o'clock. The primary Sunday-school teachers meet Saturdays at three P.M. Medical students' prayer-meeting Saturday evenings in their parlor at half-past seven o'clock. Deaf and dumb hold social and religious services alternate Saturday evenings at eight o'clock. Monthly business meetings, the first Tuesday evening of every month; and the anniversary of the association is held on the first Tuesday evening in November. The Young Men's Christian Association Quarterly Reporter is issued regularly. Employment and boarding houses are found free of charge. Open on week-days from eight A.M. to ten P.M. The whole is open free to the public. The membership comprises 1,400 ladies and gentlemen. Active and associate members pay $2 a year each. Active members are male members of evangel-

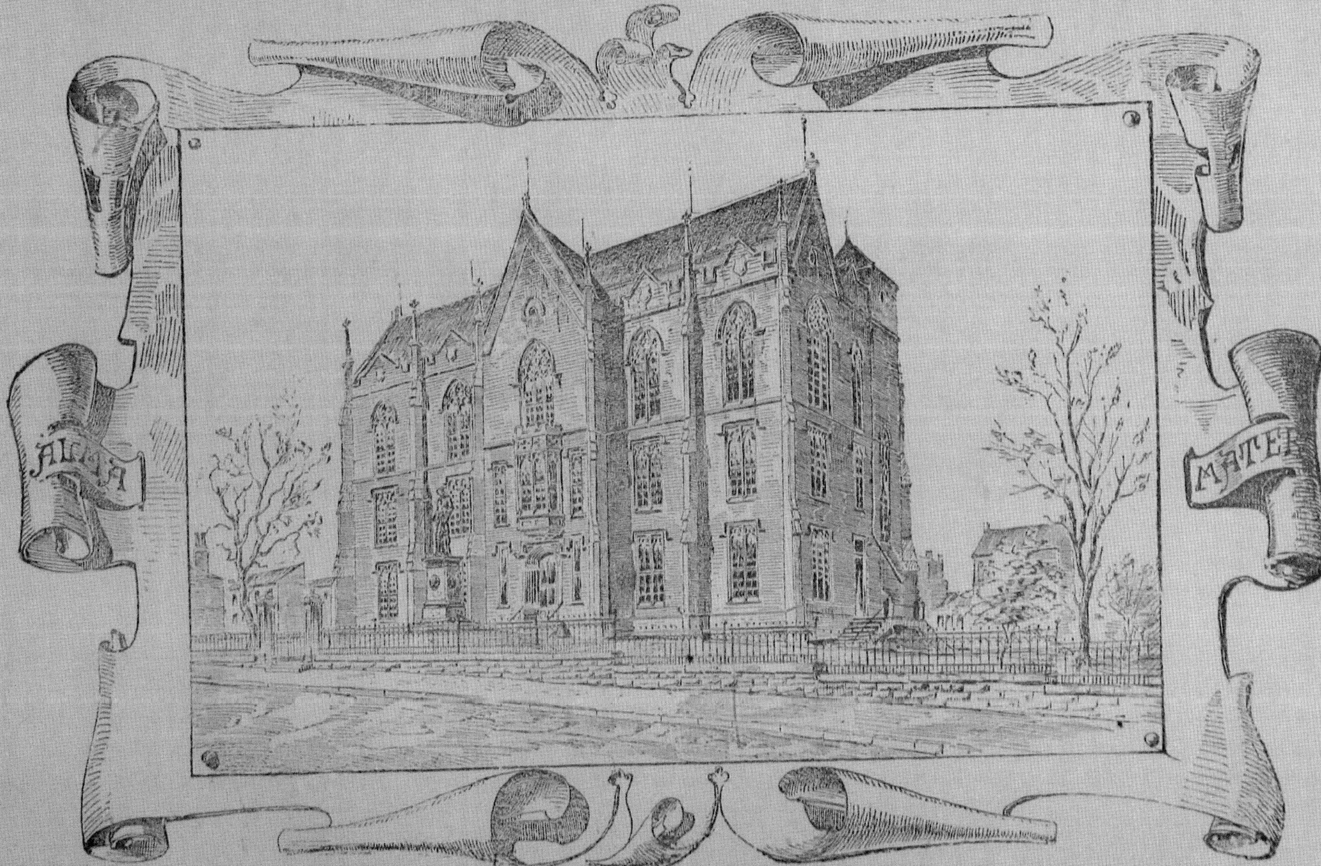

Woodward High-School.

ical churches; and associate members comprise men not members of evangelical churches, and women, whether church-members or not The members are privileged to enter the classes for instruction. The expenses are met chiefly by contributions. A contribution of $10 a year is called a *sustaining-member;* and $500 paid at one time, or $100 each year for five years, makes a *life-member.*

Young Men's Hebrew Association occupies rooms north-east corner of Eighth Street and Central Avenue. It has a reading-room, gives literary, musical, and social entertainments, and aims to secure employment for the members. Dues. life-membership, $50; initiation, $1.50; annual assessments, $4.00.

Young Men's Mercantile Library Association, in College Building, has 40,000 volumes, 5,000 pamphlets, fine statuary, paintings, etc. The reading-room is comfortable and cosey, and contains upwards of 200 papers and periodicals. Terms, $5 for yearly, $50 for life, and $100 for perpetual membership. Open every day from eight A.M. to ten P.M. Strangers admitted. H. B. Morehead is president, and John M. Newton librarian.

Zoölogical Society of Cincinnati owns the largest and finest zoölogical gardens in the United States. The buildings are as costly and as substantial as those of the zoölogical gardens in Europe. The grounds include 66 acres beautifully improved. There are 830 specimens of animals and birds, from all parts of the world. Frequently there are balls, picnics, and special attractions, and on Thursday evenings there is a "*fête.*" The restaurant inside the garden furnishes good food at moderate prices. The gardens were opened in 1875, and since that time about $300,000 have been expended. They are situated in the south-west corner of Avondale, and front on the Carthage Pike. Admission, 25 cents for adults; 10 cents for children; free for stockholders. *Horse-cars,* — Elm-street, Vine-street, or Main-street lines. Ask for coupon-ticket to "Zoo;" fare, 10 cents. The success of these gardens is due chiefly to the liberality of A. Erkenbrecher and Julius J. Bantlin, to the ability of Frank J. Thompson the superintendent, and to the enterprise of Neil C. Kerr the excursion manager. The officers are, S. Lester Taylor president, Otto Laist vice-president, Frank A. Thompson secretary.

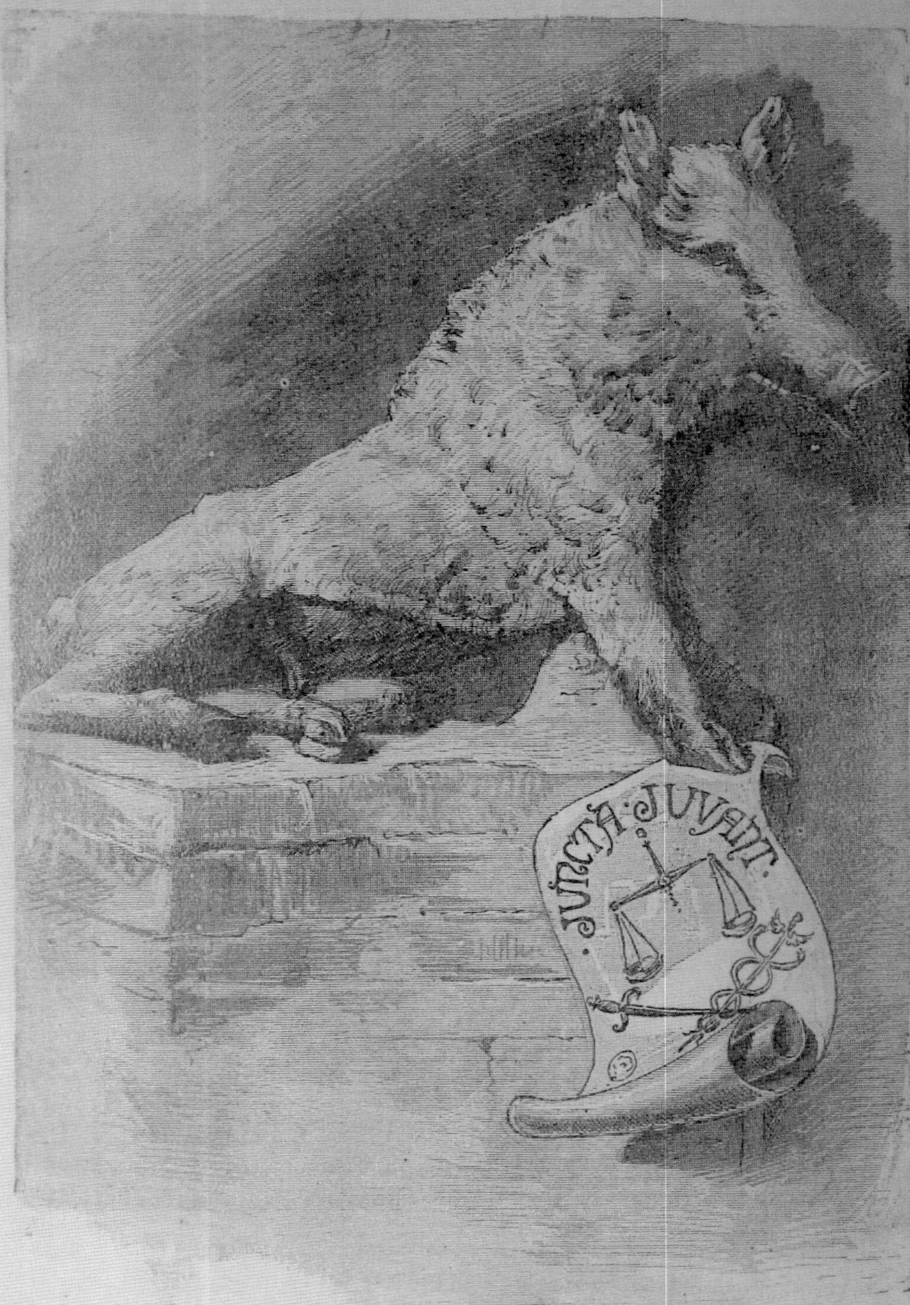
·JUNCTA·JUVANT·